SOCIAL WORK WITH CHILDREN

SOCIAL WORK WITH CHILDREN

Florence Lieberman, D.S.W.

Hunter College of the City University of New York,
School of Social Work

HUMAN SCIENCES PRESS
72 Fifth Avenue 3 Henrietta Street
NEW YORK, NY 10011 ● LONDON, WC2E 8LU

Library of Congress Catalog Number 78-23287

ISBN: 0-87705-255-7 case
　　　0-87705-257-3 paper

Copyright © 1979 by Human Sciences Press
72 Fifth Avenue, New York, New York 10011

Printed in the United States of America
9 987654321

Library of Congress Cataloging in Publication Data

Lieberman, Florence.
　　Social work with children.

　　Bibliography: p.
　　Includes index.
　　1. Social work with children.　2. Child development.
3. Child welfare.　I. Title.
HV713.L54　　　362.7　　　78-23287
ISBN 0-87705-255-7
ISBN 0-87705-257-3 pbk.

CONTENTS

Preface
PART I. CHILDREN: AN OVERVIEW
    1. **Birth through Adolescence**   **19**
        Infancy   **19**
        Early Childhood   **23**
        Cognitive Ability   **24**
        Fantasy and Play   **26**
        Coping with Sexual Differences   **29**
        Coping with Racial Differences   **30**
        At Six   **31**
        Latency   **32**
        Adolescence   **36**
        Puberty   **37**
        Crisis of Adolescence   **37**

5

2. Children and Their Situation — **40**

The Family — **40**

Parents — **41**

Siblings — **42**

Extended Family — **43**

Family Problems — **44**

Separation and Divorce — **44**

Multiproblem Families — **46**

Child Neglect and Abuse — **47**

Foster Care — **52**

Family Crisis — **56**

Death — **56**

Illness — **59**

The Family In Society — **62**

Economic Pressures — **62**

Changing Families — **64**

Cultural and Societal Influences — **65**

PART II. CHILDREN AGES 6 TO 12

3. Early Latency — **71**

Growth and Physical Development — **71**

Games Children Play — **72**

Drawings and Stories — **76**

Peer Groups — **79**

Sex Differences — **80**

Cognitive Ability — **83**

Psychology of Early Latency — **86**

4. Middle Latency — **92**

Growth and Development — **92**

Play — **94**

Peers and Group Activities — **98**

	Cognitive Ability	**99**
	Psychological Growth	**103**
	Sexuality	**105**
5.	**Late Latency**	**108**
	Physical Growth	**109**
	Peers and Play	**112**
	Cognitive Development	**117**
	Sexuality	**119**
	Psychological Development	**125**
PART III.	PROBLEMS	
6.	**Underneath the Symptoms**	**133**
	Adult Complaints	**133**
	Symptomatology	**136**
	Depression	**142**
	Aggression	**147**
7.	**Learning Problems**	**155**
	Hyperactivity	**156**
	Hyperkinesis and Minimal Brain Damage	**158**
	Problems of Ability	**161**
	Learning Disabilities	**162**
	Mental Retardation	**164**
	Underachievement	**166**
	Absence from School	**172**
	School Phobia	**173**
	Other Phobias	**177**
8.	**Mind and Body**	**180**
	The Psychosomatic Concept	**181**
	Hypochondriasis	**189**
	Tics	**190**

Eating Disorders	191
Obesity	192
Anorexia	194
Disorders of Elimination	199
Enuresis	201
Encopresis	203
Sleep Disorders	206
Disorders of Self-Preservation	209
Suicide	209
Accidents	210
Self-Mutilation	211
Disorders of Communication	212
Stuttering	214
Mutism	215

PART IV. TREATMENT

9.	**Beginnings**	219
	First Contact	221
	Family Diagnostic Interviews	223
	Parents as Collaborators	224
	Children as Collaborators	227
	The Contract	228
	Biopsychosocial Diagnosis	229
	The Facts	231
	Diagnostic Formulation	238
	Clinical Diagnosis	240
	From Diagnosis to Treatment	244
	Goals	245
	Types of Treatment	247
	Duration of Treatment	252

Concrete Services 256

Teamwork 256

10. Communication 259

Communicating with Parents 259

Resistance 260

Listening 263

Playing with Parents 264

Giving Advice 268

Communicating with Children 271

The Worker's Problems 273

Children's Resistance 275

Listening to Children 277

Talking with Children 281

Peek-a-boo; I Hide, You Seek 286

Playing with Children 287

Play and Therapy 287

Play Equipment and Setting 289

Cheating at Games 291

Fantasy Play 293

11. Leaving and Being Left 295

Being Left 296

Vacations and Illness 299

The Worker Leaves the Agency 301

Transfers 303

Leaving 304

Planning a Termination 304

The Process of Leaving 305

Looking Back 307

References 311

Index 335

PREFACE

The twentieth century is the century of children—a century that is addressing the needs and rights of children as well as the child as future citizen. Yet concern for the future of children does not differentiate our era from earlier ones. Throughout the history of child care in western civilization, the childhood years have been viewed as training for adulthood, with all the roles, obligations, and privileges entailed, as defined by a particular society. What is new is the emphasis on the child as different from the adult and the growing exposition of the child's inherent rights—rights that are similar to those of the adult and differentiated only by the existence of special needs.

Although it has always been clear that children cannot care for themselves, the age at which childhood ends has varied, depending on the complexities of society. For example, in the small, closely knit communities of the preindustrial era, the end of infancy often heralded the beginning of family, community, and economic responsibilities. In today's highly complex societies, childhood often extends into the late teens or early twenties.

Social workers have long recognized that children have the right to be born of a healthy mother into a secure family and, after birth, have the right to basics such as food and shelter and to all that society views as essential to produce active, healthy, contributing citizens. Social problems such as poverty, discrimination, and unequal opportunity and political decisions concerning taxes, housing, education, and welfare not only impinge on the family's strengths and stability but directly affect the development of the next generation. Because of Mary Richmond, social workers have also long known that "social reform and social treatment of necessity progress together."

Social workers have always seen more children than have all other mental health professionals combined. They see children who are abandoned, neglected, and abused; they see children in their own homes and in foster homes, in day care centers and child guidance centers, in settlement houses and neighborhood service centers, in courts and juvenile detention facilities, in hospitals and other institutions, and in myriad other places. The largest group of children they see are recipients of Aid to Dependent Children.

Social work is *the* professional group that works with children. It provides the only therapeutic and emotional assistance that most children will ever receive. Social workers were the pioneers in child guidance, the first to acknowledge the need for special knowledge and education when working with children. And in the days of specialties in education for social work, child welfare was an important area.

In 1917 Mary Richmond deplored the fact that many family agencies failed to individualize children of families under their care. By 1922 she viewed casework with difficult children as a well-defined specialty. She also noted an all-too-familiar problem: workers were so often overburdened that they could not possibly do well! In the late 1950s, Selma Fraiberg noted that "thousands of children with emotional disturbances ... are being treated by social workers in agencies, juvenile court clinics and child guidance centers" and concluded that if community and mental health agencies wanted social work to care for disturbed children, the profession would have to establish the proper conditions, supervision, and controls for this work.

Children still suffer because too often the services they receive are inadequate and those who attempt to help them are poorly prepared. As Richmond pointed out years ago, going through the motions is not the same as getting things done. Despite the burgeoning of new services and the development of community psychiatry, we lack workers with the experience, knowledge, and skill required to work with children. In the words of Paul Adams, children are the "parapeople, the recipients of paraservices, assigned to paraprofessionals." In many instances, no one sees them on the mistaken assumption that they will be reached indirectly through others. Consequently, the needs of individual children and their families are often neglected, or the most complicated human problems are left to harassed, untrained staff.

In 1969 the Joint Commission on Mental Health of Children charged the helping professions with the responsibility of advocating for the child's right to "developmentally oriented therapeutic help and facilitation of growth as a developing human being." Yet, in the child welfare field, too many persons called social workers lack professional training. Current services for children are skimpily provided for and skimpily served. In other words, anyone can do well enough for children (and the poor).

The problem of providing second-class services to the powerless is not new. Note the author of the following statement:

There are physicians, and again there are physicians' assistants, who we also speak of as physicians. All bear the name, whether free men or slaves who gain their professional knowledge by watching their masters and obeying their directions in empirical fashion, not in the scientific way in which free men learn their art and teach it to their pupils. . . . The slaves . . . are treated by slaves, who pay them a hurried visit, or receive them in dispensaries. A physician of this kind never gives a servant any account of his complaint, nor asks him any; he gives him some empirical injunction . . . in the brusque fashion of a dictator, and then is off in post haste to the next ailing servant—that is how he lightens his master's medical labors for him. The free practitioner, who for the most part, attends free men, treats their diseases by going into things thoroughly from the beginning in a scientific way, and takes the patient and his family into his confidence. He does not give his prescriptions until he has won the patient's support, and when he has done so, he steadily aims at producing complete restoration to health. (Plato, *The Laws*, Book IV, 348 B.C.)

Although advocacy and reform are essential aspects of social work with any age group, there is no group for which they are more important than children. But the basic needs of children and their right to have those needs met cannot be handled by the social work profession alone. The entire society must involve itself in concern for its young, examine the opportunities it offers them, and think through the many ways in which those opportunities can be enhanced and extended to all children and families.

The focus of this book is social work with latency-age children—children ages 6 to 12. Children in this age group (or in any age group) cannot be viewed in chronological isolation; they are the product of all the biological stages and situational experiences in their past and present. Therefore, Part I attempts to place the target group in perspective. The first chapter contains a brief review of all the developmental stages of childhood, from infancy through adolescence. The second describes the situational factors—familial, cultural, and societal—that influence the child's development and personality. Part II discusses in detail the three stages of latency: early, middle, and late latency (or prepuberty). Part III outlines a variety of emotional, learning, and somatic disorders that bring latency-age children to the attention of social agencies. The final section of the book, Part IV, is devoted to treatment of children and their families. The three chapters of this section cover the following topics: initial contacts with children and their families, use of the biopsychosocial diagnosis in formulating a treatment plan, methods of communicating with clients, and termination. Case histories are used throughout the book to illustrate various problems and methods of treatment.

The material in this book is derived from my own work with children and parents and from teaching others how to work with them. The theoretical rationale is derived from ego psychology, the concept of epigenetic development, and a dynamic view of personality. The focus is on health as a state of physical, mental, and social well-being; the problems of coping and adaptation are the primary concern. As Heinz Hartmann pointed out in the late 1950s, some adaptive behavior is actually maladaptive for the individual. In essence, this book is based on the recognition that there is mutual interaction between children and their environment and that human beings of any age need support from others.

Social work values the uniqueness of the individual, and its goal is the enhancement of life through meeting of basic needs. The profession also empathizes with human frailty and pain. It is these values that the interventions described in this book attempt to reflect.

CHILDREN: AN OVERVIEW

Chapter 1

BIRTH THROUGH ADOLESCENCE

Middle childhood, the ages 6 through 12, is a transitional period between early childhood and adolescence. It is referred to as latency because sexual interests during this stage are unlike those of preschool children and adolescents. Infants and preschool children express their sexuality in autoerotic activities, while the sexual interests of adolescents are similar in nature to those of adults. Sarnoff (1976) suggests that latency is the result of inhibition rather than diminution of sexual drives. In any case, the fact that most societies initiate formal schooling when children reach the age of 6 seems to indicate an almost universal recognition that a new phase of growth and development has been reached.

INFANCY

Erikson (1963) believes that during the first year of life, the child establishes a sense of basic trust through a process of mutual regulation with its mother in an environment that facilitates appropriate ways of meeting the child's needs. This experience of constancy and caring from an adult lays the foundation for the child's subsequent psychological development and socialization.

The child is born with the capacity to adapt to life outside the womb. Feeding is facilitated by sucking, head movements, and grasping. Yawning, hiccuping, and sneezing cleanse the respiratory system. Discomfort is expressed through crying or through the startle reaction to loud sounds and abrupt movements. Because its mouth and skin are sensitive and easily stimulated, the infant is responsive to being held and cuddled. In a now famous experiment, Harlow and Harlow (1966) presented baby monkeys with two types of surrogate mothers: one was made of wire and dispensed food; the other was made of terry cloth and did not dispense food. The monkeys clung to the terry cloth mother and went to the wire mother only when they were hungry. The findings of numerous studies of human children (e.g., Provence & Lipton, 1962; Spitz, 1965) attest to the need for warm contact and active stimulation as well as food during infancy.

Human children are dependent on adults for their survival far longer than any other animal. Parens and Saul (1971) suggest that the mutual give-and-take between mother and child which develops during infancy is a significant determinant of behavior throughout life. Initially, the infant is only dimly aware of its mother and perceives her merely as an object that satisfies its needs. But as the mother comes and goes, her image is organized in the infant's mind through memory imprints of the visual, auditory, and tactile sensations she provides. When it is two or three months old, however, the infant will respond to its mother's attention by smiling, which usually makes the mother even more attentive.

Infants explore their mothers visually and then manually. When they are five or six months old, the mother alone receives a special smile that Piaget and Inhelder (1969) term "attention to the object." By manipulating the mother's body and by exploring and playing with their own bodies, infants establish their physical bodies and body ego as separate from others.

As the baby slowly differentiates itself from its mother, the attachment to her becomes less dependent on the immediate gratification of needs. The baby's vocalizations begin to parody human speech and thus represent an attempt to communicate. The baby distinguishes between its mother and strangers by staring at them, then checking back at the mother's face. Mahler (1963, 1971; Mahler, Pine, & Bergman, 1975) terms this the stage of differentiation. When the baby is approximately nine months old, it will experience separation anxiety until it learns that mother will return. The peek-a-boo game is a milestone in learning at this time because the baby can practice the notion that objects exist even when they cannot be seen (Kleeman, 1967).

The physical ability to crawl, climb, and walk enables young children to practice leaving and coming back to mother. When she is absent, they will turn to a transitional object such as a blanket or a stuffed toy for comfort (Winnicott, 1975). By returning to her, they refuel themselves emotionally (Mahler, Pine, & Bergman, 1975).

Siblings and father are the first outposts in the child's widening practicing space (Abelin, 1971). Within the first months of life, babies begin responding enthusiastically to siblings and other small children. Before they are six months old, they recognize and smile at the father. At nine months of age, they can be attached to him, especially if he has participated in their care. During this period of exploration, the father is especially important because he is another person to turn to and explore and thus aids the process of individuation and separation. When tired, however, babies tend to return to mother to be comforted.

During the stage of rapprochement, which occurs between the ages of 14 and 22 months, children develop an even greater awareness that they are separate from mother. Thus they become more active about gaining her attention and requesting that she participate in their activities. During this stage, children usually demand attention from both parents, sometimes playing one against the other, which reflects ambivalent feelings toward the mother. The father at this time is a stable island of external reality. As their ability to understand verbalizations develops, children begin to understand that everyone is "I" to themselves and "you" to others. "This capacity to take himself as an object among objects and to symbolize this state marks the beginnings of rationality and a new order of intelligence (Fraiberg, 1968, p. 80)."

Piaget (1963) calls the stage between birth and age 2 the sensorimotor stage. Beginning with the use of innate reflexes of sucking and grasping, then assimilating their expanding sensations and, through accommodation, modifying the sensorimotor sequences, children build a series of new schema that enhance their mental development and expand their knowledge of the world. The process of looking at objects and assimilating the visual sensations those objects produce, organizes new visual schema. By assimilating their own movements, they learn the feel of the body, and their movements, manipulations, reflexes, and habits lead to the assimilation of new objects into old patterns. By the time they are seven or eight months old, babies begin to differentiate objects and learn that objects are permanent. During the final phases of the sensorimotor stage, children explore and experiment by trial and error and then apply familiar patterns to new circumstances with the help of mental combinations—which enhances the ability to use symbols and internalize symbolic acts.

Walking and talking herald a new stage in learning, acting, and relating. But when children learn to say "I" and "me," they also learn to say "no." A struggle to achieve autonomy then ensues between the ages of 2 and 3 and involves mastery over objects and the body.

EARLY CHILDHOOD

Erikson (1963) terms the stage of development that occurs between the ages of 2 and 3 as the period of holding on and letting go, which is characterized by ambivalence and is typified by opposites. This period is also called the anal stage because it coincides with the physical ability to control the sphincter muscles and with toilet training in many cultures. The socializing process of toilet training introduces more frustration into young children's lives; their negativism and their ambivalence about pleasing the parent or being autonomous also causes anxiety about the possibility of losing mother's love. Later the control imposed by adults becomes self-control, which children accept because they identify with their parents and want to be like them. Learning this control increases their sense of autonomy and independence, but feelings of doubt and shame and of right and wrong also emerge during this struggle against parental demands.

Cognitive and physical development both facilitate and limit this expanding autonomy and independence. The ability to delay gratification, to exercise control over bodily functions and aggressive impulses is facilitated by the ability to translate needs and affects into words. However, verbal communication is restricted by childish thinking and a limited understanding of what words mean.

By the time they are 4, children have learned that they exist without the mother, that the world includes other adults and other children. Though they still rely primarily on body language, they are able to verbalize some of their own needs and to understand some needs of others. As a result, they are better able to tolerate delays in obtaining what they want. At this age, children have internalized an image of mother and have achieved what Piaget and Mahler term object constancy—the mother-child relationship is stable and positive and is not dependent on whether the mother is physically present or has satisfied their needs. This enables children to complete the process of separation-individuation.

Cognitive Ability

The thinking of preschool children is characterized by primary process thinking (Fenichel, 1945). This type of thinking resembles dreaming: it is illogical; disorganized; ruled by emotions, wishes, and fears; and tolerates and condenses contradictions. It is based primarily on pictorial, concrete images rather than words (which are the basis of secondary process thinking). Analogy, allusion, displacement, condensation, and timelessness are all elements of primary process thinking.

Piaget categorizes children between the ages of 2 1/2 and 6 or 7 as in the preoperational stage: a transitional stage between the sensorimotor period of infancy and concrete operational intelligence, the thinking mode of latency. In the preoperational period, children's thinking is egocentric: i.e., their ideas about causality, logic, and how others feel are limited by their own viewpoint, limited knowledge, and lack of experience. Children of this age believe that the world is as they perceive it to be and that their explanations for external events are true. In other words, their thinking has a magical quality. Wishes are real and equated with deeds. Giants, ogres, and witches exist and can inflict pain and injury. Their interpretations of their own psychological processes tend to be concrete and strange, and they invest their wishes, thoughts, and dreams with concrete reality because they are unable to understand the personal nature of these abstractions. Indeed, not until adolescence are children capable of dealing with abstract ideas in any meaningful way.

Life and death are incomprehensible abstractions to children. They cannot distinguish between what is alive and what is not—between the stuffed dog and the real dog, the doll and the baby, the tree and the person. All are alive, and all feel and think as the child does. The family includes all living things in the immediate physical environment, including pets.

Young children are also incapable of differentiating objects according to their attributes or of handling more than one variable at a time. This, plus the absence of adequate categories, the inability to distinguish the subjective from the objective and delineate between fantasy and reality, and the inability to comprehend time leads to global reasoning and limited understanding. As a result, the same words will mean different things to children and adults (Piaget & Inhelder, 1969). This childish reasoning is illustrated by the following recipes, which were dictated by children kindergarten pupils to their teacher. (The author wishes to thank Mrs. Jill Desmond, teacher at Indovino Sachem School, Long Island, New York, for permission to reprint these recipes.)

Fried Eggs by Lisa: You crack the shell open. Put it on the stove. Cook it for 5 hours and turn it over. When you finish you go and play.

Chocolate Cake by Susan: First you put in chocolate mix. Then you put in the white stuff inside the cake. It cooks for 17 minutes or 2 minutes. When it comes out of the oven you put chocolate on it.

Hamburger by Frank: Take them and mush them up flat. Then you put them in the oven for 16 hours. Then you put it in a roll and eat it.

Pancakes by Aaron: All you have to do is get some pancake
mix and put them on the stove. You mix water, then stir it.
Try it with milk and see if it works. You can put eggs on them
if you want to. Cook till 3 o'clock.

Fantasy and Play

Fantasy and play help preschool children work through
some of the world's mysteries. Their thoughts and conclusions are real to them, and fantasy is a form of thinking,
whether or not adults view it as such. Children's fantasies
include theories about the real world that will influence
their actions, thinking, and behavior, and generate additional fantasies. As a result, sexual explanations develop
from their own infantile sexual interests. For example, if
told that the baby grows within the mother and is then
pushed out, children easily conclude that it must be pushed
out through the anus, like feces. The notions that pregnancy is accomplished orally and that intercourse is sadistic
and violent also seem reasonable to a child. When children
are able to comprehend what actually occurs, they may
reject these notions consciously, but unconsciously the
themes persist and are expressed during play.

Children also indulge in daydreams—conscious, wish-
fulfilling fantasies that they recognize as unreal. In Sandler's view (1975), daydreams represent a compromise
between conscious and unconscious thoughts and begin
during play. Daydreams can be a temporary respite from
the harsh demands of reality, but if real life is too frustrating, children will daydream excessively. When secrecy
seems essential, daydreams will be substituted for play.
Daydreams contain past impressions, current wishes, and
enable children to make the past or future more satisfying
than it was or may be in reality. Although daydreams and
fantasies help children deal with frustration, they can also
prevent children from learning how to obtain genuine satisfaction.

Play is the universal method that children use to assimilate experiences which are too difficult to understand because of their limited experience, knowledge, and coping abilities. By repeatedly assuming a variety of roles and doing in play as grownups do, children can deal actively with situations they may have experienced passively and make the outcome more satisfactory (A. Freud, 1936). As anxiety is played out, it is assimilated and alleviated; in this way, play serves as a catharsis and a safety valve. Danger seems less dangerous when children can play out imagined or real dangers and conflicts between wishes and prohibitions.

Sometimes the conflict or anxiety seems so obvious that it is difficult to believe that children are unaware of it. But they must be unaware of it; otherwise the anxiety would become too real and overwhelming and would intrude on the play, stopping it, as demonstrated in the following case:

John, age 4, had been in foster care since he was 2½. He had been removed from his own home by the court when he was hospitalized with two broken legs, a fractured left hand, a broken nose, multiple bruises, malnutrition, dehydration, lice, and evidence of previous fractures of the ribs and lower extremities. Now, a social worker was preparing him for his return home through play sessions.

During his third visit to the playroom, John suddenly stopped filling the water tank with toys and began playing with the baby doll. He treated it lovingly, wrapping it in a blanket and feeding it a bottle. "You feed the baby," he demanded, and placed the doll in the worker's arms. "I'm a baby," he said watching the doll. "Sometimes it would be nice to be a baby again, wouldn't it?" the worker asked. John began shouting "A baby, a baby" and ran around the room. Then he took the doll and threw it face down in the water tank with the arms and legs in distorted positions. "Everything's a mess," he said, looking sadly at the tank. Then, "I'm a big boy," a pause, "I want to go now." Another pause: "You play with me don't you?" When the worker replied, "Yes, we play together, and you are a big boy now,"

> John said nothing but clutched her shirt and pulled her from
> the room.

When John tried to repeat the experience of being a baby and change the outcome, the impending return to the baby's actual environment recalled the anxiety and trauma he had experienced. It would have been helpful if John and the worker, together, had made everything nice for the baby doll. But John needed to play through, again and again, the horror of having lived in a home where parents had made such a mess of a baby. Of course, John was not ready to return home.

In more normal situations, the gratification that children obtain in play compensates for daily frustrations. By fulfilling wishes in play, they achieve pleasure with a minimum amount of risk. Dangerous sexual and destructive wishes can be transformed and disguised in play roles, which is a step toward sublimation. In play the ego commands, and in satisfactory play, the ego feels no conflict and therefore no anxiety.

Play that involves phobic defenses and obsessional rituals seems to be a defensive activity rather than a means of coping with daily anxiety. This type of play does not bring mastery or gratification, it does not aid growth of the ego, and the child is unable to stop it at will.

The anxieties that accompany the conflicts which are typical of each developmental stage are reflected in play and in the style and manner in which play develops. The themes that appeared in play at an earlier age will reappear in more complex and lengthy versions.

At age 4 or 5, children are concerned about oedipal relations and defenses against them; their anxiety is related to being small and to anger about being excluded from what the grownups are doing. The compensating fantasies are "I can do these things" and the family romance (S. Freud, 1909b). At this age, children play with dolls a good deal and act out a wide variety of events involving father, mother, and substitutes for them. The props are the implements and roles of the adult world. This play is creative and imaginative and provides children with a sense of omnipotence and success. Time is telescoped; other children assume or are assigned roles; daily frustrations are easier to manage (Peller, 1954). The need for this type of play is recognized in nursery schools, kindergarten classes, and even in the first grade, where pots and pans, dolls, doll clothes, beds, and other items that are part of the child's world will be found in the classroom.

Coping with Sexual Differences

In play, it is possible to be mother or father, to have a baby or be a baby and thus work through one's love for and identification with parents as well as accept one's own sexual identity. At this stage, parents become idealized and are accepted as role models. When they are understanding, loving, and supportive and do not complicate their children's fantasies by involving them in parental conflicts, the children will be able to cope more easily with oedipal conflict.

The oedipal conflict is resolved through love as well as fear. Love and need for the parent of the same sex makes children want to be good and loved. But parents are big, strong, and omnipotent, and bad boys and girls lose love and are punished. To young children, castration and physical injury are the logical consequences of bad wishes, thoughts, and dreams because the conscience is neither reasonable nor flexible, nor can children differentiate between actual deeds and thoughts at this age. In this childish way, children entering latency solve the first oedipal crisis, which will reoccur again in adolescence for a final working through and resolution.

As a result of identifying with the parent of the same

sex, sexual identity, an important part of ego identity, becomes firmly established and permits children to learn the sexual roles and behaviors that the culture expects of them. This identification also aids the growth of the superego, which functions whether or not parents are present. Thus children now possess an internal watchdog consisting of incorporated parental commands and values.

Coping with Racial Differences

Children notice racial differences, particularly differences in skin color, as early as age 2. How they explain these differences will reflect age-specific logic. To notice the differences is normal; however, their meaning will be consonant with how individual children explain other differences, including sex differences.

Discoveries about sex differences and differences in skin color are visual ones that disturb children's equilibrium and generate anxiety about the body. McDonald (1970) reported the reactions of children in an integrated nursery school when a white child returned from a vacation well suntanned. She and the other children, both black and white, became upset about the possibility that the color was permanent. Black children who cut or scraped themselves were worried about scar tissue that would be a different color.

Being black, white, yellow, red, or brown is part of one's identity. In some societies, especially in American society, skin color has significant social meanings. How children will deal with anxiety about racial differences and how they will integrate them will depend on the responses of significant adults. The values that adults place on a particular skin color will be communicated to children and contribute to their confusion about what is good and bad. What may appear to be expressions of prejudice among prelatency children are more likely to reflect lack of knowledge and understanding and identification with adults. If children are older when first confronted by racial differences, they will be able to think more logically and arrive at a judgment based more on fact than on irrational anxiety. They also will be more open to contamination by adult prejudices.

Although completely segregated communities still exist, children are unlikely to be isolated from the knowledge of racial differences for long because more nursery schools and day care facilities are integrated today and television is a strong influence in children's lives. Thus, at some point, they will try to understand. Young children of any race who deny or seem not to notice racial differences have usually identified with their parents' prejudices and are unconsciously aware that the subject is dangerous.

AT SIX

When children enter latency, they are slightly more than twice the size they were at birth and their physical proportions are similar to those of adults rather than infants. They have all their baby teeth and a few permanent teeth, and their nervous systems have developed sufficiently so that voluntary movements are under greater control.

At age 6, children seem quite grown up; they can talk, think, dress and undress themselves, draw, construct things, and sometimes are able to write. They are aware of their immediate neighborhood and have a sense of their place in it. They know their family name as well as their given name. Despite all these accomplishments, however, they are still extremely dependent on their parents. To cope with their inadequacies and problems, children this age rely on the mechanisms of denial, projection, incorporation, and isolation to limit their anxiety and master important social tasks and learning. Fantasy and play help them to work through inner conflicts as well as conflicts related to the outside world.

At this age and throughout the greater part of latency, children continue to express affects—especially anxiety, fear, and depression—predominantly through actions despite their increased vocabulary and verbal abilities. Repetitive behavior tends to be symptomatic of an internal or external danger, as filtered through the limited cognitive understanding of an individual child. Pre-latency and latency-age children simply do not have the complex language required to describe their feelings. Their relatively weak egos, limited coping ability, helplessness, and dependency converge to create dangers and worries. When they are in stressful situations, their behavior will say more than their words.

LATENCY

The achievements of latency are formidable. Between the ages of 6 and 12, there is growth of physical and intellectual abilities, expansion of interests, mastery of even wider and more diverse circles outside the home, and the growth of sexual and personal identity.

In latency, the egocentric thinking of the younger child is replaced by the orderly, logical processes that characterize secondary process thought. This enhances verbal ability, enables the synthesis of a variety of experiences, and the establishment of moral and ethical standards. Although physical activity remains an important means of expression, its predominance declines as verbal expression increases. The world becomes more comprehensible as children develop the ability to understand cause and effect. As talking becomes a major means of expression, the capacity to cope with more experiences becomes possible, impulses are more controllable, and conscience and morality are more reasonable.

The competitive games so typical of latency provide acceptable outlets for aggression. Playing and relations with peers foster competition but also help develop social competence and the ability to compromise (Sullivan, 1953). As physical skill increases, there is less dependence on others. This expansion of the child's world helps the child learn to differentiate between the inner psychological and egocentric world of early childhood and the external world of society.

Latency-age children who have successfully introjected parental values and love can be away from home for longer and longer intervals. Certain of parental approval and caring, they can move out to seek the approval of others by becoming more socialized and more in control of their own actions. The social approval that comes from doing, making, and completing bolsters their self-esteem. Playing enhances mastery by providing children with opportunities to think out and work through difficult experiences. As Erikson (1963) has pointed out, children achieve a sense of mastery through planning, sharing, meditating, doing things well, and being useful.

Identity is clarified during latency through the sexual role stereotypes provided by adults and enforced by peers. Because latency-age girls and boys engage in separate and different activities, they avoid sexual stimulation that they are ill-equipped to handle. It is in adolescence that the stereotypes, proscriptions, and distance between male and female are questioned and changed.

Too often we forget how much children accomplish between the beginning and end stages of latency. The following statements written by three siblings—Robbie, 7; Elizabeth, 10; and Dana, 14—illustrate the tremendous amount of growth that occurs. Robbie is the only boy in a family of five children; the statements of his two eldest sisters (Sue, 16, and Kathy, 18) are not included here. The children produced their statements at the request of their mother, who at the time was a graduate student in social work and was preparing a paper about siblings. She asked each child to describe the other siblings.

Robbie, age 7 (who printed on lined paper)

LIS	1	WHEN I CRY SHE TRIES TO CHEER ME UP AND SOMETIMES SHE YELLS AT ME.
DANA	2	WHEN I COME HOME *FROM* SCHOOL SHE YELLS AT ME SOMETIMES SHE DOESN'T
SUE	3	SHE PLAYS GAMES WITH ME.
KATHY	4	SHE LIKES TO TALK TO ME
TERRY	5	[The family dog]

Elizabeth, age 10

Sue gives me lots of imaginative ideas. She tells me a lot of things. But she also yells a lot. She gives me things that she had when she was my age and things I like too. Sometimes it takes a long time for Sue to do things because she always has to do something else first. And she compliments me a lot.

Dana never tells me much about her stuff. And she likes to play around with me sometimes. She's always sorry when she hurts me. But she yells at me sometimes when I do something she doesn't like. And she compliments me a lot.

Kathy always talks to me about things and I learn a lot from her but sometimes she makes me do something specially for her friend. She tells me about when I was little sometimes also when she was. And she compliments me a lot.

Robbie is my buddy and he likes to do things with me, but sometimes he gets grumpy and yells at me. He likes to do stuff for me and gives me things. And he says my stuff is better than his.

Dana, age 14

All my sisters, and my brother, have affected me a great deal. *Kathy*, 18, is someone I feel close to, although we are not with each other often. For the past few years she has been very busy with things in her own life. We can talk for a long time about a lot of things, or just joke around. I enjoy being with her. She's moody, and I am too. . . . Since she's been away from the family, we rarely fight. . . . When she lived with all of us, she'd get angry and take it out on everyone. But now that she is on her own, she's happier. I think she has made it easier for the rest of us to be more free. Now that my parents have raised one child, they . . . have a better idea of what . . . [the rest of us] want and should be allowed to do.

Sue is the sister I am closest to. In 4th grade, I began telling her things that happened each day. I needed someone older to confide in, and she was very understanding. She would tell me some things, too. This has continued through now, at a larger scale each year. We try to give each other advice when we need it, without forcing it. . . .

Elizabeth is someone who I watch a lot. I always think about what she is doing in her life, now, and compare it to my life when I was the same age. . . . She is a good person to be with when we are both in a funny mood. She. . . . is also very creative. She inspires me by showing me things she's made and showing me how to make them.

Often she gets impatient or frustrated and upset over things that don't really matter. I try to reason with her, and make her understand. I always want her to change these ways while she is still a child, before they get set in her. . . . She is the first child I have seen from the time she was a baby, and watched her grow. Now I'm doing that with Robbie too.

Robbie is someone I'd like to be closer to. Often I find myself yelling at him, and he tells me this. He is fun to be with, he has a lot of that child's innocence that I envy. When he's in a good mood, I can talk with him, play with him, ask him things. . . . He's very artistic, and I like to encourage him. The problem is, when he is in a bad mood. He's very stubborn and insists on getting his own way. Then it is impossible for me to communicate or feel close to him. He is happiest when people notice him and are with him. When they don't, he is bad, to get attention. This *frustrates* me and

> I am trying to learn how to. . . . control my *anger,* and be good to him, find other ways for him to be happy. Then, I think, he will get rid of some of his annoying tactics. Because he is often a very sweet and lovable person, and I want to help him bring this more out in the open.

Obviously, the culture of this family encourages verbal expression. Robbie is the most egocentric, yet he is competent in the use of language. Elizabeth, too, seems to relate to others primarily from a personal viewpoint. Dana, well into adolescence, exhibits greater conceptual and empathic ability and takes flight into abstract concepts of family life and altruistic concern for her siblings, especially the "children." It is Dana who clearly delineates the difference between 7- and 10-year-olds as she describes the activities of her brother and younger sister.

ADOLESCENCE

Dana and her older sisters illustrate the great changes that occur throughout adolescence. In fact, Sue and Kathy wrote so lengthily and philosophically that it was impossible to include their statements. Kathy, the eldest, expressed the greatest abstractions, idealism, and view of her family from the outside, almost as though she was no longer a part of it. Indeed, she was in college and was far less dependent on her family than were her siblings.

Blos (1967) calls adolescence the second stage of separation-individuation, the period when children finally separate from and shed their dependence on the family and become members of the adult community. This is also the time when a new sense of identity is established. Adolescence is a social term for the period of transition between childhood and the responsibilities of adulthood. In some societies and socioeconomic and cultural groups, adolescence is relatively brief. In others, schooling prolongs the time allowed before an individual must assume adult responsibilities. Erikson (1968) has suggested that the tasks of adolescence include consolidating one's identity and learning to establish intimate and meaningful relations with others. Children who have doubts about their ethnic and sexual identity or are confused about their roles have difficulty consolidating their identity during adolescence. And intimacy becomes possible only when identity is established.

During this second separation-individuation process, disengagement from parents is aided by the adolescent's emphasis on peers and the peer group. Often, the group serves as the adolescent's security blanket during the separation process. New loyalties, ideas, fads, and shifting allegiances and interests are the revolutionary aspects of adolescence.

Puberty

The terms adolescence and puberty are not synonymous. Puberty refers to the physical growth and sexual maturation that take place during adolescence, while the term adolescence is used for the social and psychological processes that take place during the teens.

The onset of menstruation in girls and the capacity for ejaculation in boys mark the beginning of biological maturity and the capacity to propagate the species. The hormonal disturbances of prepuberty initiate a process of change that will continue for several years. Sexual capacities are accompanied by growth of secondary sex characteristics and alterations in the body's form and size. At the end of puberty, the child is physically an adult.

Crisis of Adolescence

The tasks of adolescence include physical, social, and psychological restructuring. Anna Freud (1936) stated that in adolescence, a strong id confronts a relatively weak ego, and the alternating regression and progression, introversion and extroversion, activity and passivity that result explain the rapid shifts in mood that are typical of this stage of development.

New cognitive abilities are a significant source of strength when working through the problems of adolescence. Piaget and Inhelder (1969) have categorized the period as one of formal operations. Now the child is prepared to think more logically and use propositional statements and hypotheses. Thinking is more abstract and conceptual, no longer bound by concrete objects. These propositional operations are the result of the ability to manipulate language more precisely, which permits the child to abstract concepts from reality and use them imaginatively to solve real problems and prepare for future events. In addition, there is a spontaneous development of an experimental spirit that fosters play with ideas and an interest in ideals and ideologies.

Adolescents are known for their astheticism, idealism, and adoration of leaders and certain other adults. Anna Freud (1936) highlighted the problems of restricted adolescents who, fearful of change, inhibit their experimentation and thus prevent the expansion of self and capacities. Other adolescents suffer because their impulses overpower the ego, which leads to impulsive, delinquent acting out. In either situation, maturity is not achieved.

Adolescence is a long period of change. During early adolescence, children are extremely changeable and often regress to earlier stages. Between the ages of 15 and 18, however, they experiment more, widen their identifications and attachments, and deepen their emotional and interpersonal lives. In late adolescence, when college or work is the issue, they are more socially involved than ever before and are capable of developing relatively mature love relationships.

The deviance, immaturities, and emotional disturbances often associated with adolescence are always significantly related either to developmental failures or to the lack of appropriate opportunities within the social milieu. Normally, latency provides the foundation for the acquisition of skills, intellectual growth, expansion of the universe, development of ego strengths, formation of character, and the learning of parental expectations, prohibitions, and rewards as reinforced by the culture. In other words, satisfactory growth during latency contributes to satisfactory growth during adolescence and ultimately to a mature adult who contributes to society.

Chapter 2

CHILDREN AND THEIR SITUATION

To understand the child in situation, the social worker must explore with the child and significant others how each perceives the child's problems, situation, and needs. Obviously, the first step in understanding the child's situation is to understand the family, but this is not enough. Normally, the lives of latency-age children include the school, peers, community, culture, and society, any of which may be a source of difficulty for children and their families, independently of individual or family problems. More often than not, there is mutual interaction among all these factors.

THE FAMILY

No child can exist without its own or a surrogate family. Even in group residences and institutions for children, the staff usually attempts to simulate a family group, small enough to enable intimate personal relationships. As Bene-

dek (1970) pointed out, the family is a child's most important psychological field: it is a haven, a source of
attachments, a source of identity and identification.

Child-rearing is only one of the family's functions. For
all age groups, from birth to death, the family unit is responsible for providing basic necessities such as food and
clothing, structuring patterns of love, friendship, and affection, meeting basic psychological needs, and imparting a
sense of worth and dignity. The family also transmits culture and values, and each has its own patterns, goals, ways
of interacting, and fulfilling its functions. And each has its
own mythology: an aggregate of conscious and unconscious fantasies and beliefs about human nature and human
relationships that are transmitted through a chain of generations. This mythology is neither false or true; it represents
an individual family's version of reality (San Martino &
Newman, 1975). The latency-age child's language and beliefs will reflect the family patterns, and much of the child's
behavior will be adaptive to these external influences,
which include cultural sanctions and prohibitions (Johnson
& Giffen, 1957).

Parents

All roads lead to parents. Recognized as essential to a
child's optimal development, parents are also held responsible for the child's deviation. In discussions of normal and
pathological child development, it appears that parents
should be perfect, that is, be able to anticipate and meet all
their children's needs; only bad parents have children with
problems. This is a childish view. Not until adolescence do
children accept the fact that their parents are imperfect,
and only mature adults realize that their parents are human.

All professionals, including social workers, were once
children: they too once believed that their parents were

omnipotent and perfect, and they too were eventually disillusioned. Intellectually, social workers understand that parents are human, but when they become advocates for children, they often forget this, regress to the magic wishes of childhood, and become angry at parents who are imperfect.

Parents too were once children. In their pasts are the vicissitudes and problems of childhood, many of which persist, unresolved, into adulthood. Often, parents have problems that are similar to their children's problems: e.g., they suffer from phobias, psychosomatic disturbances, depression, and interpersonal difficulties such as loneliness and despair. Parents too suffer from neglect, abuse, and lack of understanding.

Siblings

Siblings are an important aspect of family dynamics and support. In most families, older children act as baby-sitters. In large families and in those where there is a considerable difference in age between siblings, the older ones play an even more important role: that of helping their parents raise the younger children whether or not their parents actually assign this role to them (Essman, 1977).

Fraternal solidarity is an important support for children whose parents have died or for those who are placed in foster care or are adopted during latency. Siblings are family and part of the roots of identity; they insure a sense of belonging to someone.

In disorganized families, siblings play many roles for each other (Minuchin et al., 1967). They provide reflected self-appraisals and assist in the crucial development of identity. They can form a defensive group against outsiders and be both socializers and interpreters of the outside world. Siblings also exert pressure on one another to conform to family or community norms. Whether they keep secrets or tattle on each other, they are intricately involved in the family dynamics (Bank & Kahn 1976). When one sibling is physically ill, emotionally disturbed, or retarded, for example, the other siblings' self-images and feelings about the future are disturbed. Loss of a sibling through foster placement or death creates myriad problems for the others.

Extended Family

Limiting the discussion to the immediate family excludes an important source of support that is potentially available to parents and children. The extended, multigenerational family is not uncommon. In some situations, several generations live together; in others, grandparents, aunts, uncles, and cousins live in the community. For all families, the parents' relations with their own parents are important (Ackerman, Papp, & Prosky, 1970).

Many cultural traditions foster the extended family. In segregated minority groups such as Chicanos, Puerto Ricans, and blacks, the extended family is a source of help, and mutual obligations exist between generations (Mizio, 1974; Temple-Truillo, 1974; Billingsley, 1969). In addition, there may be a network of other relationships, not necessarily of blood ties, many of which are long-standing and have a deep emotional impact. Self-help among neighbors and a sense of community may offer more support than outsiders realize. In recounting the destruction by flood of Buffalo Creek, an old Appalachian mining community, Kai Erikson (1976) describes the individual and collective trauma that occurred when neighbors lost neighbors, and temporary housing did not consider community ties, old neighbors, and family groups. When the survivors found that their community no longer existed as a source of support, an important part of the self disappeared. Many lapsed into apathy and helplessness when they realized that they were isolated, alone, and completely dependent on their own resources.

FAMILY PROBLEMS

Because the family is a complicated system, the problems of individual members and problems between members will offset the developing child. Frequently, the family system is so disturbed that the child's environment is tenuous or even dangerous.

Separation and Divorce

When parents separate, the event is usually the culmination of a prolonged period of disharmony. In any case, the child loses the daily presence of a significant person. If the parents have involved the child in their battles, the child may feel responsible for the breakup (Lewis, 1974). During custody battles, children feel insecure about the future. Often these children become "yo-yo" children, shuttled from one parent to the other (J. G. Moore, 1975). In familys headed by unwed mothers, the real father or an informal stepfather may be a significant part of the family's life. If he leaves, the child not only experiences the same sense of loss that the child of legally separated or divorced parents does but has fewer legal rights (see the case of Tomaso in Chapter 8).

Although children will experience a sense of loss and even abandonment, especially when they have no contact with the parent who leaves, it is not uncommon for them to be angry at the parent who stays, blaming her or him for failing to hold on to the other.

The findings of a study of children with divorced parents indicated that how well children will cope with divorce depends on their age (Kelly & Wallerstein, 1976; Wallerstein & Kelly, 1976). The preschool child feels responsible when the parent leaves and attempts to cope by denial and fantasy, tenaciously clinging to the idea that the parent will return. Seven-and 8-year-olds will respond with shock and denial, reactions that resemble those that occur when a parent dies. Initially, these children are sad, tearful, afraid, and preoccupied with the loss and the wish for reconciliation. They may express these reactions affectively and symptomatically rather than verbally. Feeling deprived and worrying about future deprivation, they may be greedy for food and for things. Despite previous conflict and even violence in the home, few will be pleased by the separation. Although they may express anger more easily at the mother than the father, they may displace this anger onto teachers, friends, and siblings if they are afraid of antagonizing the mother. Children of this age do not want to choose between parents, and they try to remain loyal to both. As in mourning, eventually they become resigned to the loss, but their hopes for a reconciliation tend to persist for a long time because, unlike the final loss of a parent through death, the parent is always out there somewhere.

Older latency-age children have a greater capacity to grasp and integrate the meaning of divorce. Although they too experience feelings of loss, rejection, and helplessness, they have more resources to fight these painful feelings. Often they will deny feeling sad by adopting an air of bravado and plunging into activities outside the home. But because they have a better sense of the future than do younger children, they are more sensitive to the disturbances in the family structure and in their own identities. Thus they often feel ashamed, hurt and humiliated, which in turn may cause them to lie about the divorce to others. They may be angry at the parent who initiated the separation, despite provocations of which they may be aware. Or they may be angry at both parents for excluding them from their considerations. Although older children also fear abandonment, their fears tend to be more realistic: e.g., they may worry about an upset or emotionally disturbed parent. A variety of somatic symptoms of tension may be accompanied by a decline in school work, aggressive behavior, or a precocious thrust into adolescent activities.

In other words, divorce is a crisis that disturbs the equilibrium of the entire family. Thus intervention in preparation for the breakup and help afterwards seems indicated.

Multiproblem Families

Poor families tend to be viewed as multiproblem families. It is true that the majority of multiproblem families are poor, but all poor people do not automatically fall into this category. All multiproblem families are not members of minority groups, nor are the majority of black families fatherless. These are stereotypes (Herzog & Lewis, 1970; Herzog & Sudin, 1969).

Although poverty makes life inordinately difficult, it alone does not explain human difficulties. Some poor people are apathetic, some are militant, some are ill, and some are mature enough to manage despite overwhelming odds (National Institute of Child Health and Human Development, 1968).

Parents who seem apathetic often have high aspirations for their children but little hope that these aspirations can be attained. The absence of a father is only one among many interacting variables that affect multiproblem families. The evil of stereotyping is that an entire category of the population, children and parents, are classified as multiproblem and incurable. In addition, far too many multiproblem families must contend with a multiproblem, fragmented system of service delivery (Selig, 1976).

When the family has innumerable social and personal problems, its functioning is disturbed, and its members are constantly involved in social crises, the label multiproblem family, though pertinent, is not especially helpful. The lives of adult members tend to be fragmented, with few unifying principles to guide goals and standards. Ego defects, impulsive acting out, and an inability to tolerate tension are common. These helpless, hopeless clients are frequently diagnosed as character disorders. Afraid to form close relationships, they are difficult to engage in a therapeutic relationship and are perceived as resistant to intervention (Reiner & Kaufman, 1959). Often, they are the parents of severely disturbed children. Because of early emotional deprivation and loss, these clients act in such an infantile manner that the professional will often react with disgust and communicate to them that they should stop acting like the babies they are (Lieberman & Gottesfeld, 1973).

Children in such families also tend to be impulsive (Malone, 1966). Acting out of impulses is a way of life for them and their families, and their actions speak louder than words. Yet these children have few pleasures and little sustained interest in anything. Often they seem to be searching for reliable contacts; they are oriented to external pressures and understand the wishes of others but are unaware of their own feelings and lack inner controls. These children are not withdrawn; they constantly look to others for attention. Like their parents, they suffer from developmental delays and immaturities (Malone, 1966).

Child Neglect and Abuse

Many parents who neglect or abuse their children are the products of generations of neglect and abuse (Fraiburg, Adelson, & Shapiro, 1975). Emotionally starved and brutalized, they repress their rage and despair as well as hope. Though they may remember the abuse, tyranny, and desertion in their own childhoods, they cannot remember the affect that accompanied these events. Thus they reenact their experiences over and over again with their own children, unable to give what was lacking in their own lives. These parents are caught in a vicious circle of apathy and futility (Polansky, Borgman, & Sax, 1972).

Although the children of multiproblem families are often neglected and abused, the problem is not peculiar to such families. Brutalization, neglect, and sexual abuse of children occurs in all income groups, but poor families tend to be reported to legal authorities more frequently because they use emergency clinics and public social service organizations more often (Newberger, 1977). Families with higher incomes usually go to private physicians, who tend to deny that their patients would act in such a manner. Other professionals, including social workers, are often reluctant to breach the confidentiality of the client-worker relationship by reporting these families to legal authorities.

Children under the age of 4 are most vulnerable to severe abuse, but a significant number of abused children are latency age or even adolescent. It is extremely difficult to determine what abuse is because the definitions of neglect and abuse vary according to the focus of the profession (usually, medicine, law, or social work) that does the defining. Most social workers view the following as indicators of child abuse or neglect: physical, sexual, and psychological abuse; emotional deprivation; inadequate care because of parental incapacity or lack of resources: and societal abuse (Kamerman & Kahn, 1976). Child abuse is rarely an isolated instance; it is usually repetitive and is accompanied by chronic neglect.

The term neglect is applied to a wide range of concrete physical and emotional needs, including supervision, nurturance, and protection. Child abuse focuses on nonaccidental injuries that are the result of acts of commission or omission and require medical or legal intervention (National Institute of Mental Health, 1977).

Cultural and socioeconomic differences in child-rearing, including differing beliefs about the nature and use of physical punishment, often compound the difficulties of diagnosing abuse. Because a variety of psychological difficulties and situational factors contribute to child abuse, it is difficult to categorize parents who abuse their children. Excessive stress (in the parent's view), social isolation, and ideation about the child's potential for evil seem to be important contributing factors. Often the parent is ignorant of the parental role, lacks empathy for the child, and perceives the child as a miniature adult, even when an infant. Because of their own dependency needs, some parents are incapable of caring for dependent children; others cannot tolerate their children's moves toward independence. Often, the children are unwanted or are viewed as competitors, as bad or seductive, or are identified with other hated and feared individuals. Other abusive parents, rather than feeling indifferent about their children, overidentify with them and repeat with them their own childhood experiences. Despite the disruption, loss, and abuse in their own lives, many abused and abusing parents are engaged in an intense, never ending effort to obtain from their own parents the approval and nurturance they never received as children. Similar behavior is often seen in children. Although no one abusive parent has all these characteristics, all suffer from a lack of self-esteem, social isolation, minimal relationships, and a sense of overwhelming stress.

Justice and Justice (1976) suggest that child abuse is the end result of a system of interactions involving husband and wife, parent and child, child and environment, parent and environment, and parent and society. This view emphasizes the family system and related systems rather than one individual: i.e., both parents are involved, no matter who does the actual abusing. Symbiotically entwined, they compete to be taken care of. Since neither can meet the other's needs, each perceives the child as the immediate source of external stress and thus as an available target. Essentially, these are fused, undifferentiated families.

In families where abuse has not actually occurred, a parent may express an overwhelming fear that he or she could hurt the child. A mother may have persistent fears, fantasies, and daydreams about hurting and killing a child even before it is born. If her fears are dismissed, they increase and so does the possibility of abuse. Often a parent's rage toward a child camouflages anger at the spouse. Such a parent must be helped to understand the underlying reasons for this emotion. If parents seem preoccupied with others who abuse children, one is entitled to wonder whether they are potential abusers themselves. This is also true of parents who believe in severe and disproportionate punishment for children (Wolkenstein, 1977).

Gil(1975) focuses on society, which condones corporal punishment of children by refusing to accord children equal rights with adults. Goode (1971) has suggested that parental rights and obligations and family patterns of force are backed by state, community, and neighbors. Parents who use force teach force and socialize their children as they were socialized. Child abuse is merely an extension of the violence in society. Furthermore, because children are dependent on and smaller and weaker than their parents, force is not synonymous with overt physical abuse.

Violent husbands and battered wives are often seen in social agencies. Marriages that contain victims and assailants are not unusual; sometimes the violence is sexual and psychological rather than physical. Often the victim is unwilling to give up the marriage, partly because of a lack of resources, community pressure, low self-esteem, masochism, or a personal history of abuse and neglect. The abuser tends to be impulsive and sensitive to slights and ridicule, feels inadequate, and usually was subjected to physical abuse as a child. Like child abusers, wife abusers and their wives usually have suffered frequent losses, are socially isolated, and when the abuse occurs are experiencing severe stress.

Children who observe violence between their parents are abused (Lystad, 1975). They usually have many physical and social problems and become pawns or mediators in the fights between parents (J. G. Moore, 1975). Often they turn the violence against themselves. Few studies have been done on the effects of child abuse on children, and little direct therapeutic work has been done with abused children to undo their trauma. Instead, remediation usually focuses on the parents, and the children are removed from the home temporarily or permanently. In foster placement, these children seem to provoke rejection and punishment, which results in multiple placements. It is as though they accept their parents' negative view and treatment of them.

Although the prevalence of sexual abuse of children is unknown, it occurs more frequently than is generally believed, not only in parental homes but in foster homes. According to Rosenfeld et al. (1977), sexual abuse of children by adults ranges from seductiveness and overstimulation to overt sex play and incest. Girls seem to be the target of sexual abuse more often than boys. Sometimes the child is petted, fondled in unusual ways, or encouraged to participate in mutual masturbation. Although latency-age children sometimes engage in sex play with peers, sex play with an adult is far more disturbing to the child because it blurs the boundaries between generations and is more stimulating. Usually, the child knows the adult involved and therefore may equate the activity with loving and caring and enjoys the feelings it arouses (Schultz, 1973; Brant & Tisza, 1977). When the adult is the child's father or stepfather, everyone in the family, especially the mother, is aware of the situation, but it becomes a family secret, a collusion. Members of these families often have intense relationships with each other and few outside social contacts.

Incest and sexual abuse are not restricted to lower

class families (Giarretto, 1976). They can occur in any family where the parents are having marital difficulties. Although the entire family is involved, the abused child becomes the family scapegoat, feels guilty, and is punished if the law becomes involved and the child is removed from the home.

Children have difficulty talking about sexual abuse because they are afraid of the adult involved and feel guilty about their own participation. Frequently, they do not comprehend what has happened until they reach adolescence or even adulthood. This new knowledge then interacts with other problems to disturb the personality. For example, in treatment many adult women with a variety of sexual and emotional problems begin talking about incidents of childhood sexual abuse for the first time.

Foster Care

Neglect and abuse are among the reasons that children are placed in foster care. Other reasons include the mother's physical or mental illness; the child's unmanageable behavior; parental desertion or death; the mother's unwillingness or inability to care for her children; and family dysfunction (Fanshel & Shinn, 1972).

Children in foster care have many emotional, physical, and intellectual disabilities. Few enter the system without emotional scars. They are as much in need of therapeutic services as are disturbed children who are placed in residential treatment. Separation from home is a serious threat to any child's emotional stability, and few children participate actively in the decision. These facts alone mean that they must be prepared for the experience and helped to work it through. Although children's reactions to separation will be conditioned by previous experiences, it is extremely important for them to understand what is happening.

Few children wish to leave home, regardless of how bad the home may seem to professionals. The child feels helpless and abandoned, which is often a realistic perception. Preschool children may feel that they will never be cared for; latency-age children may believe they are being punished for bad thoughts or behavior. Anxiety about their angry feelings will lead to denial, repression, and idealization of the parents. However, they will demonstrate their hidden feelings by their behavior. Feeling rejected and punished by their own parents and expecting to be rejected and punished by the foster parents, they may precipitate actual rejection and punishment (Rochlin, 1961; Littner, 1956).

Too often, these children are expected to establish a relationship with the new parents before they have grieved for the loss of the old. Many have experienced other unresolved losses. Repression of affect and an inability to grieve and protest will disturb any child's ability to develop normally.

A foster-child syndrome resulting from long-term placement can be carried into adulthood (Murphy, 1974). As adults, some foster children fear that society will hurt them, and they harbor a hidden wish to hurt back. This may be accompanied by excessive concern with self-control, which will lead to constriction of personality and expression. A precipitous desire for marriage and a family will be accompanied by a low tolerance for the demands involved. Because these individuals search constantly for someone who will meet their own unmet childish needs, they will compete with their own children for attention. Too often, they become the parents of children in foster care, as did their own parents before them.

Regular visits are extremely important for both child and parent. If the family can be helped and if all parties cooperate, the child may experience a new, more protected situation. In addition, frequent visiting expedites a child's early return home (Fanshel & Shinn, 1977). Most natural parents do not want to sever ties with their children; many feel guilty about their inability to care for their children and most want their children to have more than they had (Jenkins & Norman, 1972). Mothers of children in foster care sometimes feel stigmatized by the placement because of the parental problems that made the placement necessary. These problems, compounded by agency practices that often cater to the needs of foster parents at the expense of the needs of natural parents, frequently act as a deterrent to visiting (Jenkins & Norman, 1975).

Foster parents do not have an easy job. They must relate not only to the child, the agency, and its changing workers but to the natural parents, who may be difficult, disturbed, and inconsiderate. The natural parents threaten the foster parents' status; often after they visit the child's behavior deteriorates. Although the child's behavior does indeed become worse, the reason is that the visits bring back painful feelings. But it is better for the child to feel and work through than to make-believe. As Perlman (1977) points out: "Children carry their absent parents alive within them, and they may fiercely fight or stonily resist being loved too much too soon by strangers (p. 137)." Parents represent a child's roots and identity, and the tenacity with which children identify with and idealize even extremely bad parents may disturb the foster parents or other adults who work with them. But one should always remember that in children's eyes, those who devalue or criticize their parents are also devaluing and criticizing them. It takes time and trust before children can relate to foster parents.

Some children are torn between their foster parents and natural parents and are afraid to make a commitment to either. How well the child will adjust will depend on the degree of agreement that exists among parents, foster parents, foster siblings, social workers, and foster child. The greater the disagreement, the greater the child's conflict (Gottesfeld, 1970).

Too often, children are placed in foster care without sufficient preparation, or the placement reflects the needs of the foster parents or agency rather than the child's needs. In addition, a turnover of workers or foster homes merely exacerbates the child's feelings of helplessness and rootlessness (Krugman, 1971; Appelberg, 1969). Sometimes the only constant in the child's life is an abstraction called the agency.

Entire families are upset when one or all the children are placed. If the siblings are placed together, their interactions may be so troubling that they are separated. If some remain at home, they may feel ambivalent and guilty. If the child who leaves dominated much of the parents' time or was hostile and disruptive, the other children may be glad, but simultaneously worried—after all, if one sibling can be taken away, why not the others (Shugart, 1958).

Foster children are special children: they are given a special label and are subjected to special expectations. Long-term placement usually means that their future will be no better than the present because, unlike other children, they can lose the foster family when they come of age, leave school, or become economically independent.

> *John*, age 18, had been in foster care since the age of 2, when his mother abandoned him in a taxi. He remained with one foster family until he was 8, when the foster mother died of cancer. Because he was unable to relate to his new foster parents, he was placed in two different homes within a year. Therapy was not recommended for him until he was 14, when his foster parents complained about his disobedience.
>
> Throughout the years, John's natural mother, father, and grandparents—all of whom lived separately—seldom visited him. Each promised that he could live with them but never fulfilled that promise. John was unable to accept the reality that his family would never take him back.
>
> At 18, John was obedient, quiet, careful, and had few

friends. Because he attended college and worked part-time, he had little time for relaxation and was not doing well in school. Thus he faced not only possible dismissal from school but the loss of his foster home because of his age.

John suffered many losses too early; rejection by his own family and the death of his first foster mother were serious disturbances in his situation. And his current insecurities threatened to upset his already restricted ability to adapt.

FAMILY CRISIS

Children such as John, who endure many crises in their lives, find separation, loss, and severe disturbances in their life patterns difficult to endure. Whenever the fabric of life is threatened, both adult and child experience a serious crisis. During a crisis, individuals discover that they must find completely new ways of coping. A crisis triggered by an actual loss may cause unbearable tension and feelings of helplessness. Anyone would recoil from these feelings, and many individuals cope initially through withdrawal and denial (Rapoport, 1965). Although death and serious illness are normal events in life, they are more traumatic for some persons than others.

Death

When John's foster mother died, his old feelings of separation and abandonment must have been intensified because death reactivates old losses. Death, after all, is but another form of separation, albeit irreversible and final (Lindemann, 1965). Death is difficult for an 8-year-old to comprehend because it is a highly abstract concept—one that challenges the comprehension of most adults. Younger children sometimes believe that if properly cared for, a dead person will come back to life. It is only as children experience the death of pets or relatives, develop a clearer sense of time, and are able to handle abstractions that they gradually begin to understand the irreversibility of death.

The task of mourning is to integrate the loss that occurs in death. This takes time; tolerance for powerful and painful affects must be developed and the reality of the loss must be tested when the natural desire is to deny it. Only when this work is done will an individual be able to reinvest feelings in others. But intense feelings are difficult for children to tolerate. Young children tend to deny both the reality of death and the emotions it evokes. Their reactions resemble those observed in pathological mourning. They also try to keep alive the relationship with the dead person. Latency-age children may not seem sad when a parent dies and may, in fact, remain active. Yet they unconsciously deny the death and expect the parent to return. They also tend to glorify and idealize the parent, even in adulthood. But anger at the death and past disagreements with the dead parent surface and are displaced onto the surviving parent or parent substitute. Some children assume the characteristics and even the responsibilities of the lost parent. Although this may enrich their personalities, continued idealization tends to reduce their self-esteem and increase their guilt about former transgressions and bad thoughts about this "perfect parent" (J. B. M. Miller, 1971).

Children need an adult who will listen and talk to them, help them clarify their ideas, and gently sort out their fantasies. They need someone who will answer their questions, understand their feelings, and reassure them about the future. This is difficult for the surviving parent to do. At these times, a close relative or a social worker can help these children.

In a mistaken effort to protect children, adults often exclude them from funeral rites, talk to them about death in a religious or philosophical way, or tell them magical stories. This only increases a child's own confusing fantasies. Children need concrete explanations of what has happened. By participating in funeral services and religious or cultural customs of mourning, children can share their grief with others, see that grief can be tolerated, and learn to tolerate their own (Furman, 1974).

Some families attempt to keep the death a secret, fearing that the children will be overwhelmed. This becomes a dysfunctional secret that isolates the children. Because of the covert family agreement to deny what is known, the children must resort to make-believe too (Evans, 1976). Families can have secrets about many things: illness, the behavior of a parent or relative, as well as death. As a result, children may become preoccupied with disease and death or feel insecure if they cannot trust what they see and hear because no one else will acknowledge it.

Latency-age children try to defend themselves against the pain of mourning. But if mourning is delayed it often leads to depression and even suicide in adulthood, especially on the anniversary of a parent's death (Schowalter, 1975). Yet children cannot be forced to mourn or accept what they are not ready to accept. All that can be done is to establish a climate of trust and honesty so that when they are, a trusted adult will be available to clarify questions and confusion.

When a parent dies, a child loses more than the parent. There are many accompanying stresses, which affect family stability and involve economics, housing, and even separation from the surviving parent. The child's future is threatened in reality and all of life may change. In this sense, a parent's death is always untimely unless the child is an adult.

The death of a sibling, too, is untimely. If this is a result of illness, there may be time to anticipate the death, mourn beforehand, and talk about the process. But if the sibling dies suddenly, all the old ambivalence is aroused. Surviving children may feel guilty, show marked changes in behavior, develop somatic complaints that are similar to the dead child's, or be preoccupied with physical damage, accidents, and rescue. They may overidealize the dead brother or sister (Blinder, 1972) or believe they were responsible for the death because they were careless or had hostile thoughts.

The untimely death of a child is also a crisis for parents. All deaths out of normal sequence throw off the inner timetable of expectations (Weisman, 1973). The death of a child is an excruciating event for parents because they must work through the question: What did I do wrong? The death of a spouse creates innumerable problems of management. If the father dies, the mother may be forced to work or ask for public assistance; if the mother dies, the father may have difficulty finding appropriate care for the children. The family may be dispersed and other changes may take place. Even if this does not happen the surviving parent needs to withdraw emotionally from others for a time to deal with emotional needs. Parents as well as children often use denial, which gives them time to assimilate painful facts.

Illness

It is unnatural for children to have a fatal illness. Confronted with this possibility, parents may be unable to accept or admit initially that death is a possibility. If the illness progresses slowly, there will be time for everyone to come to terms with bitter grief. Siblings will need to help care for the dying child, and even the ill child must be allowed to participate, understand as much as possible, and accept some of the realities of the illness. If family members and medical staff pretend or indulge in make-believe, the ill child will sense the undercurrents of grief and concern. Appropriate professional help to work out these problems and support from relatives and friends may reduce the despair and helplessness of both family and patient (Futterman & Hoffman, 1970).

Illness involves myriad physical, financial, and emotional problems. Hospitalized children face separation from home, pain, frightening medical procedures, and, often, future consequences. Specific problems accompany different illnesses, and the social worker must be familiar with these problems if he or she is to assist the child and family. Some illnesses result in death before adulthood; other require special appliances, diets, school arrangements, limited physical activity, or isolation (Travis, 1976).

Families of sick children feel angry, guilty, and grief-stricken and may resort to magical beliefs to keep hope alive. Chronic grief and sorrow are part of the fabric of life for parents of chronically or seriously ill children.

Long-term illness creates burdens for the entire family. Interruption of sleep, financial problems, special housing needs, medical crises, and other difficulties disturb the family's life-style. A mother may be overinvolved with the sick child, the father may feel left out, and communication between the parents may become so painful that they avoid each other. The parents will feel guilty if the disease or disability has been transmitted genetically, and in all cases they will wonder how they failed. Siblings may worry about their own future, act as though nothing is different, or be overprotective. Unless some of their questions are answered, the siblings may feel abnormal.

The sick child's reactions will depend not only on environmental supports but the severity or noticeability of the disease, and the child's age and developmental capacity. The preschool child may perceive mobility as punishment. The school-age child may miss school, former activities, and friends. All children need help in handling their denial, regression, depression, and underlying anger.

Young children often perceive hospitalization as abandonment unless their mothers are allowed to stay with them constantly (more and more hospitals permit this). The latency-age child who is put in a crib or a bed with sides is disturbed about being treated like a baby again. Surgery threatens a child's body image and sense of intactness. The young child will perceive anesthesia as an attack or smothering; the older child will feel out of control. Even a simple operation such as a tonsillectomy will awaken strange fears of losing sexual organs (Jessner, Bloom, & Waldfogel, 1952).

It is helpful if adults, especially parents, can deal calmly and clearly with the events, prepare children with the doctor's assistance by explaining all the procedures, possible feelings, and the expected results clearly and concretely. It is extremely important to clarify physical aspects such as pain or loss of function because these will be the most frightening. Temporary symptoms and regression are not unusual before or after an operation.

Latency-age children often accept surgery with a deceptive stoicism that adults sometimes misconstrue as maturity and understanding. But repression of affect is a common coping mechanism of children who are confronted with imminent physical assault. Thus explanations will be necessary before and after surgery so that the child can relive and work through the fear (W. T. Moore, 1975); if this is not done, the repressed affect will persist even into adulthood.

Serious illness or disability in a parent will disrupt family routines, interactions, roles, and often realities. Disabilities such as severe physical incapacity or mental illness may cause radical changes in the parent's personality. Marital relations may change as a result or already-existing difficulties may be intensified. The emotional and physical demands on the adults will affect the demands made on the children. Sometimes children will be expected to take on inappropriate roles. In any event, all family members will reflect the family's difficulties (Anthony, 1970).

The Family In Society

A family's transactions and methods of coping are only part of the child's context. The neighborhood, the school, the media, and the variety of other forces also impinge on the family and the child (Minuchin, 1970). The family is never static; it is continually involved in a series of transactions and reciprocal relationships with other systems. Just as the child is only one individual within the family, so the family is only one system in a series of systems. As a subculture of the larger society, the family is affected by the political decisions, economic policies, and attitudes about different socioeconomic, ethnic, and racial groups that exist in that society (Anthony, 1975a). The frustrations that family members experience in relation to other systems affect how the family functions and interacts and exacerbates family tensions. As a result, it is not unusual for family members to react against one another rather than together against external strains.

Economic Pressures

Families are directly affected by the economic policies and opportunities of society. For example, lack of employment, or poorly paying employment limits what a family can provide for its children and creates tension in all family members. Conversely, when parents feel economically successful, their optimism will influence the child's sense of self and hopes for the future (Kagan, 1977).

According to the National Research Council (1976), 15.5 percent of American children live in families with incomes below the government-defined poverty level. But the federal government uses two definitions of poverty: "economy" poverty and "true" poverty. The economy poverty level is derived from a formula based on the amount of food required for subsistence, family size, and the consumer price index—i.e., this level barely sustains life. The true poverty level is based on the median income of families of a similar size: in other words, 50 percent of these families live at or below the poverty level.

In 1974 the true poverty level for a nonfarm family of four was $7,500, which was similar to the minimum income standard established by the Department of Labor (National Council of Organizations for Children and Youth, 1976). The economy poverty level, on the other hand was $5,038. (Most public assistance budgets are derived from the formula used to obtain the economy poverty level.)

The number of families living at or below the economy poverty level is increasing each year, and in many of these families, both parents work! Current welfare policies encourage fathers to leave their families, and even food stamp policies encourage working members to leave home because the family is better off economically without them (Blaydon & Stack, 1977).

The number of working mothers has increased radically, reflecting economic need and the structural and philosophic changes that are taking place in families. As a result, many children lack formal care after school because day care facilities are unavailable (National Research Council, 1976; Harris, 1977).

The lack of jobs in many localities has caused many families to leave their extended families and customary social networks. In addition, many families continue to emigrate to the United States in the traditional quest for opportunity and advancement. All these families must adapt to new customs and social groups. Whether these changes will precipitate a crisis may depend on a family's strengths and ability to make the necessary contacts. If a family or individual has already-existing problems, a move may exacerbate them. Some children, particularly preadolescents and young adolescents, find it difficult to enter new peer groups. Mothers of preschool children may miss former social and family supports and feel isolated and home-bound (Tooley, 1970). In areas where services are scarce, geographic uprooting can cause serious difficulties.

Changing Families

The sharp increase in geographic mobility over the past decades has severed relationships with the extended family and with racial, cultural, and ethnic groups that families traditionally have relied on for support. In addition, contemporary marriage seems to emphasize male-female relationships rather than family unit, parenting, and child care (Rossi, 1977). Thus another outstanding change on the American scene is the increase in divorce at all income levels. In 1975 one out of every six children under the age of 18 lived in a single-parent home, and more than one million children were involved in divorce. Fewer children are involved in remarriages, however, because the rate of remarriage among divorced women is far less than among divorced men and because more children remain with their mothers. Ninety percent of single parents are women—the result of the increase in divorce and the rise in out-of-wedlock births (National Research Council, 1976).

Women earn considerably less than men. As a result, a substantially larger and increasing proportion of families with incomes below the poverty line are headed by women. Single mothers under the age of 25 and those living in large cities have the lowest incomes. Black women predominate in this category.

Inadequate income is only one of many difficulties that separated, divorced, and unwed mothers face. Often, they have no help in carrying out family tasks that normally involve two adults. Many of their personal and social needs, including the need for affection and sexual gratification, are unmet except under difficult and temporary circumstances. Yet these solitary women, who are likely to be deprived emotionally, physically, and economically, are expected to meet their children's needs—and many of them do. Some, however, turn inappropriately to their children, not only for help with tasks in the home, but for emotional support (Glaser & Navaree, 1965).

Cultural and Societal Influences

In all societies, goals are achieved through culturally acquired behaviors. Culture consists of a system of beliefs, social forms, prescriptions for behavior, traditions, and rules for regulating communication among individuals of a particular racial, religious ethnic, or social group.

> [These rules] . . . are not universally or constantly obeyed, but they are recognized by all and they ordinarily operate to limit the range of variations in patterns of communication, belief, value and social behavior in . . . /a particular/ population. . . . From the viewpoint of the individual his sociocultural environment is made up of situations, roles and institutions that represent normative pressures on him for correct performance and also offer opportunities for personal expression and satisfaction (Le Vine, 1973, p. 4).

Different cultures have different views about children's psychological requirements, depending on their perceptions of the nature of children and what will assist growth. These perceptions are influenced by the larger society's view of the type of adult that is required. According to Erikson (1963), parents are the culture-bearers: their conscious and unconscious values will determine the child-rearing practices they will view as proper and healthy. The physical environment also influences this view to a significant degree. For example, Kagan (1976) studied the Eskimos of Hudson Bay and observed that because they are confined to a small living space nine months of the year, they must begin inhibiting their children's anger, hostility, and aggression in early infancy. Children's needs and developmental patterns cannot be separated from the environment in which children grow nor from the community's needs and the demands that the community will make on the child to become a useful adult member of society.

American social work's clients come from widely diverse cultures and physical environments, not only in the geographic sense but in the sense of rural versus urban areas and in the sense of individual family's living conditions, facilities for play, and so forth.

Despite these differences, all families are affected by the larger society to an increasing degree because many functions previously accepted as the function of the nuclear or extended family have become the responsibility of the state. Consequently, the expectations and values of the larger system and those of the family or subculture may not coincide. For instance, the American educational system's extreme emphasis on I.Q. and intellectual achievement reflects national concerns and values rather than individual and familial values and needs. The same can be said for negative views about certain ethnic and racial groups, which have created feelings of inferiority in a significant percentage of the population and have even elicited expected, devalued behavior (Goffman, 1963).

Although many studies have been done on the effects of culture on beliefs and customs, and child-rearing practices, these have not produced definitive information about the influence of culture on individual performance, values, and the like. Although some sexual differences may be culture-bound, many differences in male and female development are found in all cultures. These differences apparently reflect genetics as well as learning and social interaction (Neubauer, 1975; Maccoby & Jacklin, 1974). (For discussions about the problems involved in cross-cultural research, see Glick, 1975; Axelrod, 1969; and Ashton, 1975.) Studies on the effects of social or economic class have been hampered by similar difficulties. Studies of differences related to class frequently find that there are more dissimilarities among persons within the same class than there are among individuals from different classes. Comparisons of a variety of studies are invalid because of methodological and conceptual differences and because the variable under scrutiny does not remain static over time. For example, early studies of the relationship between child-rearing practices and socioeconomic class in the United States concluded that lower-class parents were more permissive concerning child-rearing practices than were middle and upper class parents. The recent results of studies, however, indicate that middle-class parents are more permissive (C. Deutsch, 1973).

There is little agreement among professional disciplines concerned with human personality, behavior, and development about the role of environment and culture in relation to individual behavior or about the process of human development. Even within each discipline, there are a variety of theoretical frameworks. Social work is not immune to these differences: "tensions exist, both among practitioners of various methods and among various individuals and schools of thought" (Keith-Lucas, 1971, p. 325). Over time, different segments of the profession differ in the emphasis that they place on the social environment. No group, however, denies the importance of society because social work is, by definition, work in society.

The biopsychosocial view of individual development seems to allow the greatest flexibility and permits consideration of all the variables that contribute to individual differences. Within this theoretical framework, the child's socialization depends not only on social models and reinforcements but on unconscious as well as conscious emotional interchange. Socialization is a cumulative process that begins at birth and involves incorporation into groups and relationships, transmission of cultural and social norms, individual capacities, and inherited constitution. This is the concept of an interactive process between person and society based on a genetic-cultural configuration of development, within which the person is an actor as well as one who is acted upon.

Children have biological and natural impulses, but specific cultures forbid and socialize against some of them. In the beginning, it is the mother and the small family unit that transmit the attitudes of the culture and the society. The family is the precursor of the larger world. The school then widens the child's social arena and is the forerunner of the adult social world. The ethogenic viewpoint suggests that, first, imagination or social "make-believe" prepares the child for social action and, second, social order is created and maintained by ceremonial means. Thus when children emerge from the family to the larger world of the school, they must discover those ceremonies and develop their own personal style of participating (Harre, 1974).

It has been said many times that a child is not a blank tablet on which culture and society write. All living things develop in a species-bound progression. In humans, this development includes physical growth, locomotion, thought, speech, memory, and other functions usually referred to as ego functions. Maturation is a constitutional characteristic—the unfolding of innate potential that is programmed into each individual at conception. The process of maturation is autonomous in the sense that it occurs independently of the environment, but environmental influences may halt or hamper the process (Hartmann, 1958). Social and psychological development also proceeds in a prescribed sequence but is brought into motion, elaborated on, and maintained or hampered by the environment.

II

CHILDREN AGES 6 TO 12

Chapter 3

EARLY LATENCY

Children ages 6 to 8 1/2 are more dependent and childlike than older latency children but more grown up and socialized and thus often more pleasant to be with than are younger children. Their abilities and skills seem to improve rapidly, and by age 8 1/2, new physical, mental, and psychological attributes are apparent. These developments contribute to the widely held impression that the latency-age child is relatively peaceful, industrious, and obedient, but this is a simplification of the actual situation.

GROWTH AND PHYSICAL DEVELOPMENT

Physical growth tends to be slow and relatively constant at this age and indeed throughout most of latency. There are individual differences, however; some children have a sudden spurt of growth between the ages of 6 and 8. Girls are generally more advanced from birth on in skeletal maturity and motor development than are boys, but boys tend to develop more and larger muscle cells than girls. In both sexes, the body's proportions change noticeably because the arms and legs grow faster than the trunk during this stage. Skeletal growth is usually matched by dental maturation: 6-year-olds can often be identified by their missing front teeth. During early latency, children show tendencies to be advanced, average, or retarded in their rates of general growth, which can be affected by racial, ecological, and psychological factors as well as by disease and heredity (Tanner, 1970).

Physiological maturation of the brain enables motility to be more purposeful. Most 6-year-olds can recognize another person's right or left. They can also throw a ball reasonably accurately but are unable to bat or catch it because eye-hand coordination, which depends on muscle development, comes later. For the same reason, their writing will not be smooth and they will be unable to scan a printed page. A sizable number of 5 1/2- to 7-year-olds, particularly boys, may not be ready for first grade, regardless of IQ and socioeconomic background, because of delayed physiological maturation and ego development, which go hand in hand (Hirsch, 1975).

GAMES CHILDREN PLAY

Learning to balance is fun at this age. Six- and 7-year-olds love to do hand stands, climb, skate, ride a bicycle. In fact, they rarely sit still for any length of time. It is as though early latency is a transitional phase from unrepressed, free motor expression to purposeful activity. Repetitive body movements such as foot and leg tapping and transitory symptoms such as nose picking, hair twisting, grimacing, stuttering, nail biting, and pencil chewing are common mechanisms for discharging tension in stressful situations.

At this age, motility is also channeled into rhythmic and repetitive games—skipping, jumping rope, swinging, hopping, running—usually accompanied by cadenced chants. Although these games provide practice in speaking and counting, permit the purposeful and refined use of muscles, and help develop relationships with peers, they also have competitive aspects. As Goldings (1974) pointed out, the words and motions are sensual and aggressive, but the sexual components are disguised, limited, and ritualized.

Many of these rhymes and games, unlike nursery tales, which are told to children by adults, have been transmitted orally for centuries from child to child (Opie & Opie, 1959). The persistence of this type of activity suggests the universality of childhood fantasies and wishes, which can be released safely in this way. Remember the rhyme "If you step on a crack, you'll break your mother's back" or "If you step on a crack you'll have bad luck"? How often do we see young children carefully avoiding cracks on the pavement? The following rhyme heard among children in the United States and Great Britain is a good exercise for distinguishing between left and right: "Left, left, I had a good home and I left/ Left, left, I had a good home and I left/ Left my wife and four fat babies, left 'em/ Right, right, right in the middle of the kitchen floor." Some readers may recall this simplified version: "Left, left, I left my wife and 48 kids/ Right, right, right in the middle of the kitchen floor."

Whereas 4- and 5-year-olds insist on having the same nursery rhymes repeated over and over again, children of 7 and 8 will parody these rhymes and popular songs, often using improper words in an innocent manner. They also like to express their aggression toward other children (and adults) by taunting and teasing. For example, a child will point up, and when the other person looks up say "Made you look, made you stare/ Made the barber cut your hair/ Cut it long, cut it short/ Cut it with a knife and fork." The following is another: "Georgie Porgie, pudding and pie/ Kissed the girls and made them cry/ When the girls came out to play/ Georgie Porgie ran away."

Many games children play—tag, hide-and-seek, guessing games—are equally traditional. These provide collective rules that enable the child to learn the ways and values of other children. Although this play is social, the child is still egocentric, still unable to understand the concepts of mutual responsibility, social responsibility, and group solidarity.

Symbolic play, or make-believe, is characteristic of children until they are about 8 years old. As early as age 2, children begin imitating adults and later shift to substitutes, such as a doll or teddy bear, and project their own actions and feelings onto these objects. Then they progress to objects such as blocks and sticks to represent whatever is needed for play. Eventually, these symbols may bear little resemblance to the objects they represent. This type of creative imagination helps children bring their unconscious fantasies into harmony with the external world (Galenson, 1971). Later, it helps them internalize actions that may represent genuine adaptations or solutions to problems (Piaget & Inhelder, 1969).

Unconscious mental experimentation precedes the actual action of play, and in this manner playing develops sublimation and mastery. Children also use play to master unpleasant, frightening, and realistic situations by repeating or simulating the danger. Thus they may pretend they are blind, crippled, stupid, or crazy (states they may have observed), make ugly faces, or play dead, often involving other children in the play. In this way, children actively reproduce a passively endured trauma to frighten others as they themselves have been frightened. As Arlow (1971) points out, children use such play to deny and defend against frightful possibilities: in other words, these possibilities can be controlled by being undone. Children commonly use disturbing parts of their lives and new life tasks as the basis for play. Although the play of an individual child will vary, it will show a continuity of themes. In the long run, play is a child's experimental research; with it, the child achieves understanding (Piaget, 1945; Erikson, 1972).

From symbolic or make-believe, children progress to play involving interactions and common rules that are accepted and promulgated by peers. Thus, by playing out social roles together, children learn society's version of reality and establish their own identity with those roles (Reilly, 1974). In Erikson's words (1972, p. 158), "play deals with settling the past and anticipating the future."

One developmental crisis that children must deal with is school—leaving the protection and familiar authority of the family for a less known, less intimate authority. When a child is ready to enter a group activity, even with only one or two other children, and is willing to cooperate and sustain an interest in play, the teacher game becomes a favorite (Ross, 1965). Children of various ages often play this game together. Perhaps an older sibling who already attends school will be the teacher while younger siblings and neighbors are the pupils. The young "teacher" may be authoritative and punitive or kind and gentle; a pupil may be a teacher's pet or a dunce. Once again, the older child transforms what is passively experienced into active mastery, while younger participants have the opportunity to act out or project their own hostility onto the symbol of authority. Thus release of tension and mastery of new demands can be achieved through the regression and progression offered by this type of game.

In early latency, children are extremely concerned about absolutes—about right and wrong, good and bad. Being good is synonymous with obedience to adults; being bad is synonymous with disobedience. The play of this period is the oedipal drama, but now the child enlists the support of peers in dealing with grownups and the new demands of the superego. Residues of an earlier period are evidenced in anal sublimations, in collections, bartering, and competition. Cheating and lying are only bad in relation to the degree of disobedience they represent. Traditional games with rigid rules provide external controls and helps resolve the oedipal conflict. Also, the competitive aspects of these games are less unpleasant than those observed in games younger children play (Peller, 1954).

The importance of make-believe continues throughout most of early latency. Although language skills improve, role playing only remotely resembles the actual activities of adults. Only at age 8 can children accurately reproduce adult roles in play; at that age, they are better able to distinguish between reality and make-believe. Indeed, as egocentric thinking declines and the child becomes better adapted socially, the amount of make-believe play declines. Symbolic imitation and representation become part of the thinking process, but the child's thinking is often inaccurate because of continued misperceptions and lack of knowledge (S. Millar, 1974).

Drawings and Stories

Children's drawings, more than the games they play and stories they tell, tend to reveal their inner preoccupations because drawings are less influenced by defenses. Drawing comes naturally to young children in all cultures, who will resort to sticks and dirt if pencils and paper are unavailable. Few cultures lack some form of representational or symbolic art associated with religious ceremony, charms, work, pleasure.

When the drawings of children in many cultures are compared, they reveal universal components and similar progressions (see, for example, Alschuler & Hattwick, 1967; Dileo, 1970). The first smears and scribbles are spontaneous expressions of feelings that cannot be put into words. The first drawing is always of a person. Even 3- and 4-year-olds will try to represent the human figure or will identify it in their scribblings. Because children tend to draw what they are most involved with or are experiencing, they begin with heads, add large eyes, and later include mouths, noses, and ears. Legs and arms grow directly from the head. (The trunk is not portrayed because its function is unfamiliar.) At age 5, they add the trunk and place the limbs relatively accurately. Although the addition of the trunk indicates a growing awareness of the lower body, genitalia are rarely depicted unless the child has had a physical problem or an operation in that area or someone in the environment focuses anxiety on that part of the body. Usually gender is portrayed symbolically by hair style, clothing, and other obvious accoutrements that differentiate the sexes in the child's culture.

Later houses, trees, vehicles, animals with human faces are added. These objects tend to be stylized: universal symbols such as the sun, moon, and stars, for example, are always drawn the same way. Until children are 8 or 9, they imbue their drawings with emotional and imaginative elements that are distorted by their own feelings, thoughts, and inner concerns. Thus drawings of family members are often more primitive than drawings of nonspecific persons because of the depth of emotional content.

In early latency, children draw egocentrically, showing what they know exists, not what they actually see. Thus their drawings resemble X-rays: e.g., a man will be shown inside the house, his leg inside his trousers. Because optical realism develops slowly, the figure in the drawings will have two legs, two arms, and two eyes, regardless of its position.

When children reach middle latency, they outgrow the X-ray technique and attempt to use perspective. At the same time, however, their drawings become opaque—and also more repressed, schematic, and conventional. But as their drawings of a person become less expressive, they begin to use objects in the environment to express an increased interest in reality and the external world.

The stories children tell deal with characters and situations in everyday life, and the main character is always a child. When Lystad (1974) compared the stories told by children ages 6 to 11, she found some interesting differences. In stories told by 6-year-olds, children and parents were friendly and loving to one another. The characters and situations tended to be simplistic, concerns seemed to be about independence and freedom, with the family supplying support and meeting the children's needs. Sometimes animals appeared in the stories; occasionally, flowers, trees, and inanimate objects were the major characters. Fantasy-oriented stories involved super-natural beings who had extraordinary powers over people.

The stories of children who were 10 or older showed greater complexity in characters, situations, and concerns. Though realistic settings, daily routines, and positive emotions remained predominant, fantasy life was expressed in dreams of glory or in characters such as ghouls and ghosts. There was more humor—silly characters, situations, and jokes. There was also more interaction with other children and with adults outside the family. Now, in addition to independence and freedom, concerns about achievement, strength, and physical safety appear. Half the stories presented problems, such as accidents, illness, and death, that had to be overcome. There was greater empathy for the needs of others and happy solutions were possible, not only through family actions but through peers and play. Good characters were rewarded while bad ones were punished.

Peer Groups

The activities of 6- to 8-year olds reflect an increasing involvement with peers and broader experiences outside the home. Acceptance by peers helps them to stabilize their roles outside the family and contributes to the continued development of their identity and values. The group represents the transition between the family and outside world.

The degree to which the adults on whom the child depends recognize and accept the peer group as an agent of socialization will influence the group's impact on the child. Some cultural groups stress the family's primary role and strongly inculcate specific values, religious beliefs, and prescribed behavior. When attending school, the child may be faced by the conflicting mores of family, school, and peer group. When family ties are strong and the child has been well nurtured, the family's values tend to be internalized, withstand the pressure of peers, and influence the child's choice of friends. If the family is less cohesive, if the parents have less control and their values prescribe conformity to external prescriptions, the peer group will be important earlier and remain so longer.

Campbell (1964) found that children who have good family relationships have better relationships with peers. When parents are rejecting, children become dependent on peers; when parents are aggressive, children will behave aggressively with peers. In addition, the younger the child, the greater his or her vulnerability to the influence of peers. In general, the less secure and less accepted the child is at home, the greater the dependence and reliance on the group will be.

Although the 6-year-old's capacity for group play is limited to small groups, subsequent development involves an increasing ability to abide by rules and cooperate with others. As a result, group activity is more important in the middle and late stages of latency than it is at the beginning.

SEX DIFFERENCES

In early latency, children tend to play most often with other children of the same sex and similar age. Although this is a function of different interests and abilities to some extent, it also reflects society's expectations. Early sex-differentiated behavior based on cultural stereotypes is reinforced not only by adults but by peers, as illustrated in the following cases:

> *Reva,* age 8, was referred because she had tantrums, fought with her brothers, and was generally unhappy. Her family had recently moved to the United States from Israel because of the father's work. Reva's mother, Reva, and two siblings —Mordecai, age 12½, and Abraham, age 5—had been born in Israel. The father had emigrated there. Both parents were college graduates, economically middle-class, family centered in their values and activities, and sensitive to the fact that Reva was unhappy.
>
> Blond, blue-eyed, agile, active, and bright, Reva matched the stereotype of the pretty little American girl. She attended a public school with high scholastic expectations in a middle-class community. Her English presented no problem because English as well as Hebrew had always been spoken at home. She was intelligent and aggressive, and her physical skills were on a par with those of boys her age. Because of her personality and physical skills, she was extremely popular among the boys in her class and ostracized by the girls.
>
> In treatment, Reva complained about being left out by the girls, but criticized them for their timidity, for the type of games they played, and for sitting around playing with dolls and talking all the time. Although Reva liked to play with boys, they didn't always include her, and anyway she wanted girl friends. Boys and girls played together more often in Israel than in the United States, and Reva thought

the girls were jealous of her because the boys liked her. Although the oedipal flavor of Reva's problem was clear and reflected subtle problems within the home, the girls were indeed jealous: Reva was a star in everything but social relations with girls. Some of her difficulties seemed to be based on differences in cultural expectations in the two countries. In Israel, she met the social expectations for her sex and age; in a middle-class American setting, she was very different from her classmates. After talking through some of these problems, Reva made successful overtures to the leader of the "opposition" and was able to gain the acceptance of the other girls.

Ruth, age 7, came from an American orthodox Jewish family and attended a parochial school. Although she did well in school, she did not get along with her classmates and tended to seek out much younger children, whom she bossed. Almost obese, she was unusually tall for her age but well-coordinated, active, and extremely aggressive. Her personality difficulties were related to the family dynamics and the continuation of earlier problems. Although intervention with the entire family created a new balance in family relations and eased some of Ruth's tensions, she continued to have difficulty making friends. When the family moved to Israel, Ruth quickly made friends with children her own age, did well in school, and was much happier.

During the early school years, the peer group tends to encourage and reward members who master the stereotyped sexual roles of class and culture. Boys in most cultures are expected to be more aggressive than girls, physically and verbally, as soon as social play begins. This contributes to the separation of the sexes during play in latency. Maccoby and Jacklin (1974) suggest that biological factors such as sex hormones may contribute to male aggression because aggressive behavior persists in males of all ages, cross-culturally and also in primates.

Sex differences are evident in school performance; overt behavior; choice of games, toys, and themes of make-believe; and perceptions of male and female adults. However, until the age of 9 or 10, girls engage in more variable activities than do boys, who prefer the masculine model from an early age. The little girl who wants to be a boy or like daddy and enjoys masculine games usually becomes "feminine" when the hormonal changes of puberty begin.

Sexual role identity is complicated and involves not only biological realities but the processes of identification and imitation. From the psychoanalytic perspective, males and females resolve the oedipal complex differently. According to learning theory, sexual roles are learned and then reinforced in interaction with adults and peers. Class differences also seem to influence the process. The lower their educational level and therefore social class, the more parents will encourage sex typing in their children's play and behavior. Differences in sex typing based on social class are greatest among girls. The middle-class girl, unlike the middle-class boy, is freer to express an interest in boys' activities and toys (Kagan, 1964). In addition, the larger culture, through its schools and teachers (who are predominantly female in the early grades), encourages "appropriate" behavior, which is also reinforced by the peer group. Thus boys develop "masculine" interests in knives, boats, planes, and trucks, while girls develop "feminine" interests in dolls, cribs, dishes, and so forth.

Sex differences in the early years are most apparent in school performance. From kindergarten through fourth grade, girls tend to outperform boys in all areas. In this age group, the ratio of boys to girls who have reading problems ranges from 3 to 1 to 6 to 1. First- and second-grade girls usually master reading, writing, and arithmetic more easily and develop verbal skills earlier. One explanation for this is the difference in rate of maturation between the sexes. However, the feminine atmosphere of the school and teachers' values of obedience, decorum, and inhibition of motor activity—all of which oppose the stereotype of the masculine role—may also contribute to these differences in performance. Furthermore, some cultural groups view the studious boy as effeminate.

COGNITIVE ABILITY

In view of young children's dependence on external support and their limited experience and cognitive ability, their acceptance of stereotypes is understandable. Not only is this expressed in sex-role expectations, but in children's moral beliefs, rigidity of conscience, and a superego that makes simplistic, black-and white judgments. Because, in Piaget's view (1963), 6- and 7-year olds are still in the preoperational stage, still egocentric and intuitive and able to deal with only one variable at a time, they are insensitive to the intentions and feelings of others.

When they enter school, children use speech to express thinking, which itself involves the attempt to fit new experiences into previous patterns. Only gradually, as their knowledge expands, can they generalize from a variety of experiences. Although children increasingly employ appropriate language, they do not necessarily comprehend its full meaning. For example, they may be able to distinguish the right arm from the left but have no notion of the concept. At this age, there are no rank orders, no relativity, no hierarchy of values; only absolutes, all good, all bad. Children will lie; how bad the lie is depends on the degree of disobedience to adults it represents.

Through social interaction with peers, continuing maturity, and widening experiences, thinking processes improve. Thus the following interrelated factors affect and enhance mental development (Piaget & Inhelder, 1969): (1) growth and maturation of the nervous and endocrine systems, (2) exercise and experiences acquired with objects, (3) social interaction and transmission of the mechanisms of self-regulation, and (4) the process of equilibrium

—a series of active compensations on the child's part in response to external stimuli, which results in adjustments that are both retroactive and anticipatory.

In Piaget's and Inhelder's view (1969), children enter the concrete operational stage at about age 7. Then they begin to view events from more than one perspective and develop the capacity to order and relate experiences to an organized whole. Because they can weigh more than one viewpoint simultaneously, yet return to their original outlook (the principle of reversibility), they become less rigid.

One important development is the ability to differentiate objects by their attributes and to observe differences. Now children can arrange objects in a series, such as small to big, which is then transferred to the ordering of numbers. A larger vocabulary and better knowledge of word meanings and culture's labels for categories enables them to think more logically and solve problems more intelligently. But their reasoning is still limited to concrete situations, not abstractions, and they are still dependent on their own individual perceptions.

This stage of cognitive development persists until early adolescence. For example, when Piaget (1970) put lumps of sugar in a glass of water and asked children of varying ages what had happened to the sugar, 6- and 7-year-olds answered that the sugar was gone and so was the taste. Seven- and 8-year-olds believed that the sugar was preserved in small, invisible grains that had no weight or value, while 9- and 10-year olds realized that each grain kept its weight and was thus part of the sum of all the elements even after the sugar had dissolved. By age 11 or 12, children understood that although the sugar was there, the level of water would remain the same. Piaget called this "spontaneous atomism": thinking that goes beyond what can be seen and involves a step-by-step mental construction. In another experiment, he presented children ages 5 to 11 with two glasses of water that differed in height, diameter, and level of water and asked them to judge which glass had more water in it. The judgments of the youngest children were based solely on an undifferentiated personal views. Seven to 9-year-olds judged equally concretely but offered better explanations, such as the glass with the most filled space was the fuller one. The judgments of the oldest group reflected the concept of proportions.

When children begin to order their experiences, a greater notion of certainty and permanence is possible. As a result, they begin to understand that they belong not only to a family but to a city and country. The unknown, however, is still understood egocentrically; each new understanding occurs at the expense of personal beliefs. When children are threatened, their thinking will regress because egocentric beliefs are always below the surface, ready to reappear.

As they slowly become independent of perceptual data, children are better able to understand more distant experiences and the physical, natural world. The loss of animism and decline of the belief that natural phenomena are made by man for man cause them to face the concepts of death and time: before and after is now a possibility. This widening awareness of physical factors precedes awareness of social factors. Thus second and third graders are incapable of predicting the feelings of others, but as they mature they can perceive richer and more complex external psychological acts and differentiate between what they and others think. According to Whiteman (1970), the child's conception of psychological causality is related to chronological age and is influenced by exposure to adult conceptions. Generally speaking, when parents are economically or educationally restricted, this conception tends to be less developed.

Adults often assume that if they explain something to a child calmly and rationally, the child will comprehend it. But in an interesting experiment in which children were presented with a stethoscope and a hypodermic needle and asked to explain the purpose of these instruments, Steward and Regalbuto (1975) found that young children are incapable of understanding such highly abstract concepts. Children younger than 8 knew that the hypodermic needle was used to give shots but did not know why and could not comprehend that it contained medicine; medicine was taken in a spoon or glass and did not hurt. They knew they did not like the needle and could offer only magical explanations about how it worked. Most children age 8 and older realized that the needle was used to prevent and cure illness, and many knew that it contained medicine. Although both groups understood that doctors used the stethoscope to listen to the heart beat, the younger children said that the doctor did this to determine whether a person was alive or dead. Older children realized that the doctor used the stethoscope to determine whether the heart was working properly, but their explanations of the relationship between the heart and circulation were incorrect. The younger group did not even understand the reasons for visiting the doctor. In this experiment, it was obvious that only gradually do children outgrow the simplistic, magical, egocentric view of the world in which they live.

PSYCHOLOGY OF EARLY LATENCY

During early latency, children are involved primarily with mother and father and the relationship between the two. Although they seem to accept the fact that they are too small and too young to become the partner of the parent of the opposite sex and although their identification with the parent of the same sex seems obvious in their play and behavior, children this age continue to work through residues of the oedipal conflict. Thus they will vacillate between babyish behavior and behavior that seems relatively grown up, compliant, and sensible. Secondary process thinking and talking become more dominant, but they will also engage in solitary talk, play out associated fantasies, and relapse into primary process thinking and talking. Frequently, they will assume babyish postures, giggle, wave their arms and legs, lose control and balance—especially in the company of other children, each prompting the others to use toilet language, dirty themselves, and spill food (Kestenberg, 1975). Because the ego in early latency is relatively weak, children will use both regression and repression against libidinal and agressive wishes in an effort to cope with anxiety. Regression to babyish behavior provides a respite from the latency task of consolidating ego and superego functions; repression eases anxiety, enables the child to comply with the rigid demands of the childish superego, and produces the coping mechanisms of denial and reaction formation.

Conflict and ambivalence in relation to impulses and commands of the superego are apparent in alternating obedience and rebellion—the latter always followed by self-reproach. Because it is difficult for children to tolerate guilt feelings, they will blame others for their misbehavior whenever possible. Statements such as "I couldn't help it; he made me do it!" are not unusual.

The castration fears and animal phobias of the oedipal child are often replaced by separation anxiety and the fear of death. Struggles against masturbation are dealt with by obsessive-compulsive mechanisms such as avoiding cracks in the sidewalk, performing certain magical rituals, indulging in magical fantasies, or exhibiting behavior such as ear pulling, nail biting, and so on (Bornstein, 1951, 1953). If the child has strong superego prohibitions or has not relinquished primitive oral and anal-sadistic wishes toward the mother, complete repression of masturbation may occur. This in turn may lead to repression of physical activity. Excessive attempts to ward off masturbation may result in symptoms such as general restlessness or in dealing with the external world in a sexualized, distorted, often compulsive way (Fraiberg, 1972). Inhibition of masturbation also may inhibit curiosity and thus affect learning and creative activity.

Children normally use mechanisms of defense constructively in the total process of coping, especially when they are in danger of being overwhelmed or are confronted with threats that cannot be mastered within the current situation. Defense mechanisms are pathological or contribute to pathology only if they interefere with a child's development and progress in coping (Fraiberg, 1972). White (1974) has defined coping as adapting under relatively difficult conditions that require new behaviors to bring about change or solve a problem. Because adaptive behavior requires appropriate information, internal equilibrium, autonomy, and the ability to handle several variables simultaneously, the child's ability to cope is limited.

In addition to sociological explanations for separating boys and girls according to sex, age, and interests, some researchers suggest that each sex goes through a different process when resolving the oedipal conflict. Kestenberg (1975), for example, believes that the girl enters latency feeling rejected by her father; although she is disappointed in both parents, she is less so with her mother, with whom she identifies but is less dependent on than earlier. Her source of narcissistic satisfaction is in being a good girl.

Latency-age girls frequently share secrets with girl friends, the most important secret being the vaginal opening, which they may explore through mutual masturbation. Although girls develop a sense of fairness based on equality among themselves, they exclude boys, calling them wild, stupid, and bad. This identification with their own sex enables them to reject the masculine role.

The boy enters latency with a strong identification with his father and strong reactions against feminine traits. In the process of relinquishing his identification with his mother and his wish to have a baby, he represses his confusion about inner genital sensations and denies the existence of any inner genital structure. As a result, his concern focuses on his external sexual organ. He repudiates femininity of any kind and denigrates the feminine sexual organ. Thus he too seeks the company of his own sex and tends to identify with and engage in "masculine" activities —those involving motion, activity, and aggression. Although he may play house when he feels relatively nondefensive, he usually prefers to play the role of father.

Because young boys are surrounded by women in American society, they face another problem. Mothers and female teachers—the dominant educators in the early years —may admire and expect stereotyped masculine behavior and reject feminine behavior in young boys. On the other hand, they may prefer to deal with quiet, "feminine" behavior. If so, the boy may have to seek out male playmates and activities even more persistently. Of course, the model presented by the father or male figure in the home also will influence how the boy expresses his masculinity (Kestenberg, 1975).

Teachers are an important influence in early latency. Children transfer their feelings about maternal figures to the teacher and in the early years react to her as all-knowing and important. In turn, through her warmth and encouragement, she helps her pupils through the crisis of learning; their identification with her aids in this process. Whether children succeed in school depends on their ability to work, which in turn is based on their ability to sublimate. The teacher who, while being warm and accepting, maintains some distance helps children repress oedipal conflicts and also represents reality by making appropriate demands (Kay, 1972).

The stories that latency-age children like to hear express the concerns of the age and the oedipal constellation.

Their reactions to a story may reveal not only fears that are covered up in everyday life but relief because others share similar feelings and troubles. Peller (1959) suggested that in early latency, children are fond of three types of stories. One type, which she called the "fantasy of the reversal of role," deals with one individual who is strong and powerful and another who is small and weak but in the end becomes strong and powerful—the hero. This type of story relates to feelings about older siblings and the big, strong father. The hero obtains the goals of the oedipal wishes in ways that are acceptable to the ego; after struggling against all odds, the hero triumphs in the end. The hero, with whom children most often identify, is fearless and frequently defies authority. In a second type called the "Bad Boy" story, the main figure is impervious to the general awe accorded the story's father image; he lacks virtue and makes a big display of his badness. The third type of story deals with a twin or an animal companion that serves as an alter ego, a constant companion, and an escape from loneliness. Another group of stories of this type involves a constant group of friends who never fight and are not clearly identified as to age or sex (e.g., Dr. Doolittle or Peter Pan). There is no competition, and when the story ends, all the characters are the same as they were at the beginning. Peller suggests that all three kinds of stories produce an excitement that is almost sexual; all are related to the child's unconscious wish to see and know what adults are doing.

The child's accomplishments in early latency show a unity and steady progression. Although the tendencies of early childhood still exist, they are gradually repressed (A. Freud, 1968a). Physical maturity and coordination enable greater independence and more experiences. Sublimation assists in learning, and learning assists the ego and produces feelings of mastery and competence. Development of the superego enables a sense of right and wrong that, although extremely rigid, is more internalized. Development of cognitive abilities is aided by all these experiences as well as by maturity. Peer relationships support children's moves toward separation from home, broaden their world, and help them learn and do. In early latency, children are busy learning many things.

Chapter 4

MIDDLE LATENCY

In Chapter 1, Elizabeth, age 10, illustrated the achievements of the latency-age child. Dana, her 14-year-old sister, described her as fun to be with, creative, and a maker of many things. But sometimes Elizabeth "gets impatient or frustrated and upset over things that don't really matter." Elizabeth's other sisters described her in a similar vein: she was sweet natured, talented, industrious, constantly making something, or involved in some project—a true latency child in the Eriksonian formula of industry and self-esteem.

GROWTH AND DEVELOPMENT

Many achievements in middle latency are the outgrowth and culmination of physical maturation. The myelinization of the corticothalamic tract that occurs at about age 8 enables finer eye-hand coordination and more purposeful physical activities than were possible before. In addition, the child continues to grow in height and weight at a steady pace and becomes sturdy, energetic, and skillful in managing his or her body. Between birth and age 10, the musculature of girls increases five-fold and shows little subsequent growth. Boys, on the other hand, continue to develop muscle cells until age 18, when they have fourteen to twenty times as many muscle cells as girls. Although the amount of subcutaneous fat increases in both sexes during middle latency, the fact that girls are developing more is soon reflected in their physical appearance. At this age, girls are still as strong as boys, but this will change as the rate of physical growth in the sexes begins to show more differentiation.

Although both sexes experience pubertal growth at the end of middle latency, here again, girls develop earlier and faster than boys (Tanner, 1970). As early as age 8½, a girl's uterus and vagina begin to develop, and by the end of middle latency, her nipples begin to bud. Preceding the onset of menstruation, which generally occurs by the end of late latency, she may undergo a spurt of growth. (A few girls will begin to exhibit noticeable pubertal changes as early as age 8 or as late as adolescence.) Although boys do not develop secondary sexual characteristics until much later, the testicles and penis enlarge and the scrotum reddens at age 10 or 11.

Normally, a child's rate of growth reflects the family genetic patterns. As mentioned earlier, however, cultural, regional, and economic patterns and even emotional factors can accelerate or impede sexual and physical maturation. Gender is an important variable in determining not only how a child will feel about his or her pattern of development but how others will react to it. Smallness and delicacy—often viewed as assets in girls—may be serious problems for a young boy. The boy who experiences accelerated growth may find that his physical prowess is an asset in relation to other boys, whereas the precociously

mature girl may be confronted by inappropriate expectations and even seduction on the part of older boys or adults
who misjudge her age.

Myopia often develops or becomes worse during this
period, and other physical "defects" such as hearing and
dental problems may be discovered because of school difficulties and mandatory physical examinations. Unless there
is great deviation from the norm, however, the physical
developments of middle latency ordinarily lead to greater
skill and management of the body.

PLAY

As children enter middle latency, they are able to pursue
an ever increasing variety of satisfying activities that involve
interaction with peers, provide a sense of competence and
skill, and channel physical and psychological energies in
purposeful and socialized directions. The increase in physical coordination is evidenced in the physical activities that
are popular at this age. Expertise in riding a bicycle, in
catching, throwing, and pitching a ball is evidence of improved muscular control and coordination. Although all
physical movements become smoother and more purposeful, perfecting of flexible body movements is a major
achievement. Continued interest in rhythmic movements is
demonstrated by an increased interest in dancing, especially among girls, and in rock and roll (Kaplan, 1965).

The end-product of activity is at times more important
than the activity itself. Through competence and produc-
tivity, children achieve self-esteem, prestige among their
contemporaries, and a sense of self-mastery. Because practice for competence requires the ability to control, inhibit,
and modify immediate desires and wait for the pleasure
that accompanies the ultimate outcome, development in
play foreshadows the ability to work. Hobbies are an impor-

tant landmark in this development; they too are halfway between play and work (A. Freud, 1963).

Although middle latency is the age of interaction with peers, solitary activities are also important. Now, special interests such as hobbies, crafts, and collections will be pursued avidly and almost exclusively for a time. One interest may be supplanted suddenly by another, just as at a later age one friend may be replaced by another. For some children, these early interests remain a part of their lives, becoming a specific area of competence or even a vocation in later life. These hobbies and crafts are pursued with a best friend or group of friends as well as alone. Through them, curiosity, previously expressed mainly in active play, is now expressed increasingly in intellectual pursuits such as working with chemicals, craft materials, models, electrical or construction equipment, and the like.

Children who maintain an interest in painting and drawing will be more realistic in their representations by age 9. They now understand perspective, can depict movement, and no longer need to represent what they know to exist in the form of X-ray-like drawings. This reflects not only increased understanding but increased repression. Therefore, art tends to be less self-expressive and often demonstrates the use of popular or schematic models that are symbolic of increasing socialization and conformity.

The stories children read and tell in middle latency also tend to be more reality oriented ones about other children and the struggles appropriate for their age. The characters become more complex and the problems depicted are more psychological, dealing with inadequacy, failure, loneliness, rejection, and the like. The basic theme involves a hero who overcomes these problems, despite great odds and adults, with the support of a constant, loyal companion. Worship of heroes and heroines who do and achieve great things assumes great importance. Children this age can weep over and sympathize with the character's tribulations and enjoy the glory of his or her success.

Real-life heroes and heroines in sports and entertainment (TV is especially important at this age) become the focus of attention and are reflected in many of children's games, jokes, and parodies. Now, in addition to making things with their hands, children "make" things with words. This is apparent in rhythmic and repetitive games, satirical rhymes, nonsense, tangle talk, puns, tongue twisters, secret languages, and tales without end. In other words, middle latency is a time for sharpening intellectual as well as physical skills. Language becomes a vehicle for controlling the behavior of self and others by channeling aggression into words. Special names are concocted for special children: e.g., brain, bookworm, dunce, copy-cat, show-off, scairdy cat, tattletale, goody goody, and the like. Words and rhymes provide an acceptable way of releasing anger (Opie & Opie, 1959). For example, nosy children will be taunted with the following rhyme: "Ask no questions/ And you'll be told no lies./ Shut your mouth/ And you'll catch no flies." A threat can be couched in this manner: "See my finger/ See my thumb/ See my fist/ You'd better run!"

Word play continues in jokes and riddles because this is an age of play on words and play with reality. Of course, adults also relish the double entendre because humor is an outlet for otherwise forbidden impulses and topics. Because children use denial as a normal part of their coping repertoire, they do not use jokes in the same sense (Wolfenstein, 1951, 1953). Although jokes permit children to express the forbidden, they cannot dismiss as nonsense a problem that seems too real because they will react directly to the latent content. Latency-age children are less able than adults to combine sense and nonsense. To them, joking is fun to the extent that it runs counter to reasonable thought. This bewilders younger children, perhaps because they will not achieve "reasonable" thought until middle latency. Comprehension of jokes increases with intelligence and age, and the rules of joke-telling are only gradually understood. Frequently, children will not understand that nonsense makes the joke until they reach adolescence.

Part of the fun of being a latency-age child is hearing others express the unacceptable. So children will trick others into saying unacceptable things. For example, they will ask a child or an adult to count as follows: "I one my mother, I two my mother" . . . until "I eight my mother"—which will be greeted with gales of laughter.

The joking riddle is a favorite in middle latency. Here again, children's riddles differ from those of adults. They are extremely simple; the joke is that another person has been conned, which makes children feel more intelligent because they have been able to fool someone. For example, "Why does a bus have wheels?" "I don't know. Why?" "In order to run."

Jokes and riddles about morons (defectives) or ghosts and spooks (death) are disguised expressions of children's concerns. Although children only half believe in the effectiveness of charms, rituals, and magic, they feel compelled to use them as a means of controlling not only themselves but an increasingly complex world. Some charms or rituals bring good luck, others bring evil, and some, such as sealing a bargain in blood, are traditional ways of pledging loyalty and entering pacts. Fears are dealt with by spitting or crossing the fingers; old superstitions, such as not walking under a ladder, are obeyed; and finding things will bring good luck. For instance, "See a pin and pick it up/ All the day you'll have good luck./ See a pin and let it lay/ Bad luck you'll have all that day."

Children share more and more of these activities with a good friend or group of friends. They invent secret codes, swap belongings, and devise rituals for special occasions such as birthdays. Rules are basic in active games and in a wide variety of board games. Observing the rules structures the activity, controls behavior, and by translating competition from the personal to the traditional, makes it less unpleasant (Peller, 1954). Although there may be some cheating, the basic expectation is that everyone will stick to the rules, which are understood and accepted by all participants. Many games are social institutions, transmitted in the same form from one generation to the next (Piaget & Inhelder, 1969).

PEERS AND GROUP ACTIVITIES

Cooperation, loyalty, gangs, cliques, and organized games are the stuff of middle latency—the age of socialization outside the family. At this age, children are preoccupied with the immediate society of the neighborhood and school. In the games, competitions, and rules of the non-primary group, the personality advances toward autonomy, though still within the confines of prescribed social roles. Now, children engage in competition that enables them to win in reality. This is different from the fantasied victories of the younger child because competitors are peers, not adults, and thus more equal, and the more realistic modest targets are appropriate to the abilities of middle latency. Although the systems of external controls engendered in group activities, codes of behavior, and value systems are more varied than those of the family, they too encourage the continued growth of internal systems of control. Empathy, compassion, and acceptance of self and others despite differences are possible outgrowths of group participation.

Children's groups are both informal and formal. Neighborhood, school, and athletic groups spring up spontaneously; sometimes the focus is a specific activity, sometimes a club will be organized, or a group will simply consist of available children who are the same sex and age.

Formal groups are usually organized by adults or organizations and generally are led by volunteers, parents, or professionals. These groups provide children with additional opportunities to identify with and learn from adults as well as peers. Socialization groups provided by Ys and settlement or neighborhood organizations are often more sensitive to children's needs than are groups led by parents or volunteers. Professionally led or supervised groups tend to focus on meeting children's needs in age-appropriate ways and foster activities that will enhance socialization and feelings of competence among individual members. In groups such as Little League, which are led by parent volunteers, parents are prone to act out their own competitiveness and aggression by pressuring the children.

Both types of groups, formal and informal, meet a variety of the needs of latency-age children by providing them with opportunities to interact and cooperate with other children, improve their skills and self-esteem, and explore new social and physical worlds. The group supports children in their continuing efforts to separate from the primary family and helps them come to grips with new problems associated with a larger world—the world outside the home.

COGNITIVE ABILITY

Play during middle latency differs significantly from that of earlier stages of development. It is more realistic, constructive, logical, and objective and also better organized and more elaborate. Like other activities at this age, play reflects physical maturation, psychological change, and cognitive growth.

The processes that began during early latency now come to fruition. A gradual unfolding and integrative process occurs, and there is a growth from the subjective to the objective viewpoint. Socialization is an obvious example of this gradual improvement in understanding. By age 11, children have progressed from an inability to differentiate between their own and others' views and needs to an awareness that the views and needs of others differ from their own. They are also able to consider several viewpoints at one time. Both developments can be observed in play with other children and in groups.

When participating in board games and team games, children this age are expected to abide by the rules and cooperate with and respect the rights of other children whether adults are present or not. By doing so, they demonstrate an ability to view one event from many different perspectives, not only their own. The use of perspective in drawings also reflects this ability to see things from more than one viewpoint.

Many games such as monopoly require the ability to sort, order, and classify many different objects, relate one move to another, and all moves into an organized whole. Thus the child must be able to comprehend a total system of interrelated parts, exploring several possible solutions—from beginning to end or from end to beginning—always returning to the original outlook. This demonstrates what Piaget and Inhelder (1958) term concrete operational thought, which is characterized by the principles of perspective, reversibility, classification, and relationship. All thought, however, is still dependent on what can be perceived and manipulated or imagined and visualized in a tangible form.

Because the ability to classify helps children connect previously unconnected thoughts and see the logical relationships between different types of related knowledge, their world becomes more ordered, comprehensible, certain, and thus less frightening. Now that they can understand more than they actually see, they can establish concepts about actual objects and subsequently about abstractions such as space, causality, and time. They also understand that dreams are personal and occur only at night, but the unreality of dreams is only gradually established.

In middle latency, relationships within relationships are also understood: family, extended family, city, state, and country assume more meaning because one can be seen in relation to another entity or to several entities, which in turn are part of a still larger unit. In school, the child's use of symbols improves in reading and writing, geography, and so on—all of which demand this new ability to understand relationships. The child's ability to remember also increases with the capacity to organize, categorize, and understand relationships.

Middle latency also brings increased sensitivity to motivational processes. For example, conflicts, arguments, and other disagreements give children some idea of not only their own psychological processes but those of others. Children of this age cannot be called introspective, however. The older child's seemingly greater ability to understand the role of intentions and feelings in personal behavior appears to be related to more varied experiences and exposure to adult conceptions.

Although 9- and 10-year-olds have a much better grasp of motivational factors in themselves and others than do younger children, they are still incapable of understanding complex psychological motivation. They do, however, have a beginning idea of subjective responsibility. In early latency, their judgments about behavior were based on the consequences: the more serious the consequences, the worse the behavior. In middle latency, they can give some thought to intentions as well as what actually occurred (Whiteman, 1970).

Because cognitive abilities develop gradually and verbal thinking is still centered on action and concrete visions, children often revert to egocentric thinking at this age.

Thus they sometimes confuse actual objects or things and the symbols used for them. Pleasurable things such as play or recreation will seem to take less time than unpleasant tasks such as homework, practicing the piano, or chores. There may be disparity between the words children use and seem to understand and adult conceptions of the meaning of those words; sudden discontinuities in communication will reveal the child's misunderstanding. This is illustrated in the following case:

> *Robert*, almost 11 and the eldest of two children, was thin and shorter than average but alert, verbal, and obviously extremely intelligent. His parents had brought him for treatment because he was lonely and unhappy. Both parents were college graduates, middle class, and professionals.
>
> According to Robert, he lacked friends because he couldn't play football and baseball as well as the other boys. He also complained that school was boring, but his father had said that if he did well in school, he would get a better job when he was older. Another problem, in Robert's view, was that when he became very angry, he went into a closet to cool off. (Robert was asthmatic, but spoke of this unconsciously and symbolically.)
>
> Because the first two problems seemed age-appropriate, the worker accepted Robert's priorities and said that being able to play ball with his friends was extremely important—maybe more important to him than school. Robert disagreed and said that school was more important because he wanted to go to a good college like MIT. (Robert was indeed at the head of his class.) He wanted to go to MIT to be a detective. He wanted to learn how to solve things. When asked what a detective could solve, he said: "A detective would look at things, notice if something is different. Then he would try to find out what is missing and try to find it." For example, "jewels."
>
> This appears to be a sensible conversation. Robert begins the interview in a grownup manner, but when he talks about college, his childishness becomes apparent. Doing well in school is important when one is ready to go to col-

lege. MIT is a good college, but, what college is all about,
Robert is too young to comprehend. In addition, some personal problem seems to be intruding on his thought processes.

The worker asked herself what jewels Robert could be
missing? When she talked with his parents, she asked
whether the child had a genital problem such as an undescended testicle. They indicated that this was not a problem
but were amazed that the worker had asked. Only a week
before, Robert had come home, confused and worried because a boy in his class had been operated on for an undescended testicle!

Now Robert's vocational interests are understandable.
His puzzlement about a part of the body that can be made
to appear or disappear reveals his inadequate knowledge,
concrete thinking, infantile fears, and age-appropriate psychological concerns about his masculinity. (Blos, 1960, discusses how boys react to the problem of undescended
testicles.)

PSYCHOLOGICAL GROWTH

Robert presented his problem with friends as caused by his
inability to play ball as well as other boys. His superiority
in school did not compensate for his shame at not being as
good as they were in activities so important to a boy's
masculine image.

Shame and a sense of inferiority and inadequacy are
common problems in middle latency. In Erikson's words
(1963): "If . . . [the child] despairs of his . . . [competence]
and skills or of his status among his partners, he may be
discouraged from identification with them . . . and consid-
ers himself doomed to mediocrity or inadequacy (p. 260)."
The child will feel shame about physical defects, exposure
of failures, and loss of control. Inferiority is frequently
coupled with shame, often traced back to earlier injuries
and failures. The feeling of shame is different from guilt,

which arises from conflict (Jacobson, 1964). The important tasks of this period are control of impulses and adaptation to the real world. To fail in these tasks or to be personally inadequate is shameful.

The ego is strengthened through learning and mastering school tasks, peer demands, and the skills required in games and play. The ego can cope with reality in reality; there is less need to fantasize and make-believe. Reality testing improves because of an improvement in cognitive abilities, more experiences, and a sense of real competence. Growth occurs in many areas of functioning: intellect, affect, and control over motility, all of which enable the child to organize and consolidate the ego. The ego's defensive mechanisms are more dependable; reaction formations are more solidified and sublimation occurs more often than ever before. Defenses are oriented toward coping with problems in the outside world rather than with internal conflicts (Bornstein, 1951). Consequently, in middle latency the child tends to defend against impulses rather than act on them (Becker, 1974).

Because of real achievements and new interests, children this age demonstrate more ability to regulate their self-esteem, which in turn contributes to a sense of self and identity. Whereas younger children are controlled by fear of external adults, the superego of middle-latency children, tempered by a stronger ego and internal representations, is better able to control behavior. Of course, these children still depend on adults for controls, but to a lesser degree. Identification with the ideals of the peer group, adherence to the rules of the game, and cooperation with others—combined with the reduction of instinctual pressures and development of a stronger ego—result in more flexibility and thus a stronger superego. Feelings of shame and inferiority tend to be more dominant than feelings of guilt because children this age seem more concerned about having their equilibrium upset than about conflict and suffering.

As a result, their defenses and symptoms tend to be ego syntonic and their capacity for introspection or thinking about their own motives is limited (Bornstein, 1951).

In middle latency, parents seem more human, less omnipotent. Thus the family romance is a new fantasy: e.g., "My real parents were rich (or noble, or unusual in some other way); I don't really belong to these ordinary people who call themselves my parents." Children at this time have fantasies about being adopted or having a twin who is raised by extraordinary parents. This begins a process of psychological separation in which the child's libido transfers from these denigrated parents to contemporaries, community groups, teachers, leaders, impersonal ideals, and aim-inhibited, sublimated interests (A. Freud, 1965). The process accelerates during late latency, culminating in the second separation-individuation phase of adolescence (Blos, 1967). Separation from parents is impossible during latency; physically, emotionally, and in reality, children still need parental guidance and support for basic security.

Development of intelligence and skills is propelled not only by maturation but also by expectations of the environment and the self through the ego ideal. The need for parents and other adults relates to the child's need to identify with them in control and modulation of drives, thinking, communication, reality testing, and other successful relations. The process of separation and the changing relations between child and parents help the child turn to others such as peers, but peers cannot substitute for parents (Parens & Saul, 1971). Children know this: they still perceive security and constancy as essential.

SEXUALITY

Sex differences are perhaps more marked in middle latency than ever before. In most societies, girls are more passive, sociable, dependent, obedient, and responsible than boys, while boys are more dominant and aggressive. The extent of these differences varies from one society to another. Whiting and Edwards (1974) suggest that in cultures where boys are responsible for animal husbandry or agriculture, differences between the sexes are greater. In cultures where boys care for infants and perform domestic chores or where girls have little opportunity for this type of activity, these differences are less apparent.

In American culture, the stereotypes of desirable characteristics at this age tend to be a pretty face for girls and height and muscular development for boys. Although all social classes permit girls to be studious, studious middle-class boys must also participate in sports and other male activities. Lower class boys tend to admire physical achievements more than intellectual achievement. On the other hand, early evidence of overt heterosexuality is less acceptable in middle-class girls of this age than it is in lower class girls (Kagan, 1964).

Neither boys nor girls actually lose all interest in sex during middle latency; its manifestations simply vary with the culture's expectations and degree of permissiveness as well as the sublimations available. In groups or with a best friend, girls always express an interest in boys and will tease one another about it. A girl will often provoke her brother to the point where hitting, scuffling, and body contact occur. This activity often disturbs parents because they fail to recognize that both children enjoy this game despite their protestations to the contrary.

Girls like to dance because the activity libidinizes the body, provides outlets for their sexual feelings, and yet helps them achieve control over their bodies (Kestenberg, 1975). Although boys tend to deny an interest in girls, depreciating them and their femininity and excluding them from group activities, they are not unaware of girls. The boy who engages in rough play with his sister is doing so voluntarily, and he does his share of provoking reactions.

Masturbation is assumed to occur at this age, but little is known about the actual activities involved because both sexes repress and deny them. It should, however, be less of a problem than it was during early latency because the ego is stronger, the sex drive is less active, and the superego is more reasonable. Greater orientation to the outside world, more gratification in reality, and deflection of sexual aim into sublimatory activities such as dancing and playing ball also should reduce sexual conflict. For example, although girls will rock back and forth or press their thighs together while watching television or will wrestle with their brothers, they are not, generally speaking, preoccupied with sex. Compulsive or excessive masturbation or guilt about masturbation is an indication of problems. According to Bornstein (1953), occasional masturbatory activity should not be too disturbing to a child of this age. Sexual interest is more likely to be expressed in disguised voyeuristic, exhibitionistic, and sadomasochistic activities.

In summary, the end of middle latency marks tremendous growth of the ego and superego and the ability to regulate one's own self-esteem. Thus affect, mood, and the ability to deal with normal tensions are more stable at this age. The increased capacity to verbalize and the broadened modes of expression permit children to express themselves in language rather than motor activity. Moreover, their ability to use allegory, comparison, and simile enable them to speak indirectly about deep concerns without feeling threatened. And finally, rational thinking and fantasy are clearly separated because primary and secondary process thinking are now sharply delineated (Blos, 1962).

These awesome achievements are essential for future development. The next developmental phase will witness an upheaval that places critical demands on the child.

Chapter 5

LATE LATENCY

The literature about prepuberty is contradictory. According to Blos (1970), children enter this phase at age 11. Others, however, believe that its onset occurs as early as 9 or 10 (e.g., Harley, 1971) or as late as 13 or 14, while still others insist that it is simply a stage of adolescence (e.g., D. Miller, 1974). This confusion is not surprising. Children vary so much in maturational tempo at this age that some seem to be adolescents while others are obviously child-like. Those who work with these children must keep this fact in mind to avoid having inappropriate expectations or using inappropriate interventions.

In late latency, most children exhibit the physical and behavioral changes that culminate in puberty. Therefore, it is helpful to call this phase prepuberty. Children this age are usually still in grammar school, and they still fall within Sullivan's "juvenile era" (1953). The prepubertal child is neither a child nor an adolescent but is somewhere in between (Blos, 1970). In other words, one must end a discussion of childhood with prepuberty and begin a discussion of adolescence with prepuberty.

Physical Growth

Physiological growth during prepuberty, more than at any other time, intensifies the differences between male and female. Observable changes in both sexes are preceded by unseen hormonal metabolic processes that not only set overt changes into motion but affect behavior, feelings, and thoughts. These processes upset the balance achieved during earlier phases of latency before the child or the family is even aware that physical change is taking place.

There is a significant increase in secretion of hormones and the beginning of adult-like steroid metabolism as early as age 8 or 9 in both sexes. Because estrogen and androgens influence neural activity, Kestenberg (1975) and others believe that their quantity quality, ratio, and rate of increase and decrease significantly affect behavior. The correlation between anatomic and hormonal change is most obvious in prepuberty because gonadotropins produce sex-specific gonadal growth. In addition, changes in inner genital structures precede and overlap with external manifestations of sexual development, and the resultant inner tensions are disquieting to children even before changes in bodily structure or the occurrence of menarche in girls and emission in boys (Fraiberg, 1972).

As mentioned in the previous chapter, girls begin the process of sexual maturation approximately 1½ to two years earlier than do boys. Thus they tend to be taller and heavier than boys by the time they are 11. Although onset of menarche can occur between the ages of 10 and 17, the mean age for most American girls is 12.6, plus or minus 1.4 years. Boys usually experience ejaculation for the first time between the ages of 13 and 16, but this may occur as early as 11 or as late as 18 (Schonfeld, 1971). Thus one can assume that some sexual maturation is occurring in both sexes at age 11 or 12 and that between the ages of 10 and 15, there will be great variation in the rate of development among individuals of the same sex.

According to Kestenberg (1975), boys of 11 or 12 have prostatic activity, and girls have vaginal secretions, gonadotropins in their urine, and accelerated secretion of estrogen (which becomes cyclical) and exhibit changes in the pelvic bone and exterior and interior genitals. At age 12 or 13, boys have some downy pubic hair and a marked increase in production of gonadotropins; girls have pigmentation of the nipples and their breasts fill in. However, menstruation, real growth of penis and testicles, production of active spermatazoa and ovum, and axillary hair frequently occur later.

Obviously, the external genitals of females do not grow as much as those of boys. But because the uterus and ovaries begin to develop even before prepuberty, girls experience inner genital tensions sooner than boys do and on a cyclical basis, phases of high tension being associated with a reduction of hormone levels. Growth of the female genitals creates a feeling of inner swelling and pressure, which, when combined with visible body changes, disturbs the girl's body image and basic equilibrium. The preoccupation with both the inside and outside of her body that results contributes to fantasies and fears about her body and its processes. Premenstrual cramps and spontaneous vaginal lubrication may make her feel dirty and different.

After an initial phase of irregularity, menstruation is usually accompanied by regular estrogen cycles, which produces a more ordered rhythm that gradually can be anticipated. Menstruation also helps to localize and organize inner sensations, providing a more realistic comprehension of the unseen sexual organs.

Although boys mature more gradually and at an older

age, changes in the degree and quality of androgen production occur throughout childhood and accelerate in adolescence. Levels of estrogen, which changed at about age 3 and at the beginning of latency, change again at about age 12. Between the ages of 10 and 12, there is a major increase in production of testosterone.

The prepubertal boy experiences inner genital tensions activated by prostatic and testicular maturation. If he associates these strange feelings with female reproductive activity, his sense of masculinity may be threatened. This frequently leads to exaggerated aggressive, "masculine" behavior. His fear of femininity is further exacerbated by initial breast development and a tendency toward pudginess in the lower torso (Blos, 1962), but with the increase in androgen production and skeletal growth, his body soon changes to the more desired masculine image.

The young boy is also threatened by erections and testicular movements that seem to be out of his control. In an effort to control these phenomena, he may manipulate his penis and scrotum by moving his body in certain ways. First emissions and spasmodic ejaculations are also overwhelming because they are beyond his control. Unlike girls, boys are rarely prepared for these events or for the internal changes taking place within their bodies. And because sex education tends to concentrate on masturbation, both sexes are prey to many fears and fantasies (Paonessa & Paonessa, 1971).

Sometimes, young boys experience orgasm before they can ejaculate, confuse nocturnal emissions with urination, or misinterpret pelvic spasms or scrotal spasms as bellyaches or—even worse—as menstrual cramps. The growth of testes and scrotum is often frightening and misunderstood. However, the sharpness of the first orgastic experience can bring relief and help the boy integrate and organize his body concepts, just as the onset of menstruation does for the girl.

Kestenberg (1975) believes that body movements and rhythms express children's attitudes about their bodies. In early and middle latency, the trunk moves in a solid, one-piece way. In late latency, it becomes more supple, especially at the waist, because of changes in the upper and lower torso. At the same time, however, the trunk and limbs grow at a disharmonious rate (which explains the gangly appearance of many young adolescents). But whether children experience changes in their bodies as pleasurable or worrisome, the body is always a focus of attention. Sexual feelings and thoughts are a driving force, and misunderstandings and fantasies lead to many anxious moments. Physical defects, even slight deviations from the norm, may create deep feelings of inferiority. For example, precocious, retarded, or noticeably asymmetrical breast development or delayed menstruation creates fears in the young girl. In addition, many parts of her body are sensitive and eroticized. A boy will worry about undescended testicles or a "small" penis. Furthermore, his thoughts, even anxieties, can trigger an erection. Yet the strengths and abilities children develop in earlier years help them deal with these changes and anxieties in age-appropriate ways.

PEERS AND PLAY

Although prepubertal children engage in many activities such as sports, reading, and hobbies, which can be shared with a friend or pursued alone, friends are more important than ever before. Both boys and girls need friends, individually and in a group, to help them deal with the new upsets. Peers are the "experts" who will explain what is happening now and what will happen later; they are also "mirror images" because the same things are happening to them— i.e., they help to externalize feelings (Kestenberg, 1975). The styles set by peers are sacrosanct: by conforming to the peer group's standards concerning clothing, interests, expressions, and hair styles, a child begins to replace the conventional, soon-to-be-repudiated standards of parents.

The best friend who is loved intensely and is sought out because of her idealized and desired qualities as well as her similarities is extremely important for the prepubertal girl. This friendship permits a girl to be close to another female who is not her mother. It is almost a love affair: a first "homosexual" love. The two girls compare ideas, bodies, and bodily changes. They cannot live without each other, yet they may quarrel frequently and then make up again. Friendships at this age tend to be exaggerated and to exclude all adults except idealized rock and movie stars, some teachers, and a few other older women.

Boys too have close friendships, but these tend to revolve around wrestling, horseplay, and body contact. Yet boys also share new interests and hobbies, exclude parents and girls, but seek out adults such as science, shop, or physical education teachers and admire athletic heroes or other men who perform special feats.

In prepuberty, the skills and hobbies that were acquired earlier develop to a higher level and new ones are added. In addition to talking, playing, and forming special clubs, girls frequently become devoted to a variety of animals, but especially to horses and horseback riding. Riding provides genital stimulation and calls for coordination that involves using pelvic and abdominal muscles in relation to the animal's movements. Like genital impulses, horses can be perceived as wild and untamed. Horses, almost universally, are considered phallic symbols but, at the same time, the acts of grooming and feeding them are maternal and desexualized (Blos, 1970; Kestenberg, 1975). Prepubertal boys show an intensified interest in playing ball, in constructing and flying model airplanes, and in mechanics, biology, and science, which coincide with the growth and movement of the penis and testicles. These interests help them to rationalize fantasies about the body, as if moving objects could help solve the mystery of body movements (Kestenberg, 1975). An interest in magic tricks, puppetry, and so on is also evoked by the body's inner machinery and movements. These activities provide opportunities to manipulate and surprise others rather than be surprised and manipulated oneself.

Erikson (1951) studied how children use blocks and space at this age and found that boys are interested in height and downfall and in motion and its channelization or arrest, while girls appear to be interested in space that is enclosed, blocked, and intruded upon. He interpreted these differences as reflecting the different anatomical concerns of the sexes. The jokes, whisperings, and secrets among both sexes reflect curiosity about the body's anatomy and function, where babies come from, and the like. But childish confusion between the eliminative and reproductive systems is reflected in smutty jokes about elimination and the buttocks (Blos, 1962). Of course, the boundaries between the sexes are not impermeable. Changing times, opportunities, and experiences increasingly call into question sex-differentiated interests. Yet it is astonishing how tenaciously this differentiation persists.

Interest in the body is also expressed in a new concern with grooming, not for the sake of cleanliness but to acquire an appearance deemed fashionable by peers. For both sexes, preoccupation with the hair represents displaced concern about other parts of the body and masculinity and femininity (contemporary hair styles tend to be more unisex than differentiated these days). Despite their intense interest in face and clothing, prepubertal children often seem sloppy and dirty to their parents. What cannot be seen is frequently not attended to; it is not unusual to see an unwashed neck beneath a carefully groomed hairdo.

Loyalty to the group and the traditions of the age are faithfully pursued. The following "poems" were taken

from two autograph books: the rite of passage from grammar school to junior high. Although written thirty years
apart, each book could easily be interchanged for the other
—the two contain only slight topical differences and perhaps less repression is apparent in the contemporary version. In both books, the first pages are reserved for parents,
siblings, and teachers. Both have a uniform style, with certain words written in the corner and repeated by every
classmate. Although some poems speak of success, of wanting to be remembered, and the like, the majority touch on
sexuality and are sarcastic or poke fun. The following were
signed by boys:

Old Book	*New Book*
Roses are red	Roses are red
Violets are blue	Violets are blue
I kissed a lamppost	You got an Ass
And thought it was you.	Like a B-42.

Ashes to ashes	Ashes to ashes
Dust to dust	Dust to dust
If it wasn't for boys	What's a girl
Your lips would rust.	Without a Bust.
Your fellow grad-u-8	
Lenny	
Interior Decorator	

When you are married and	When you get married
Your husband gets cross	And then get divorced
Pick up the broom	Come to my stable
And say, I'm the boss.	And marry my horse.

Both books contained the following poems signed by girls:

When Cupid shoots his arrow
I hope he Mrs. you.

When you are married
And have twins
Come to me
For diaper pins.

The peer group's impact on individual children varies according to the degree to which the group functions as a reference and how strongly each member identifies with it and desires to belong to it. Sex, age, school status, ethnicity also determine membership in many groups. Group norms become increasingly important with increasing age, but they are not static, not perpetuated indefinitely. As changes occur in individual members' interests and attitudes, the group changes.

The younger latency-age child tends to be bound by the rules of the group. But as the development of a more relaxed superego brings about more flexible attitudes, children recognize that rules are devised and enforced by humans and thus can be changed by democratic methods. Despite the growing tendency to conform to group norms, however determined, peer norms do not override other social values, such as those of parents, at this time. How prepubertal children will respond to conflicting pressures from peers and parents usually will depend on which values and behaviors are perceived as more salient for the situation at hand. As Hartrup (1970) points out, consistent, unrelenting conflict between peer and parental norms does not appear until adolescence.

One important function of the peer group is to help its members externalize disturbing inner sensations or feelings. Thus there may be a contagious spread of excitement and incidents involving loss of control, followed by seemingly unrelated shallow affects. Although group rejection of social convention is beginning, group control is simultaneously exerted in the areas of fashions and conventions concerning hair styles, clothing, poses, mannerisms, and the like. The group mirrors the feelings of its members, and each individual mirrors the feelings of other members. It also permits the phenomenon of shared or projected guilt: in other words, guilt and responsibility for certain activities can be shared by the group as a whole or projected onto the leader or another member. Blos (1962) states that this is one explanation for the increasing significance of gang affiliation at this age.

COGNITIVE DEVELOPMENT

The wider range of interests at this age and the ability to make finer distinctions concerning rules, norms, values, and so on reflect cognitive growth. According to Piaget and Inhelder (1969), a final, fundamental decentering occurs— a liberation from the concrete and movement toward a more future-oriented stage: adolescence. Thus cognitive development, as well as other areas of change, can be viewed as preparation for adolescence.

A greater notion of proportions and a beginning ability to draw conclusions from possible, nonconcrete truths, allow children to think beyond what can be seen and perceptually verified. This ability to manipulate propositions and appreciate finer implications, incompatibilities, and disjunctions lifts the imagination above present perceptions and knowledge to the possibilities of what might be. The disconnection of thoughts from objects and the liberation of relations and classifications from concrete or intuitive ties culminate in the ability to combine a variety of relations or classes, which is of prime importance in extending and reinforcing the powers of thought. When reasoning about reality can be enhanced by explanations based on a wide variety of related propositions, that reality can be considered beyond its limited and concrete aspects and therefore the deductive powers of intelligence are greatly reinforced.

The development of new operational schemes is related to a more precise and flexible manipulation of words. Both abilities improve not only the understanding of reality and experience but the capacity to formulate ideas more clearly. Piaget and Inhelder (1969) suggested that the spirit of experimentation which appears at this age is made possible by this new cognitive capacity. The essential difference between this new mode of thinking and the thinking of younger children lies in a shift of perspective. Young children concentrate on reality, but as they mature and can grasp possible transformations, reality can be expanded to include imagined or deduced events. Consequently, the world of possible value is enlarged to include many new interpersonal and social possibilities, among them future experiences for which children prepare by experimenting with their new deductive capabilities. Although prepubertal children are not yet fully capable of abstract thinking or of anticipating or even fantasizing fully about the future, they are capable of relating new ideas and values to plans for the future. Sarnoff (1976) suggests that by age 11 or 12, fantasy is not only a means of discharging drives but a mechanism for integrating reality, which assists in planning for the future.

Cognitive development and use of the intellect are no more immune to conflicts at this time that at any other. Confusion about body image and attempts to control new anxieties and impulses can interfere with these newly developed capacities. Thus prepubertal children may have problems in school—especially in math; subjects that involve spatial relations, such as chart and map reading; or creative activities—because of inhibited feelings. Sometimes children this age will refuse to handle paints, clay, and the like (Harley, 1971). Their daydreams are solitary and secret because it is difficult during the throes of change to communicate freely about fantasies. To express creativity, children must be free to draw on their inner resources in a variety of ways; to express and sublimate conflict through play, drawing, and language; and to think symbolically about absent objects and invest events with symbolic meanings. But the capacity for abstract thinking is not fully developed in prepuberty; verbalization, though advanced, has not reached its peak. Thus physical and sexual changes tend to inhibit the self-revelations of children this age, even though their daydreams and fantasies are already rich in symbolic content (S. Millar, 1974).

SEXUALITY

Sexuality cannot actually be separated from other aspects of development. But because the child's physical, cognitive, and psychological development are affected by sexuality, its very scope and influence demand that it be isolated for study.

The processes of sexual growth and differentiation that accelerate at this age are part of ongoing maturational and emotional processes which will not reach completion until adulthood. Although children are interested in sex and sexual behavior before prepuberty, the basic structure of their attitudes and patterns reflects infantile preoccupations and knowledge. Therefore, behavior and language that may seem sexual to an adult may have no such meaning for the child until the adult communicates the meaning. Consequently, dirty jokes and words that were once infantile become related more specifically to adult sexuality in prepuberty. What is new now is the capacity to comprehend, however incorrectly, some of the meaning of adult sexuality. With the development of adult genital apparatus and the upsurge in hormonal activity, sexual excitement becomes more than an accompaniment to oral, urinary, or bowel preoccupations. The child is better able to understand genital sexuality, but earlier preoccupations have a tenacious influence on sexuality through life, affecting foreplay and often interfering with the attainment of free sexual expression.

Thornburg (1974) suggests that one's peers are the primary source of sexual information and that most of the information they provide is incorrect. In a study of the adequacy of sexual knowledge among lower class boys, Thornburg found that only 15 percent had received adequate information. Sixty-six percent had been given inadequate information, 13 percent had distorted information, and 6 percent had no information at all. The boys knew little about masturbation, venereal disease, nocturnal emissions, and menstruation. (As mentioned earlier, girls are better informed about menstruation than boys are about seminal emissions.)

Though prepubertal boys and girls are more interested in one another than are younger children, much of this interest is covert, often expressed through insults and pushing. Many youngsters, especially girls, fall in love with children with whom they have little contact. Some years ago, when socials were organized for children of this age, it was common for the boys to be on one side of the room, indulging in horseplay and mischief, while the girls were on the other, whispering and giggling about the boys. Today, children are stimulated by the media and so-called enlightened adults, who, not understanding the prepubertal child's inadequate emotional preparation and lack of ability to cope, foster dating or other heterosexual activities prematurely. Some prepubertal children are not shielded from sexualized contact with adolescents, or their environment may provide little physical privacy.

The sex play that occurs at this age is more exploratory than genital. A boy may try to handle and explore a girl's body, and although she may be a passive participant in this behavior, she may have provoked it in some way (Blos, 1970). Homosexual-like body contact is more common at this age and is often induced unconsciously through rough-

housing and wrestling among boys or cuddling and closeness among girls. Despite this similarity in boys' and girls'
overall sexual interests, however, the differences between
their inner and outer sexual organs, identifications, and
social expectations result in different behavior and fears.

Anyone who has worked with prepubertal children has
noticed this preoccupation with sex. The following description of the behavior of girls in an activity therapy group
(Lieberman, 1964) illustrates the changes that occur during
prepuberty and early adolescence:

> The group met after summer vacation and contained five
> girls ages 11 and 12, one 13-year-old, and a new member
> age 10. All the girls were in the sixth or seventh grade. The
> club room was designed and equipped for four boys'
> groups, which used the room at other times.
>
> During the first few meetings, the girls talked about
> their summer vacations, school, friends, and the group's
> needs in the coming year. As time went on, they began to
> leave provocative signs for the boys they never met and
> expressed anger at their teachers.
>
> Gradually, two subgroups developed: the chronologi-
> cally older girls in one and the more disturbed and younger
> girls in the other. The older group talked about clothes,
> appearance, and hair styles, and the younger group engaged
> in active games. Sometimes a member would drift from one
> group to the other as if uncertain about where she belonged.
>
> A year before all the girls except the youngest began to
> menstruate, sex became the dominant theme. The girls
> compared their waistlines, hips, and bosoms and talked
> about physical fitness programs, bras, and sometimes boys.
> One day Edith was upset because a man had followed her
> onto the bus, asked her if she wanted to see something
> interesting, and opened his fly. He wore a false penis; she
> knew because she had seen her brother's penis. Some girls
> began dancing around; later they sat, one behind the other,
> chanting a rhyme and blowing down the dress of the girl in
> front.
>
> The following fall, six members had different figures,
> which they compared along with their hairdos. They talked

about a magazine article that described dating practices among 12-year-olds and were both shocked and delighted by pictures of boys and girls lying together on the floor. They huddled together and kept secrets from the worker, began saying "Fuck" and laughing hilariously.

When the meeting room was changed to one that was adjacent to the bottom of an airshaft, they explored the airshaft and then danced the Limbo, a dance that involves rhythmic pelvic movements. In the new meeting room, the girls criticized their mothers, talked about how to be pretty and about their feelings of inadequacy, boys, pregnancy, and relationships between men and women. When all the girls had begun to menstruate, they became increasingly curious about birth and conception and in talking about these topics resolved some of their confusion. For example, "Babies come out of the mouth." "What do fathers do to mothers?" "What is a pussy?" "What does a girl have?" "If the baby dies, will the mother die?" "What if a baby is born retarded?" "How does a baby get there?" They asked about hysterectomies, deformed babies, abortion, circumcision, "dicks," open flys, seeing their father's "ding." They discussed their fantasies about sexual intercourse, describing the penis as a bone. They talked about the thrill of dancing close and said that closeness caused pregnancy.

On one occasion, Phyllis was pinched while riding in the subway. Another time, a man attempted to assault Ruth. New questions arose about "What is a bitch in heat?" rape, early marriage, how to prevent rape, what fun it was to have fake fights with boys! Phyllis, an adopted child, said there were three ways to have children: the foster way, the adoption way, and the other way. When the therapist said "the fucking way," Phyllis nodded.

The progression of themes produced by this prepubertal group included the repertoire reported in the literature (see, for example, Blos, 1962). The group also illustrates the difference between girls in middle latency and prepubertal girls: the former are more action oriented; the latter, more concerned with the body's appearance and functions. They turn away from and criticize adults, have secrets. Their interest in phallic symbols becomes a direct interest in the phallus; they indulge in homosexual thrills, pelvic movements, fear loss of control, and finally investigate the "inner room" and then the reality of the vagina, uterus, and pregnancy.

Fantasies and concern about rape are not uncommon among young girls as they attempt to master the idea of intercourse, which they view as a passive experience, wished for as well as feared. The seemingly homosexual experiences are more narcissistic than homosexual, and the partner is as similar as possible to the self, which includes being of the same sex (A. Freud, 1965). It is as though the cherished doll of early and middle latency is replaced by a cherished girl friend (Kestenberg, 1975).

Girls tend to be aggressive and possessive and initiate contacts with boys. Yet their masturbatory activity may still be less conscious than that of boys, which tends to be more focused, conscious, and related to internal feelings. Girls become interested in heterosexuality earlier, whether in reality or fantasy, than boys do, and they tend to be more preoccupied with their relations to other children of both sexes. Boys continue to be more action-oriented and concerned about dominance over the physical environment, including their own bodies. But they, like girls, look to peers and older boys for sexual information, including new forms of masturbation. Prepubertal homosexual practices, exploration of oneself through another, are additional attempts to externalize genital sensations. Rough-housing and wrestling stimulate genital contact and excitement and become forms of mutual masturbation (Blos, 1962; Kestenberg, 1975).

All kinds of thoughts and affects, both erotic and aggressive, can trigger an erection in boys, and the feelings of loss of control that result intensify their fears of castration and their body image becomes confused. In seeking release from tension, they often explode into episodes of unprovoked aggression, chase or tease one another, grab

each other's testicles, and tease and frighten girls, especially sisters. Hypochondriacal preoccupations may develop as a reaction to strange spasms that are confused with
bellyaches or menstrual cramps. Although boys seem to
deny the existence of the testicles and scrotum, pejoratively
calling them "balls," "eggs," "breasts," they are simultaneously viewed as "jewels" (see the case of Robert in Chapter 3).

Despite sex education, prepubertal children have distorted fantasies and ideas about the body. Both sexes often
liken the erect penis to a bone. But, as Fraiberg (1972)
pointed out, the penis remains the dominant sex organ in
adulthood, whereas maturity demands that the girl shift her
attention from the clitoris to the vagina. Girls' knowledge
of the vagina may be distorted or denied, usually because
of the need to cope with enlargement of the labia and
clitoris and the genital tensions that increase as the clitoris
and breasts become more sensitive and eroticized (Blos,
1970). Masturbation usually involves the clitoris and finger
play with the hymen, and when the feelings spread to the
vagina, they can be frightening. Yet masturbation is a unifying experience that helps girls integrate the internal genitals into their body image. Later, the menses help to
complete this unification.

The new inner swellings that create pressure and disturb prepubertal children are also pleasant. Thus children
often intensify this pressure by overeating and retaining
feces and urine. This induced pressure is frequently accompanied by fantasies about babies growing inside or about
passively submitting to penetration (rape). Boys counteract
their unconscious wish for a baby and "feminine" passivity
by exaggerating their masculinity. Girls have less difficulty
since they usually have more opportunities to play out this
wish for a baby by baby-sitting. However, infantile ideas
about birth will reoccur, and they may view intercourse as
dangerous, or bloody like menstruation. Yet the anxiety it
arouses has pleasant, erotic aspects (Harley, 1971).

Psychological Development

Puberty, including the stage immediately preceding it, is a significant developmental crisis that imposes special tasks on children (Erikson, 1953). Rapport (1965) has defined crisis as an upset or a series of discontinuities which disturb a homeostatic state to such a degree that the individual's habitual methods of solving problems do not result in the rapid restoration of equilibrium. The changes that induce a sense of crisis tend to be viewed as threatening either because they conflict with fundamental instinctual needs and a sense of integrity or because they evoke a feeling of loss and deprivation. Anxiety is a natural reaction to the former threat, while depression is the natural reaction to the latter. In either case, the threat tends to reactivate unresolved conflicts and old memories: i.e., the individual unconsciously links the new situation to an old one.

The increase in tension, anxiety, and feeling of helplessness leads to attempts to relieve the discomfort; the greater the threat and feeling of helplessness, the greater the possibility that efforts to cope with the new demands will evoke maladaptive behaviors such as disorganization and somatization and defense mechanisms such as repression, denial, magical thinking, excessive fantasy, regression, and even withdrawal from reality. In many cases, an individual will initially exhibit maladaptive behavior and then rally and move forward in a more productive way. Some persons will perceive the situation as a challenge and mobilize their energies to meet it. In the latter case, ego abilities enhanced by new knowledge, skills, interpersonal relationships, and even new models can be used for the purpose of identification and solution (Rapoport, 1965). Although success in managing some aspects of the situation will lead to hope, progress does not occur in a straight line: the person in crisis struggles back and forth, regression and progression are intertwined.

Prepuberty is not a sudden crisis; it creeps up on the

child and heralds a period of much greater upset that continues for a longer period. Although the nature of the tasks and changes of prepuberty can induce feelings of anxiety, helplessness, loss, and disorganization as well as maladaptive behavior and regression, the process of trial and error helps the child develop adaptive, flexible coping mechanisms that in the long run produce a strong, capable, adult.

Prepuberty represents an upset in the steady state that characterized early and middle latency. The decisive physical changes of puberty that are beginning to take place involve general appearance as well as specific genital changes and functions. Although instinctual needs increase with the increased production of hormones, youngsters lack adequate outlets for the tensions that those hormones arouse. When menstruation or ejaculation occurs, it is spectacular enough to be a body crisis that affects a child's sense of reality, self, and identity. And because there is so much variation from child to child, an additional difficulty arises: though deviation from a fictitious norm is the norm, this is difficult to explain to youngsters. Feeling different from others, they feel hopelessly ugly and different. Children who are in treatment at this age frequently are discontented with their appearance and wish they could change it.

Hormonal upsets and changes in the body lead to physical and psychological diffusion. Just as the growing child's arms, legs, and trunk seem to be out of proportion, so the body image loses its firm boundaries, which affects the ego's functions and identity. Narcissistic self-involvement increases with the need to reassess the body and its changing image and boundaries. All impulses, not only sexual ones but hunger and aggression, increase. Greediness and overeating are common during prepuberty, and children this age seem to delight in dirt and disorder. Modesty and sympathy are often replaced by exhibitionistic tendencies and even cruelty, not only to peers but to animals. Although the ego and superego are firmly consolidated by prepuberty, there is a struggle against these frightening impulses and an intensification of reaction formations, and the superego seems to fall apart. To preserve it and to fend off anxiety, prepubertal children will resort to all the methods of defense that they used in earlier stages (A. Freud, 1936).

There is often a conscious feeling of loss—loss of control over the self, the body, and old relationships. The much-awaited physical maturity will herald not only the end of childhood, forever, but the end of the appropriateness of depending on parents. Loss and recovery are played out in many ways in the beginning of this second stage of individuation and separation. Although children need help and guidance at this time, the struggle between dependence and independence makes it difficult for them to ask for it. In addition, they turn away from familiar adults before they have formed the strong new attachments and impersonal ideals that are so characteristic of late adolescence. Ironically, the absorbing narcissism of prepuberty interferes with relations with others, even with peers, and children become less accessible to the help of others, especially adults, at a time when they need it most.

This rejection of parents occurs with much ambivalence and backward and forward movement; more complete separation will not occur until adolescence. Renewed disappointment with parents who are not omnipotent is related to the loss and security of past beliefs and dependencies. In daydreams, children correct reality, and the reawakening of the family romance is only the forerunner of more complete disillusionment (A. Freud, 1968b). Children's fantasies about having better parents somewhere contain an unconscious erotic component that removes the parent and sibling of the opposite sex from the incest taboo. As a result, their imagination can consider a wide variety of erotic situations and relationships, including secret infidelities and love affairs, especially involving the mother (S. Freud, 1909b).

The fact that sexuality linked to parents begins to be disturbing is revealed in children's unconscious fantasies, particularly dreams. In real life, children react by being "repelled" by their parents' bodies, and every parental approach frightens them. For both sexes, the mother is the link to a dependent, infantile past; she is the preoedipal mother who dominated them and on whom they were dependent. Thus there is a return of old oedipal conflicts that were repressed in earlier stages of latency.

The prepubertal girl is more ambivalent about her mother than is the boy. Though she fears dependency, she has a real need for her mother's approval and help in becoming a woman. In an effort to counteract the wish to be cared for, the girl will sometimes develop a crush on an older woman or be "in love" with a girl friend. She may evidence heterosexual interests, but fathers, other men, and boys are actually less important than her activities seem to suggest. What is important is the entry into womanhood; for this, the young girl needs a female ally and helper.

Boys as well as girls of this age are fascinated by breasts, the most overt sign of womanhood, as attested to by boys' glances and snickers when their female classmates begin to develop. Boys are also interested in their mother's breasts, which symbolize not only their new sexuality but their old dependency. In reaction to the wish to be taken care of, which he perceives as passive and "feminine," a boy will shy away from expressing interest in girls and women. The father is viewed as an ally, not an oedipal rival, and the boy seeks a good relationship with him. The mother is threatening, not only because of the boy's passive, "childish" wishes but because she revives old fantasies about the castrating mother. As a reaction to feeling weak, the boy seeks to develop social competence and physical prowess and to engage in male, team-oriented contests—

all of which ensure emancipation from mother (Blos, 1965).

In addition to all the changes described in this chapter so far, the environment outside the home becomes less stable. For example, the 11- or 12-year-old may have to change to a new school farther from home, and one teacher may be replaced by several teachers who make new demands (Berger, 1975). Because these changes increase tension, physical activity becomes an age-specific manner of discharging that tension. There is a rush to activity as well as a predisposition to act out (Greenacre, 1975), which may be expressed in school as mischievousness, restlessness, and inability to concentrate, or even insubordination.

The growing distance from parental support, frightening fantasies, loss of control, and inner disharmony make children feel and act out of tune with their environment much of the time. Yet the strengths they acquired before prepuberty do not disappear. Children of this age are still capable of secondary process thinking and social understanding, have strong ego functions, and need less assistance from others. All these factors help prepubertal children to use their environment and to think through some of their day-to-day problems. And much of their distress vanishes overnight when the specific situation that elicited it disappears.

Latency is the only stage of life in which individuals do not make sexual demands on themselves or others. Latent sexuality is a necessity if a child is to develop the capacity to cope with the turbulence of adolescence and the demands and responsibilities of adulthood. But it must take place in an expectable environment, which is generally unavailable to the child who lives in a disorganized, crowded environment. In other words, development never proceeds in a vacuum. Many children will not achieve the expected growth nor exhibit the expected behavior of latency. Children are sensitive to fluctuations within their environment, and this sensitivity will manifest itself in their behavior more often than not. It is never sufficient to study a child to determine what is wrong *with* him or her. A true understanding of what is wrong requires an equal emphasis on determining what is wrong *for* the child.

III

PROBLEMS

Chapter 6

UNDERNEATH THE SYMPTOMS

Children come to the attention of a social worker in many diverse ways. Usually they are brought to a clinic or agency by their parents (customarily the mother), either because the parents are having difficulty managing the child or because someone in the community such as a teacher complains about the child and suggests treatment. In some cases, the court insists on evaluation or treatment because of a child's disturbed or disturbing behavior. In others, children come to a social worker's attention when they are removed from their homes because of parental neglect or abuse or when foster parents or other caretaking officials are concerned about them.

ADULT COMPLAINTS

Latency-age children rarely request help for themselves. It is difficult for them to express their unhappiness in words, and they are likely to express their problems through behavior. Although their behavior gets them into difficulty, they tend to be less aware of the suffering their behavior causes than are their families. Unless they are overwhelmed by anxiety, the behaviors and symptoms that concern clinicians and parents will not concern them. Instead, they will worry and complain about external stresses and frustrations and want them to be changed. They seldom accept the idea that they themselves must change.

The behaviors that prompt adults to decide that a child needs help tend to be those that disturb them. Thus their complaints frequently reflect their own needs rather than the child's; at times, they object to behavior that is typical at certain ages. For example, when Long (1941) examined parents' complaints about undesirable behavior in their children, he noted the following. Disobedience was the major complaint about children ages 3 to 10 and ages 14 to 18. Parents of young children often complained about temper tantrums, thumb-sucking, and bed-wetting, whereas parents of older children did not. Parents of 3- to 5-year-olds never mentioned that their children were shy or uncommunicative, whereas parents of teen-agers often complained about these behaviors. Fears were listed as undesirable traits in children up to age 10; the frequency of this complaint then declined steadily.

In a comparative study of mothers', teachers', and clinicians' views of the behaviors of children in Woodlawn, a black community in Chicago, Kellam et al. (1975) asked mothers of first graders whether their children had the following symptoms: nervous habits, sleep problems; hypochondriasis; problems with toilet training, eating, or learning; sexuality; fears; and the like. Almost all mothers listed at least one symptom, and as many as two-thirds of the children had a large number of symptoms. Although many of these symptoms were similar to those usually included in psychiatric referrals, others seemed to be related to social and cultural contexts. Parental reactions to symptomatic behavior also seemed to play an important role in these behaviors.

To obtain objective information and help parents organize their thoughts about their children's problems, some agencies ask parents to fill out a questionnaire. Using this technique, Arnold and Smeltzer (1974) studied parental complaints about 351 children ages 2 to 18 who were being treated in a child psychiatry clinic and found that some complaints were similar for all ages: e.g., school difficulties, somatic symptoms, disobedience, and other behavior problems, problems in relating to others (fighting, bullying), restlessness, and affective problems such as sadness, loneliness, and feeling disliked by other children. Complaints about running away overnight were rarely made about younger children, while behaviors such as fears, crying easily, and speech difficulties were less prevalent among teen-agers. On the other hand, some parents of younger children mentioned rapid and extreme mood changes—which are typical of adolescents. Thus prejudgment, selectivity, and a recognition that some behaviors were atypical for their child's age group were probably involved in the parents' complaints.

According to parents and teachers, latency-age boys present more difficulties than do girls. In Arnold's and Smeltzer's study, 70 percent of the patients ages 2 to 12 were boys, whereas only 52 percent of the children in the older group were boys. This difference is typical of referrals to child psychiatry and child guidance clinics; perhaps the greater motor activity of latency-age boys is more disturbing to adults. The similar percentages of male and female referrals in adolescence often reflects sexual acting out among young adolescent girls or parents' fears that this will happen.

Neubauer (1975) reported that boys and girls under age 8 are referred for different reasons. Boys tend to be

referred because of reading disorders, speech disturbances, lack of bowel control, hyperactivity, and aggressive
behavior. Girls, on the other hand, are referred for overdependency, emotional overcontrol, bowel retention, and
anorexia; are brought for help at an earlier age; and show
more oral and withdrawn behaviors. Neubauer concluded
that parents become more upset about mood swings and
withdrawal in little girls than about aggressive, outward
directed behavior in boys, apparently interpreting the former as evidence of greater pathology. Although quiet behavior is common among girls in general, the degree of
withdrawal that characterizes clinic populations is unusual
for very young children, and the parents' referrals seem to
reflect an awareness of this fact.

SYMPTOMATOLOGY

Parents and teachers are not the only persons who focus on
specific behaviors. Many professionals use referral symptoms and other descriptions of behavior to categorize and
diagnose children's difficulties. But as Anna Freud stated
(1970), symptoms can be the result of many causes: they
"are no more than symbols, to be taken merely as indications that some mental turmoil is taking place (p. 19)."
Symptoms can either be transitory responses to developmental or environmental stress or deeply imbedded in the
personality and thus injurious to development.

Latency-age children seldom verbalize their problems,
first, because they are incapable of verbal abstraction and,
second, because they usually do not know *consciously* what
the problem is. For these reasons, they naturally tend to
express their discomfort, anxiety, fear, depression, and
helplessness through their behavior. Indeed, children
rarely complain, even about the bad things that happen to
them—especially if their parents are to blame—because at

this age, they are dependent on parents and need to identify with the parental viewpoint. As a result, they are likely
to interpret an unpleasant event as punishment for bad
behavior, thoughts, or wishes. The younger the child, the
more natural this reaction.

Because children have less ego strength and ability to
cope and are more dependent and helpless than are adults,
they are in greater actual danger. What adults judge accurately as maladaptive behavior may be the only way children can express inner conflicts and problems. In fact, their
behavior, although unconscious, is a personal and specific
message to the adults who are most important to them.

Because latency-age children are not introspective,
i.e., they rarely scrutinize their own thoughts and feelings,
they move naturally from psychological concerns to environmental realities, externalize their problems, and expect
their caretakers to solve them, either by punishment or by
removing the difficulty. No person lacks problems; children
simply exhibit symptomatic behavior more often than
adults do and in more varied ways. There is rarely a single,
simple cause for a child's symptoms, nor is there a single,
simple solution. Symptoms will appear in isolation or in
combination, they will appear and disappear (A. Freud,
1965).

Symptoms are the end result of children's attempts to
cope with a variety of discomforts and conflicts that produce anxiety. When the symptom reduces or eliminates the
anxiety, children see no need to change their behavior. The
underlying anxiety may be related to unmet needs or to
external demands and prohibitions that cause anger, guilt,
or fear of punishment or loss of love. The problem may be
an internalized one based on fantasies and misunderstandings, but usually internal and external problems are combined.

When adults react unfavorably to symtomatic behavior, children become anxious unless the secondary gains

outweigh the ramifications of adult displeasure. All children experience anxiety. Because many of their conflicts are specifically related to different phases of development, their anxiety and symptomatic behavior are transitory and will dissipate, with help or in the normal course of development. For example, going to school for the first time evokes some anxiety in all children. The degree of anxiety and the behavior that results will reflect an individual child's history, the amount of security at home, the ability to cope, and the family's method of dealing with anxiety. The realities of the school experience, of course, will either assuage or increase the anxiety. How successfully children will deal with this new situation will depend on their individual capacities and the degree to which the situation is congruent with their individual abilities and needs.

Throughout latency, children are confronted by a variety of new situations that create tension. How individual children will react will reflect the demands of the situation, the influences and anxieties of their parents and culture, and their own unconscious tendencies (Johnson, Szurek, & Falstein, 1942). An anxious child may regress, stop achieving, or exhibit aberrant behavior.

Children become anxious when the level of functioning that is appropriate for their age meets with disapproval, when there is dissonance between their behavior (normal or deviant) and environmental expectations, or when new situations call for new behavioral patterns. The anxiety can either push children to change in the desired direction or produce a variety of symptoms. As Chess (1973) pointed out, however, identical symptoms can be produced by diverse events, situations, needs, and pathology.

Although many generalizations about behavior have been derived from studies of children and from a variety of clinical and theoretical reports, the worker must apply these generalizations in relation to a specific child's unique situation within a biopsychosocial-historical context. Only then will the worker understand the child and the private communications of the presenting symptoms. If the behavior is a recent development, it is probably a reaction to a current threat. Why a situation is threatening can be understood only when the child's viewpoint and circumstances are understood.

A variety of "developmental interferences" disturb the normal course of development. For instance, gross environmental interferences such as parental neglect, abuse, and lack of interest and inadequate stimulation place impossible demands on children. Other interferences, including those that are culturally or socially determined, impose unhealthy restrictions on them. Accidents such as death or illness also affect the environment's ability to meet children's needs (Nagera, 1966a). How children will react to any of these interferences will depend on the nature of the stressful event and their individual capacities, including developmental age as opposed to chronological age. For example, one would ordinarily expect 7- and 12-year-olds to react differently to events such as their own illness and hospitalization or the illness and hospitalization of a parent or sibling. But if older children have a history of serious difficulties and developmental problems, their reactions may be similar to those of younger children.

Most children manage to cope with entry into school —a normal developmental crisis that calls for new ways of dealing with many new experiences; for others it is too much. For example, children who have unresolved developmental conflicts that were appropriate at an earlier age, then school will revive these conflicts. Normal developmental conflicts can become serious developmental problems when the environment has been traumatic or has grossly interfered with the child's rights and needs.

Often, parents will not request treatment for a child until a problem becomes disturbing to them. Thus, although they view the problem as recent, the problem has obviously existed for a long time. Far too many children who are placed in foster care live in a series of foster homes. Because these children rarely have the opportunity to work through the first separation, not to mention subsequent ones, a progression of symptoms, ranging from simple and specific reactions to complex symptomology can be found in their histories. Other children, who have suffered a traumatic experience at some point in early life, have not been helped to work through the old anxiety. Any of these developmental interferences can cause difficulties later, as illustrated in the following case:

> *Helen S,* age 15, was the eldest child of an intact, middle-income family; there was one brother, age 13. She had attended a special school for children with learning disabilities since she was 11. Despite an apparently normal IQ, Helen performed many years below grade level, and there was evidence of serious emotional problems. A psychological evaluation at age 12 indicated strong oral needs, lack of sufficient nurturance, and the diagnostic impression of schizophrenia in remission. Although Mrs. S had sporadically sought help, she usually complained about her husband or about Helen.
>
> Helen's teachers described her as quiet, controlled, and attentive. She completed assignments and was doing rather well, but still performed below grade level in most subjects. Helen came to the school social worker's attention when Mrs. S complained to the teachers about Helen's tantrums at home, which disrupted the household to such a degree that she talked of residential treatment for Helen. It was obvious that many things Helen did provoked her mother.
>
> During her second interview with the worker, Helen agreed that she had difficulty with her mother, but only because her mother asked her to do things at times that weren't convenient for Helen. Her brother didn't have to do anything. He just laughed at her. Helen said that after the first interview, she had done everything her mother wanted her to and that everything was O.K.; her mother, her father, her brother were all O.K. The only thing that was not O.K. was one of her dogs. The big one was O.K., but the little one was in trouble. Sometimes he peed in her bed; one day she

noticed a stain. "Maybe it would be better if we get rid of the dogs; they disrupt the household. It was really my brother's fault. He threw the dog against the wall, and I think that's why the dog is like that. It was when the dog was little, and I don't think he's forgotten. And then I spilled nail polish on my bed. I was really mad, but I didn't let my mother know. She got really mad at me, yelled, but I wanted her to. I guess I felt I deserved it for what I did."

In the next interview, Helen complained about her difficulty in choosing between two hi-fi records and how confused she got when making a decision. She also bought an almanac because it contained lots of facts. Then she complained that her father broke her rocking chair. Well, actually it was several years ago, but he didn't fix it then and now it was too late and he had to get her a new one. After all, it was his fault.

When Mrs. S was asked for some developmental history, especially whether Helen had had some physical problem, she said that Helen had been an inquisitive and creative child until she was about 3 or 4, when she became defiant and antagonistic. She lost interest in things quickly and seemed to have an insatiable need for new toys and so forth. She was always indulged. However, when her brother was toilet trained at about age 2 and Helen, at 4, was not, Mrs S consulted her pediatrician, who told her not to worry, it would pass. But Mrs. S did worry and sent a sample of Helen's urine to a lab, which reported that Helen had a severe urinary infection that needed immediate attention. Mrs. S changed pediatricians immediately.

Helen could not urinate routinely; she would have accidents whenever her bladder became full. As a result, she was hospitalized four times. The first time, she was examined with a cystoscope (a slender, cylindrical instrument that is inserted into the bladder through the urethra) and had an operation. Mrs S slept in a chair for three nights in Helen's hospital room, not wishing to leave the child alone. The three subsequent hospitalizations also involved surgery.

Helen's maternal grandmother was the first to detect aberrant behavior in Helen (at age 5). She felt that Helen was not doing things other children did: she never went far from home, had few friends, and had learning problems in school.

Helen's severe urinary infection, which occurred during the oedipal period and involved manipulation and surgery in the genital area, represented a serious developmental interference. How could a 4-year-old be expected to cope with this? Despite the best preparation and her mother's presence, the procedures must have awakened fantasies of mutilation, castration, sexual penetration, and more. Staying in bed and being deprived of home and familiar food are traumatic enough for a little child. When oral deprivation and physical assault are added to this, a child can easily believe that parents who allow these things to happen are not protective and are punishing her for bad things such as oedipal wishes, masturbation, sibling rivalry, bed-wetting, and so on.

When accidents or other traumatic experiences are combined with a child's limited cognitive ability, they create a critical incident that must be worked through. When these conditions are not handled at the time they occur, they become elaborated and extend into many areas of life, causing aberrant behavior, restricted activity, fears, and complex problems. After her experiences, Helen was undoubtedly afraid to participate in many activities, including learning. The experience was buried in her unconscious but not forgotten. As Helen said, even dogs remember things that happened long ago.

DEPRESSION

Spitz (1946) and Bowlby (1960), among others, have described depressive reactions in infants and young children. Between the ages of six months and 4 years, children become progressively aware that their mothers are separate objects. If the mother disappears for any reason, it is a serious loss. By age 3, children's sense of self and awareness of mother and father as separate individuals is relatively firmly established, and at this age the father's disappearance is also a severe loss. When the loss is permanent, children tend to search persistently for the lost object. According to Jacobson (1971), it is this type of loss that underlies many adult depressions.

As children grow older, their reactions to loss become less direct and more complicated. They mask their depressive feelings with a variety of symptoms that essentially are attempts to cope with the loss and feelings of helplessness (Glaser, 1967; Toolan, 1969). The loss does not have to be an actual separation. Even when parents are present, they can be psychologically absent if they are neglectful; preoccupied with their own environmental, physical, or economic crises; or are depressed. Rejecting or overdemanding parents make children feel inadequate, and the loss of self-esteem and feelings of hopelessness and helplessness that result contribute to depression (Bibring, 1953). In other words, if children experience loss, whether in fact or fantasy and for whatever reason, they may exhibit depressive affect.

Because parents are extremely important throughout latency, those who are unable to provide the necessary supports and relationships will produce feelings of helplessness, inadequacy, and frustration in their children. Although peers, teachers, and other adults can augment parents, they rarely can provide the constancy that parents are expected to provide (Parens & Saul, 1971).

Latency-age children also judge themselves. During early latency, immaturity and limited knowledge and understanding about cause and effect contribute to a superego that imposes unreasonable conditions. As children grow older, knowledge, mastery, and a more flexible superego help them maintain their self-esteem despite failure and disappointment, but environmental support is still essential.

When children do not love themselves or feel unloved

by others their frustration naturally leads to anger. But anger directed against oneself is uncomfortable, and anger directed toward one's parents is usually perceived as dangerous and produces guilt. The common method of defense in these situations is denial of dependency and loss and displacement of anger onto inappropriate objects, including the self.

Some professionals believe that until adolescence, personality structure, ego abilities, and object relations preclude depressive illness in children. Even young children, however, exhibit depressive reactions or their equivalents. Mendelson (1974) reviewed the literature about depression in children and concluded that sustained states of depressive illness do occur during childhood but are overlooked or are diagnosed as something else. Social workers and others who work with children observe anxiety, sadness, and many symptoms of depression, which usually are reaction to external circumstances and internal conflicts that children perceive as threats to their well-being. Cytryn and McKnew (1972) described children who have a persistently sad affect; seem hopeless, helpless, withdrawn from social contact; move unusually slowly; are anxious; fail in school; have social problems; and sleeping and eating difficulties. These symptoms may appear singly or in combination. Often they are evident for several months before parents seek help.

A child who usually functions well may become acutely depressed after a traumatic event. When there is no immediate precipitating factor and the depression is chronic, children tend to have marginal emotional development. They are clinging, helpless, dependent, and lonely, with a history of past depressions and at least one parent who suffers from recurrent depression.

During middle and late latency, children view crying as babyish. Thus they rarely cry or express feelings of guilt. Instead, they commonly resort to a variety of behaviors and symptoms such as withdrawal, listlessness, hyperactivity, regression, temper tantrums, poor school performance, phobias, somatic symptoms, eating and sleeping disturbances, and enuresis (Malmquist, 1972). Many of these behaviors are actually a means of self-punishment; others, especially provocative behaviors, also induce punishment from adults and scapegoating by other children.

Choice of symptoms will reflect the cultural milieu, personality, and experiences in reality. For example, Coles (1967) and Meers (1975) noted differences in the symptomatology of middle-class children and lower class children. Middle-class children tend to have more overt fears and anxieties and their symptoms seem to be attempts to control violence and anger. Lower class children often seem freer, more outgoing and spontaneous, and less controlled.

Although poor children tend to experience more loss and have more needs, their families are often warmer, closer, and more indulgent than are middle-class families. At the same time, however, they may be subjected to more physical punishment and strict moral training. Although the home may teach strict obedience, these children are also subjected to sensuality and sexual stimulation because of crowded living quarters and lack of privacy. Thus at home and in the street, poor children are frequently overstimulated, underprotected, and exposed to violence and frustration. Consequently, they tend to express the violence and rage around them and within them through violent or masochistic activities (Meers, 1975).

Some poor children and their families escape the confusion and deprivation of their communities through religious activities. For example, the church has assumed an important social and cultural role for many black families (Comer, 1974). For others, parental inability to live up to the moral codes and the influence of the streets and peers creates an ambiguous atmosphere. This ambiguity is apparent in all classes; in more affluent circles, however, the ambiguity is more closely related to parental pathology than to community pathology.

Schools in severely deprived communities tend to have a higher percentage of what seems to be intellectual and academic retardation. Confusion, noise, extreme acting out, and lack of control are also more common in these schools than in middle-class schools. Many children appear to doze, lost in daydreams and fantasies and seemingly unaware of the bedlam around them. They are apathetic, depressed, and have little energy or interest in learning and therefore look and act retarded. Intellectual and academic retardation are often reactions to frustration caused by a nonsupportive and confused home and school and hopelessness about the future (Meers, 1970).

Depression is not ordinarily listed as the primary symptom when latency-age children are referred for treatment. Adults are usually concerned about loss of control, hyperactivity, deliberately negative and even teasing behavior because they seldom understand that these behaviors may be attempts to cover up depression (Posnanski & Zrull, 1971). In other words, adults are often more concerned about how children behave than how they feel.

Latency-age children defend against depressive feelings in myriad ways. Obsessive, magical control can be used to defend against feelings of helplessness. A lack of energy can be masked by hypomanic excitement. Sadness can be mastered by reverse affect. Denial or withdrawal can be used to avoid unpleasantness or to put distance between oneself and the disturbing experience. And antisocial behavior and somatization will distract attention from unpleasant internal conflicts. Because children are extremely dependent on and susceptible to external influences, particularly their family situation, their reactions are more variable and temporary than are those of adults. Furthermore, depressive affects in children do not last as long as the underlying disturbance, which in the long run determines the intensity and nature of the child's real difficulty (Anthony, 1975 b).

AGGRESSION

Although adults worry about aggressive behavior in children, aggressive play and activities are not unusual. Cruelty can be observed in many games children play, and they frequently tease and are unkind to one another. (Extreme cruelty to younger children or the killing or torture of insects and small animals is a different matter.) (Lebovicci, 1973).

Aggression is normal in all animals, including humans. However, human children learn to control their aggressive feelings because of their love for mother and their need to keep her love and approval. As the ego and superego develop, expressions of aggression are modified and children can channel their aggressive energy into constructive tasks such as learning and mastery (Buxbaum, 1970). According to Anna Freud (1968a), fusion of the forces of sex and love and aggression and destruction makes it possible for children to love and to be assertive simultaneously—to compete, satisfy their curiosity, and learn many things.

Loving and caring and identifying with loved persons are the result of adequate nurturing during childhood, particularly the early years. In this way, children learn to control their impulses and to sublimate their aggressive feelings into purposeful activity. Through loving and being loved, they also learn empathy for others. When children have been unable to fuse love and aggression, their destructive wishes are extremely frightening to them; if a parent is destroyed, they are abandoned. Caught in this dilemma, children tend to project their anger, which makes the once-loved person the aggressor and persecutor. To alleviate this intolerable situation, they then project their aggression onto persons outside the family, even complete strangers.

Latency-age children who function at this level have developmental problems. Their low tolerance for frustration produces chronic tension and anxiety, which demand physical expression. Sometimes these states occur as a reaction to frustration of a basic need to be cared for; sometimes they occur in children who are so tied to their mothers that without them they feel helpless and strike out. Yet these children can relate to people and care about them. Children who have not been mothered cannot love anybody and thus do not fear that their aggressive activity will result in loss of love. Others, even less related, withdraw from life and are absorbed in fantasy (Rank, 1949; Buxbaum, 1970); in this sense, acting out is less pathological than complete withdrawal.

Aggressive and violent activity can be triggered by fear or anger related to new or old experiences. some new experiences actually are threatening, but the dangers involved in others are imagined. New experiences can also reactivate old, unresolved problems. The greater the past problems and the greater the deprivation, the more likely that the slightest pressure from current circumstances will precipitate agressive or violent behavior. The greater the pressures in the current situation, the fewer the previous disturbances that will be required to precipitate these activities (Littner, 1972).

Most children learn from their families how to control violent feelings. But in families where violence is the primary method of solving problems, children learn to translate their violent feelings into violent acts. For example, in families where there is severe psychosocial pathology, such as alcoholism, neglect, brutality, illegitimacy, delinquency, and crime, violence is not a matter of personal feeling or fantasy, it is real, and the children live in a normless world where actions speak louder than words. These children usually experience little pleasure and have little energy for sustained interests or constructive functioning. Under stress, they communicate physically rather than verbally, their lives are dominated by external influences, and they lack a sense of stability and constancy. Because they are unable to depend on or believe in permanence and security, they spend their time trying to understand what others want of them. (Malone, 1966; Littner, 1972; Reiner & Kaufman, 1959).

In families where action is the primary form of communication, the development of mature mental and intellectual processes is not facilitated. The children cannot understand verbally expressed concepts and need physical demonstrations to understand many things in life that normally are expressed verbally (Malone, 1966). Like their parents, they act out against others and themselves in a variety of aggressive, violent, provocative, and antisocial ways.

Antisocial behavior is the expression of aggressive and sexual impulses that conflict with society's norms and often are the actualization of murderous, aggressive fantasies. The Group for the Advancement of Psychiatry (1966) terms this type of behavior "psychopathic", "impulsive behavior disorder," or "conduct disorder." As Robins (1974) pointed out, antisocial behavior rarely begins in adulthood; usually some kind of acting out and antisocial behavior occurs during childhood or adolescence.

Socioeconomic status, culture, and community influence the manifestations of behavior in children, including aggression. When Paternite, Loney and Longhorne (1976) studied groups of boys ranging in age from 4 to 12—all of whom had been diagnosed as "hyperkinetic/mimimal brain damage"—boys from upper and middle-class families tended to show less severe aggressive interpersonal behavior than did boys from lower class families, apparently because their parents were firmer, more consistent, and more competent in enforcing rules.

Violence within the family is frequently translated to the community, which in turn encourages children to express their impulses and feelings through aggressive behavior. Because television has enlarged the meaning of community, the models available for imitation, and the experiences to which children are exposed, the violence shown on television has concerned experts and parents alike for many years and is the subject of ongoing research. Television seems to encourage aggressive behavior in children (boys more often than girls) who are already predisposed to act out their aggression. According to the Surgeon General's Scientific Advisory Committee (1972), films of violent news events are more disturbing to children than are programs that contain make-believe violence, and they lead to violent behavior more often. And the younger the child, the less ability there is to differentiate between real and make-believe.

So far, the predisposition to violent behavior has been discussed in relation to poverty and deprivation. In any socioeconomic group, however, parents who are extremely disturbed, inconsistent, neglectful, or seductive may produce a predisposition for violence in their children. In Littner's view (1972), children from so-called better, more stable communities are more likely to express violence in covert ways such as argumentativeness, an unusual interest in guns or weapons, and hostile, violent, and sadistic fantasies and daydreams. As adolescents or adults, these individuals are the ones who "suddenly" act in violent and antisocial ways. The following case history illustrates this type of child:

> *Philip R* was referred because of his failure in school. His teacher believed that he tried to work up to his grade level, but he wasted time fidgeting and wandering around the

room. In addition, he was isolated, fearful, stammered, and had no friends. He was the youngest of three children and the only boy. Although Philip was 11 years old when he began treatment, his favorite toys were miniature soldiers and war equipment. Philip was preoccupied with violence but did not act violently. In reality, he was so well behaved that he seemed constricted and strange.

When Philip's abilities were tested, his verbal performance was normal, but his scores on graphomotor and visual memory tests suggested some minimal organic deficit. His reading comprehension and arithmetic ability were above average, and he had no difficulty comprehending verbally presented problems. Accordingly, the examiner concluded that anxiety, emotional immaturity, poor judgment in interpersonal relations, and an inability to control his impulses were primary interferences in Philip's case.

During treatment, it became apparent that violence was a family affair. Mr. R. would frequently become so enraged that he pulled the phone from the wall. He believed that many people did such things, and on one occasion asked whether other people ever became so angry that they felt like killing someone. Although he had never acted on it, he sometimes felt this way. Mrs. R masked her aggression toward Philip, who had not been a planned child, with oversolicitude, calling him the "Redeemer." In joking but bizarre ways, however, she revealed her underlying feelings. For example, when she was getting Philip ready for summer camp, she said that camp was like a concentration camp. Thus treatment involved active work with the parents to curb Mrs. R's seductive behavior and Mr. R's distant but frightening behavior.

In individual sessions with Philip, it took many hours of playing war games to overcome Philip's fears. Slowly, he began to be involved with other children. Although he no longer received such good marks in conduct at school, his academic grades improved. He was no longer a failure. His parents noticed that the boys he became involved with tended to be aggressive and not well behaved. With them, Philip threw snowballs at passing cars and killed birds in the park with a huge slingshot. He also became enamored of piranhas, a flesh-eating fish that he saw in the pet store. Although he was both fascinated and frightened by the piranhas and wanted to buy one, he also wanted to buy a kissing fish.

Many factors, both internal and external, seemed to contribute to Philip's preoccupation with violence. But the neighborhood in which he lived was middle-class and did not augment the violence in his home. Because his parents masked their aggressive, violent feelings, Philip was unable to fuse love and hate: i.e., he wanted to have both the flesh-eating fish and the kissing fish and was conflicted about his aggressive feelings. His anxiety diminished when some of his parents' frightening seductive and aggressive behavior was eliminated. And through play and symbolic communication, his fears were reduced and he was able to devote his energy to learning and social activities.

Because provocative and aggressive children are often unpopular with teachers, peers, and parents, there is a self-punishing component to their behavior. At the other extreme are children who are so frightened by their aggressive feelings that they cannot compete actively, are oversolicitous and anxious about a "loved" person's safety and health, can express only positive and loving feelings, and are excessively gentle. These children defend against their bad thoughts through reaction formation and inhibition and thus prevent themselves from learning. If their aggression is internalized to an excessive degree and repressed, or if they are unable to contain their aggressive thoughts, organic illness, harsh self-criticism, feelings of worthlessness, and even self-destructive acts such as accidents and self-mutilation may result (A. Freud, 1968a).

When confronted with similar problems, different children will exhibit different reactions; conversely, different problems will produce similar symptoms in different children. The problem is to understand and see beyond the symptoms that concern parents, teachers, and others and even beyond those that seem to concern children (although it is essential to understand what concerns them). Only a multidimensional understanding of a child's total situation will enable the worker to obtain a picture of a flesh-and-blood child rather than a set of pathological symptoms. In other words, the worker must know about the child's development, behavior, progress through life, and what that life has been. Although the current situation is the most urgent element, the picture must also show the past because a child's past is never far away.

Chapter 7

LEARNING PROBLEMS

Learning problems and school difficulties are often the primary reasons for complaints about children, and it has become popular to label children with learning problems as learning disabled. However, the term learning disability has become a catch-all diagnosis for a wide variety of perceptual, motor, developmental, emotional, and environmental handicaps.

Realistically, not learning is a disability. But observers may notice only that a child is unable to perform age-expected school tasks (Hobbs, 1975). In other words, the difference between actual learning and satisfactory completion of work in the classroom has not been stressed adequately. For example, Philip R had learned more than he was able to demonstrate in the classroom, but he had not learned enough. His (and Helen's) learning and emotional difficulties were interrelated.

Learning problems can be caused or accompanied by other problems such as disturbed relations with parents and peers, insecurity, guilt, shame, inhibited learning or inhibited use of learning, and even fear of succeeding. In many, many cases, learning problems are symptoms of other problems that must be attended to before learning can take place (Pearson, 1952). Some of these problems are emotional while others are related to ability. But in all cases, the inability to learn as others do creates emotional problems for latency-age children because they fail to meet expectations in an important sphere of life. School failure often becomes a vicious circle: when faced with any kind of learning task, a child will experience great anxiety, which in turn may result in aggressiveness, hyperactivity, or withdrawal. For all children, there is a fundamental relationship between learning, growing, feeling, and psychological development—a circular process in which feeling and thinking are closely related, each reacting on the other (Sapir & Nitzburg, 1973).

HYPERACTIVITY

Because hyperactive, aggressive children disrupt the classroom, are difficult to control, affect other children, and frustrate their teachers, educators and other professionals are trying to determine what causes this condition and how to manage and treat it. In addition, they are concerned about the labels, diagnostic judgments, and treatment measures that are applied to these children.

Children are labeled hyperactive when they exhibit the following specific behaviors to a greater extent than is generally considered normal: motor activity, brief attention span, distractability, impulsiveness, explosiveness, and the inability to delay gratification. These symptoms are usually accompanied by poor school performance despite adequate intelligence. Forty percent of all children referred to mental health clinics have been labeled hyperactive by the referral source. According to Zentall (1975), approximately 20 percent of all American elementary school pupils are labeled hyperactive. (Eight percent of all pupils are labeled as such in the first grade.)

Frequently, teachers apply this label and then demand parental action, even suggesting medication at times. Parents may ask their physicians for an opinion. Sandoval, Lambert, & Yandell, (1976), in a study of medical practice in this area, concluded that no consensus exists among physicians about the physical problem. The majority of them rely on behavioral symptoms—physical activity, impatience, poor response to parental discipline, history of disturbed eating and sleeping habits, conflicts with peers and teachers, academic failure, and family pathology—for diagnostic clues. "Hyperactive learning behavior disorder, etiology unknown" was the most frequent diagnosis, followed by minimal brain damage (MBD) and hyperkinesis. As many as 70 percent of the physicians in the study prescribed ritalin or some other brain stimulant, although they viewed the problem as behavioral, not neurological.

The confusion in labeling is evidenced by the blurring of differences among the terms hyperactivity, delinquency, MBD, learning difficulties, hyperkinesis, impulse disorder, and the like—all of which are pseudoscientific labels, not diagnoses. Heavy reliance on drugs as the preferred treatment has also caused controversy (Schrag & Divorky, 1975; Renshaw, 1974; Grinspoon & Singer, 1973; Cole, 1975). And the fact that these pseudoscientific labels are applied to lower class and black children far more often than to other groups has led to accusations of discrimination.

Hyperactivity, restlessness, and distractability are normal under the age of 4 or 5, and even older children express excitement, fatigue, and emotional tension through motor activity. Many young children react to the new experience of school by showing off, clowning, and constant motion. Since hyperactivity tends to be an evaluation, in this case the teacher's, children's expectable or normal behavior will vary, depending on how authoritarian or liberal the particular teacher and the culture happen to be.

The reactions of immature, hyperanxious children to the developmental crisis of going to school are often misunderstood. Children may express their fear of separation from home and their reactions to a variety of internal and external conflicts through tantrums; running out of the classroom; or disruptive, aggressive, neurotic, and even psychotic behavior (Renshaw, 1974). All children respond to and frequently misunderstand even small fluctuations in the environment, parental situations and demands, and the expectations of teachers.

Some children who exhibit hyperactive behavior are reacting to current or past overconstraint of physical activity, whether imposed for disciplinary reasons or as a consequence of serious illness. In any case, latency-age children must be physically active, not only to facilitate their physical growth and development, but to discharge tension. When they are unable to be active in appropriate ways for whatever reason, they will find inappropriate ways.

HYPERKINESIS AND MINIMAL BRAIN DAMAGE

The hyperactivity of some children is so extreme that they seem almost compelled to be in perpetual motion, and incapable of paying attention, or being quiet. When their impulsiveness, low tolerance for frustration, and aggressive activity is combined with poor school work and motor difficulties, they are frequently diagnosed as suffering from hyperkinesis, hyperkinetic impulse disorder, or MBD. The so-called hyperkinetic syndrome is vague both as a diagnosis and in etiology. Amphetamines are usually the preferred treatment, although the medical profession is unclear about why these drugs help. Furthermore, the judgment that certain children suffer from hyperkinetic disturbance or MBD is often based on the fact that amphetamines slow them down. Because of this specious reasoning and because few long-term studies have been done on the effects of amphetamines on young children, the controversy continues. Some adverse effects that occur when drug treatment is initiated are poor appetite, insomnia, gastrointestinal distress, dizziness, tremors, cold extremities, and pallor. Although these symptoms tend to diminish over time, growth and weight are affected (Cole, 1975; Grinspoon & Singer, 1973).

The diagnostic categories that were originally intended to differentiate among hyperkinetic, perceptually handicapped, and emotionally disturbed children are now blurred and confused. Too often, a diagnosis is based solely on observations of behavior. Electroencephalograms seldom provide evidence of a disorder in the central nervous system, and frequently no history of cerebral damage exists. MBD is usually defined in operational terms according to the following symptoms: short attention span; distractibility; hyperactivity; impulsiveness; labile emotions; poor motor coordination; perceptual deficits involving space, form, movement, and time; disordered or delayed development of language; and diminished ability to experience pleasure or respond to positive and negative reinforcement. Because multiple etiological factors can be responsible for any one behavior, these signs of "organic damage" may mask serious emotional disturbances, including depression. Thus a diagnosis of MBD should alert the diagnostician to further study of the specific disability, not excluding emotional disturbance as a primary factor. If such children do not receive special support in the form of a structured environment, special education, continuing diagnostic evaluations, and so on, emotional problems will be the inevitable outcome in any case (Lewis, 1976).

Ritalin, a drug commonly used to treat hyperkinesis or MBD, does not necessarily reduce hyperactivity and make children more attentive. Furthermore, drug treatment in itself has an emotional impact. In a study involving two groups of children diagnosed as hyperactive (Rie et al., 1976), one group received drugs and the other received placebos. (The parents and teachers of children in both groups were informed that the children were receiving drugs.) Parents and teachers were then asked which group was learning more. Although teachers believed that both groups had improved significantly, they noticed more improvement among the children who received drugs, apparently because they were less active than the controls. Parents of the children receiving drugs concurred with the teachers. When the children's actual performance was tested, using standard measures of achievement, no real progress was observed in either group. However, the children who received drugs were less spontaneous than the controls; rarely expressed aversion, surprise, or pleasure; and were devoid of humor. True, they were less troublesome, but they certainly were not in less difficulty.

The population to which all these labels have been applied is poorly defined, and few longitudinal studies have been done. Grinspoon and Singer (1973) studied adolescents who had been diagnosed as hyperkinetic or as suffering MBD in childhood and found that although they were less restless, they were still unable to concentrate, were impulsive, defiant, lacked self-esteem, and had other severe difficulties. As Wepman and his colleagues point out, unless children are carefully evaluated, they will derive little value from treatment that relies primarily on drugs and overlooks individual needs. More attention must be paid to providing services that will eliminate the causes and remedy the deficits related to these difficulties.

Latency is the age of industry, of learning and preparing. Although hyperactivity and learning disabilities indeed may be rooted in congenital, constitutional, or neurological defects, they can also have their roots in old, unresolved conflicts or new problems with which children are unable to cope. Unless they receive help, these children will attempt to cope through acting out or withdrawal.

PROBLEMS OF ABILITY

Emotional difficulties are not always the *primary* reasons for learning problems. A child who cannot see what is on the blackboard or hear what the teacher is saying cannot learn what is being taught. A child who is exhausted, hungry, or undernourished will not have the energy needed for learning. If the home environment is disturbed because of financial difficulty or illness, a child will not be able to pay attention in the classroom. If these conditions persist, the child will fall behind. Crises and persistent tension interfere with the "expected" environment, and children's reactions to them are normal, expectable, and often result in school problems.

Congenital lags in development also result in delayed or slowed maturation of certain physical and cerebral functions. Children who experience such lags will be behind others in class in reading and writing. Organic illnesses such as cerebral palsy; brain dysfunctions that are acquired before, during, or after birth; and a variety of other mishaps can affect a child's development. These accidents create critical problems for the child and the family.

Many of these dysfunctions affect only a limited area of functioning, such as visual coordination, fine eye-hand coordination, or speech, and may surface only when children enter school and are unable to read, write, or coordinate as well as other children their age. This type of problem is viewed as a subtle disturbance or immaturity of the nervous system rather than as brain damage.

Learning Disabilities

The terms learning disability syndrome and neurologically based learning disability syndrome are sometimes more accurate than the diagnosis MBD (Silver, 1976). A diagnosis of brain dysfunction, mimimal or otherwise, helps neither parent nor child. There is, after all, something about the term organic brain dysfunction that seems irreversible and frightening. It is more helpful to the teacher, parents, and child if the specific disability or problem is clearly identified. The alternatives are emotional problems and continued failure, which are triggered by insecurity, low self-esteem, and family disappointment. The dysfunction may cause a severe crisis in the family, particularly if there is a heavy emphasis on learning and achievement. In any case, children who are different from their peers and are the target of teachers' complaints will be troubled, and their parents will feel that they have failed in some way. This situation resembles being blind and knowing there is something to see or being deaf and knowing there is sound. These children know something is wrong but do not understand what it is or why.

Because the effects of these disorders can often be reversed by special education if children are motivated to work on the problem, they as well as parents and professionals who work with these children must understand the problem. If their communications are unclear, the children will be confused and fearful. If testing is done, the purpose and nature of the tests must be discussed with the children in advance; the children are also entitled to know the test results and what efforts will be made to help them.

The problem should be discussed in the same matter-of-fact manner in which one would discuss a common disability such as nearsightedness. This will minimize the difficulties inherent in being different. Testing and remediation should be specific and be done by knowledgeable professionals. Evaluation must be ongoing to check progress and to determine when a change in treatment is needed. When learning disabilities are identified early, many children learn to compensate for them. If they are neglected and only identified at an older age, the accumulated frustrations and failures will inevitably lead to emotional problems. These should be handled simultaneously with the learning difficulty, if not before.

Clues that suggest learning disabilities can often be found in a child's history and should be supplemented by the worker's observations during interviews with the child. The history will often reveal inconsistencies or delays in the development of language or motor skills, an unusual degree of motor activity, behavior problems in the early grades, or poor academic performance.

Silver (1976) lists a number of other clues that should alert professionals to the fact that certain children need careful evaluation. For example, some children seem clumsy, have poor manual ability, or rely on one sensory mode to an unusual degree. Some do not respond to questions or will answer questions incorrectly. Others walk around talking to themselves, naming objects as if attempting to get thoughts into their minds through their ears. They may have difficulty organizing their activities and be easily distracted by sounds in other rooms. In other words, their behavior suggests that something is wrong.

No evaluation of a child with learning disabilities is complete unless it includes the following: a physical examination by an understanding physician and a battery of psychological tests administered by a specialist who works skillfully with children. The psychological evaluation should include tests of general intelligence, motor functions, achievement, visual and auditory perception, language skills, memory, and emotional development.

Children enjoy taking tests when they understand the reasons for them and when the person administering them is encouraging, understanding, and feels comfortable with children. (Obviously, parents also need to understand the purpose of the tests; otherwise their ignorance and fears may contaminate the process.) If possible, the worker or parent should introduce the child to the person administering the tests.

Testing can be frightening to some children who have a history of failure or if some of the projective material awakens repressed, unconscious material and produces anxiety. For these reasons, as well as the child's right to know, the procedures, the results, and what will be done with the results must be discussed with the child immediately before and after testing and later, if the child still seems anxious or unclear about the tests. But this information must be geared to the child's viewpoint and ability to understand.

MENTAL RETARDATION

Diagnoses of mental retardation have traditionally been based on IQ scores. Scores below 70 are considered evidence of retardation, ranging from mild to severe. On this basis, 3 percent of the American population is estimated to be mentally retarded. Tarjin et al. (1974) suggest that this estimate is faulty because the statistics are computed from data that were obtained from children in infancy and are based on the assumption that retarded individuals have the same life-span as the general population and that their situations do not change. Although severely retarded chil-

dren can be identified early, they usually have other obvious abnormalities and a shorter than average life-span.

Seventy percent of children who are diagnosed as
midly retarded are identified between the ages of 6 and 12.
They seldom show somatic signs of retardation, and the
majority come from economically, socially, and educationally underprivileged families. As Spitz (1945) pointed out,
children who lack adequate care and mental stimulation are
usually retarded in many areas of development. In a follow-
up study of twenty-five individuals who were diagnosed as
retarded in infancy, Skeels (1966) found that those who
received individualized, stimulating home environments as
children improved and became self-supporting in adulthood. Those who remained in institutions showed ine-
reased retardation.

Children who actually are retarded may be subjected
to demands that, although appropriate for their chronological age, are inappropriate for their developmental age.
This creates tensions and emotional problems. Chess and
Hassibi (1970) noted that children with limited abilities
become restless, anxious, and engage in repetitive, aimless
activity when confronted with intellectual or social expectations they cannot meet. If the reasons for these reactions
are not understood, the behaviors may be attributed to
emotional problems rather than to an inappropriate environment.

Any degree of retardation affects the entire family as
well as the child. The higher the family's educational level,
social position, and aspirations, the greater the crisis will be
upon learning about the child's defect. If the diagnosis is
made when the child reaches school age or if the retardation occurs because of infection or illness, parents may be
virtually incapable of accepting the fact. In any case, parents who are overwhelmed by feelings of hopelessness and
guilt cannot help the child.

When a child is obviously defective at birth, the parents are faced with a life crisis. Normally, pregnant women wish for a perfect child, yet fear the birth of a damaged one. If the child is born defective, they will mourn the loss of the longed-for healthy child, but their reactions will depend on the type of the defect, its severity, and their own past experiences and personalities. Inevitably, they experience a sense of failure, disappointment, and helplessness, which may interfere with their ability to accept the child and meet its needs. All family members need time to accept and work through their disappointment, loss, and guilt. This process is similar to mourning the death of a loved one: it is slow and painful and requires successive translations and clarifications. If they do not complete this process, they may distort reality and deny the problem. The mother may devote herself exclusively to the defective child and neglect her other children, or she may feel defective herself and withdraw from the child (Solnit & Stark, 1961). Thus the child's parents and siblings need help to work through the inevitable question, "What did I do?"

How siblings will view the problem will depend on their age and whether they were born before or after the retarded child. If they are older, they may feel that their jealousy and rejection of the new rival caused the injury. If younger, they may feel tainted, perceive their parents' fears that they too will be damaged, or feel they must make up for the loss.

Some parents overprotect the damaged child and displace their anger onto the other children. Siblings, not understanding the meaning of retardation, may relate it to sexual and aggressive fantasies, which will lead to guilt about many activities. In some cases, they will identify with and imitate the retarded sibling's behavior, especially if the child seems to receive more attention from the parents (Martino & Newman, 1974). Some will carry the fear of having a retarded child into adulthood.

Retardation is similar to many other childhood prob-lems. The child is not the only one affected. Inevitably, the entire family will need help in working through and opti-mizing its opportunities.

UNDERACHIEVEMENT

Children who do poorly in school despite adequate intelli-gence are labeled underachievers. Frequently, these chil-dren present no disruptive behavior; they are simply unable to pay attention or concentrate. They also seem restricted in other activities and lack self-assertiveness. Yet they may choose younger children as playmates and act bossy and bold with them. Their facade is one of the good child, but underneath are many frightening, angry feelings. Normal aggressive activities and impulses are con-taminated by the great anger these children feel; their defense is to retreat into passivity and compliance. Be-cause they must devote most of their energy to controlling their anger and unhappiness, they are unable to com-pete or perform adequately (Dudek & Lester, 1968; A. Freud, 1968b). The following case history illustrates this problem:

> Kate A, a slightly built 11-year-old, was making poor aca-demic progress in sixth grade and risked being held back at the end of the year. She achieved a Full Scale WISC IQ of 97 (verbal, 103; performance 92) but was performing at the third-grade level in reading and math. She also had difficulty relating to peers. Kate felt that she was made the scapegoat for anything that went wrong in class, which in fact seemed to be the case. Although these problems had recently become more pronounced, they had been present for sev-eral years. Kate had always been a slow learner , and Mrs. A had taken her to a pediatrician four years earlier, suspect-ing that Kate's problem might be related to a birth injury. The pediatrician found no organic impairment, but no neurological examination was done at that time. At home,

Kate did not get along well with her siblings (she was the eldest), especially Helen, who was closest to her in age. Kate also had a history (since age 4) of stealing small sums of money from her parents to buy candy for her friends.

Kate arrived for her first interview accompanied by her entire family—mother, father, and three sisters, who sat in the waiting room. When the interview was over, her family behaved as if Kate had undergone major surgery; they seemed frightened and anxious.

Although somewhat anxious herself, Kate had good presence during the interview. In the playroom she said she preferred to talk. When asked if she knew why she was there, she said yes, her parents had explained that it would help her get along better in school. Then she said she had had a bad day. The day before, a boy in the neighborhood who didn't like her and always teased her had taken her bike and had broken it. When asked why the boy did this, she said her father told her to ignore him when he teased and he would stop. Usually, she responded by getting excited and trying to grab her bike away from him, but from now on she would act as her father had advised.

When the worker suggested that Kate must be extremely angry when this happened, Kate said she sure was. She then began talking about her pets. She had had two cats and some fish and in describing them expressed much affection and interest. That summer, one cat had been killed by a car in front of her house. She was usually careful to see that the cats did not go into the street, but she was home alone that day watching TV and the cat had gone into the street. Some neighborhood boys saw the accident and reported it to a policeman, who brought the cat back to her house, and neighbors offered to get her a new one. Since Kate was alone (her mother was in the laundromat), she handled the situation by herself and told them she'd have to ask her mother because they would have to be sure the new one would get along with the other one. When asked if she felt responsible for what had happened, she said she was always careful with the cats and this was just an accident.

In response to a question about what she liked to do, she replied: "A lot of things, like tap dancing." The previous year, she had entered a contest with another girl and they had won third place. Kate was pleased, but the other girl was disappointed because she had wanted to be first. When asked whether she would like to come in first, Kate said "No, because there are too many booby traps in being first." She couldn't explain further.

Kate liked art and gym class best, but was extremely knowledgeable about her other school subjects and seemed to know what was going on in class. She said she was last in school. When asked why, she said she wanted to be: "There is too much hassle in the front of the line." In talking about her three sisters, she said she liked the younger ones, who were helpful, but Helen was not so helpful and they fought a lot. Though small for her age, Kate seemed older than she was when she talked. She fidgeted, did not show appropriate affect, almost intellectualized.

Mrs. A accompanied Kate to the second interview. Because Kate seemed uncomfortable, the worker asked her if she had had any feelings about last time. Kate said "Yes, I felt a little funny," but she couldn't explain.

During the first interview, the worker had suggested that she bring in a picture of her cats. Kate brought several pictures to this interview. The first picture was of a fat cat with a big brown spot, which Kate described as always hungry and eating a lot. Kate said she was never hungry and didn't eat much, except when she had to stay in the house because she was being punished. The second picture showed a skinny, sad-looking cat in a dark narrow alley surrounded by signs that said "Don't. . . ." "Fragile," and so on. There was garbage all over the bottom of the page, and the cat was gnawing on a fish bone. She said he could just barely taste the flavor on the bones. The third picture was essentially the same scene but its perspective was different. There was no alley; the sky, though dark, had a big smiling man-in-the-moon; and a huge streetlight illuminated the entire area. A fatter cat was in the center of the picture with a plateful of scraps, most of which were bones. A sack of potatoes was the cat's bed. According to Kate, the two newspapers in the picture signified two different times. There were no signs saying "Don't" or "Fragile." Kate talked about games and said she was just like a cat because although she wasn't very strong, she could hold on. She was not a fighter, however; she didn't like fights. Her friend thought she was chicken.

Kate was tested for neurological damage, and later, when asked about the tests, she could not remember and looked frightened. However, when the worker explained their purpose and said nothing was wrong, Kate seemed relieved.

As Kate began talking about her angry feelings and learned she was not bad for having them, she was able to experiment with assertive behavior in games, competition, and learning. With her friend, a girl two years younger, she entered a contest for the best Halloween costume. Her marks improved, and she began to look more relaxed. She then won in chess and was the best in Annihilation. She beat up a boy who tried to take her candy. She also was no longer a school failure. She actually received a grade of 100 in several tests, received all satisfactory grades on her report card, and no longer had to do extra assignments. Slowly, the underlying reasons for her repression of normal assertiveness unfolded: sibling rivalry, feelings of rejection, fear of being damaged, fear of her father, and feelings that her mother did not protect her or care for her. There were strong unresolved oedipal themes and sexual confusion. Although inhibition of aggression interfered with Kate's performance, her inhibitions with regard to learning were related to the fear of knowing. This seemed to be the result of fantasies based on misunderstandings, which were fueled by her parents' problems and ambiguous communications.

Too often, adults protect a child from information that they believe is disturbing. For example, Kate's family was worried about her slowness, fearing that she was "damaged." Kate recognized the ambiguity of their communications and interpreted them in a childish way. (Other family secrets that are kept from children are crisis situations, death, sex, physical or mental illness, separation, adoption, and so on.) Kate told the worker about a dog who was thrown out by his owner because his ears were *too big* and he always stumbled. Children who hear what they are not supposed to hear often feel they are bad. Their unconscious conclusion may be hear not, see not, know not. When parents attempt to keep children "innocent," they also impose pseudostupidity; otherwise the family secret would no longer be a secret (Stein, 1970).

Pseudobackwardness is sometimes observed in children who have the potential for normal development. In some cases, parents do not take pride in their child's accomplishments or encourage and reward the child for achievement. In others, the mother cannot believe she produced a normal child, either because she feels damaged or because there is a damaged child in the extended family. Although these children learn to fit the role they are assigned, they feel damaged and inferior and often cling to infantile autoerotic pleasures such as soiling and wetting and excessive masturbation in addition to not learning (Berger & Kennedy, 1975).

Sometimes children will inhibit or restrict certain abilities because they believe they cannot do as well as they want to do or are expected to do or because they fear the consequences of winning. Unresolved oedipal problems are usually behind their inhibitions (Klein, 1949). Other children who seem to be extremely well endowed intellectually may be academic failures because they have never learned to do involved tasks that require planning and integrated, sustained effort. These children tend to be immature, physically clumsy, and inept. Rather than use speech to communicate their thoughts and emotions, they use it for narcissistic, exhibitionistic gratification and for impulsive affective discharge: i.e., they act out through words to defend against anxiety and shame. In many cases, they reflect family patterns that reward and eroticize verbal communication and passivity and tacitly forbid the activity and curiosity so essential for growth. For these children, words are empty, unrelated to feelings and reality, and mask serious developmental deficiencies (Newman, Dember, & Krug, 1973).

Retardation in the process of separation and individuation also interferes with learning. For instance, some children are symbiotically tied to their mothers, either because of their own unmet needs or because their mothers need mothers themselves. In the latter case, the mothers expect their children to know intuitively what they mean and want; the children in turn expect to be understood without communicating appropriately. Although nonverbal understanding is useful for infants, it interferes with the older child's learning and development. In other cases, infantile speech, baby talk, and secret language continue into latency, fostering a special private communication, mutual dependence, and erotic stimulation between child and mother. This pattern is often accompanied by problems in eating and elimination, which require the mother's constant attention, including handling and cleaning of the child's genital area.

Children with problems of separation and individuation have difficulty learning because magical thinking and infantile omnipotence persist. Thus they are prevented from learning about reality and how to cope with life. In situations where mutual dependency is not so extreme, there is less differentiation than appropriate. The mother views her child's successes and failures as though they were her own and constantly checks the results of tests and homework, sometimes completing the work herself (Buxbaum, 1964).

Serious ego deficits and psychological immaturities and conflicts will interfere with learning. To learn, latency-age children must be able to think logically and differentiate between reality and fantasy. If learning is imbued with sexual or aggressive overtones, it becomes an arena for the expression of other emotional conflicts.

ABSENCE FROM SCHOOL

Children who are depressed, preoccupied with problems, or are unable to pay attention or sit still are figuratively absent from school, though physically present. Some children are physically absent for extended or repeated periods. Kahn and Nursten (1962) state that children fail to attend school, literally or figuratively, for either social or phobic reasons.

Truancy

Truancy is more common among adolescents than it is among younger children because the latter are less able to be alone and function without formal structure and care. Adolescents, alone or in groups, will stay away from school as a lark or as a gesture of rebellion. Dissatisfaction with school or with parents may contribute to extended absences, even among younger children. If the community or peer group devalues school, children have no compelling reason to attend. Children who are truants from a variety of social obligations and are unwilling to accept restrictions, responsibility, and organization of their time are deficient in socialization and character development.

Some children are absent from school because of distress about parental pathology. Most parents in such cases will obtain help if the problem persists because they recognize the child's need for an education and accept the sociolegal requirement that children attend school regularly. In grossly disorganized families, however, the parents cannot or will not enforce their children's regular attendance in school. Some parents rely on their children to help manage the home, refusing to accept their social obligations and not understanding children's needs. Sometimes these parents are overwhelmed by crisis and misfortune; often they need parents themselves.

School Phobia

While truants spend the time they should be in school on activities outside the home, children with school phobias stay home and refuse to return to school. Because school seems to be associated with intense terror, they will feign illness, fatigue, and so forth to avoid it. But the real problem is not school; the problem is acute anxiety, which these children cannot explain. Their reasons for fearing school are usually rationalizations, and by displacing their anxiety, they externalize an internal conflict or problem, which can then be avoided by avoiding school. This permits them to stay home and check on the situation that is actually causing the anxiety (Johnson et al., 1941). (Even when the phobia occurs in late adolescence, the unconscious purpose is to return home. The onset, usually masked by somatic symptoms, may mark the beginning of a severe emotional breakdown.)

At any age, the acute onset of a school phobia may occur because of some precipitating event that appears to threaten the child's ability to control reality. This event may be the real or *feared* illness or death of a parent or the child's illness or surgery. The problem is the understandable wish to control life and death, accompanied by a fear of the ultimate separation that is inherent in death.

All children who experience such crises do not resort to school phobia. The phobia usually occurs in children who are narcissistic in orientation, still engaged in magical thinking, and whose object relations are extremely ambivalent. These children, at an older age than is usual, have an awesome sense of omnipotence and still equate unconscious death wishes with reality. The intense anxiety they feel increases their need for magical control, especially if no other means of control seems available. The phobia is an attempt to achieve this control.

In Sperling's view (1967), a direct, analytic approach is best with these children, regardless of their age. This approach includes retracing the circumstances that led to the first anxiety attack and linking the fear with unconscious aggressive wishes and fears through generalizations about children and their angry wishes. By airing these unconscious death wishes, the magical qualities attached to unconscious thought processes tend to be devalued. Acute school phobia requires crisis intervention, which should be initiated as quickly as possible after the phobic behavior appears.

Hostile dependency between parent and child is a common underlying dynamic of most school phobias. Although phobic children have learning difficulties, are isolated from peers, and suffer from somatic illnesses, they also achieve the goal of controlling and punishing their parents, especially their mothers, because the parents' mobility is restricted and they have problems with school authorities. Generally, the phobia is complemented by the parents' problems and unconscious encouragement of the phobia. In a study conducted by Gittelman-Klein and Klein (1975), children with school phobias were treated with either imipromine or a placebo for six weeks and their parents received counseling. At the end of the experiment, the findings indicated that the drug was more efficacious in inducing the children's return to school. The authors concluded that if parental counseling had been neglected, the children, who were less anxious because of the drug, would have been happier whether they returned to school or stayed home.

Separation anxiety during latency is fed by long-standing hostile, dependent relations between child and parent. If parents do not understand that love and anger can coexist, their children will never learn that one can be angry, yet love and be loved. Disturbed communication between parent and child and alternating seductiveness and hostility on the part of parents often precedes the emergence of school phobia. Anxiety about loss and abandonment, triggered by unconscious aggression and ambivalence about closeness, usually exists in both child and parent. The separation problems tend to support the child's regressive behavior (Coolidge et al., 1962).

Sperling (1967) coined the term "induced school phobia" for situations where children become phobic in the absence of a manifest external precipitation event. The pathological interaction between parent and child is related to parental needs as well as identification with the child and the phobia. Parents may be repeating their own experiences with their own parents, thus perpetuating a long history of separation difficulties. The phobia also limits parental freedom and may be used to control and punish one or the other parent.

Chronic or recurrent school phobias are often symptoms of severe personality disturbances, including symbiotic ties between parent and child. In these cases, a therapeutic alliance with the parent is essential. Working with the child alone will engender resistance in the parent, who will terminate treatment once the child returns to school.

When Coolidge and Brodie (1974) did a follow-up study of children with school phobias and their parents after ten years, they concluded that although these children had returned to school, they tended to be constricted in adolescence and early adulthood. Many mothers still communicated the safety of psychological symbiosis, the danger of autonomy, and the notion that anxiety should be dreaded because it cannot be mastered. The parents fell into three groups: (1) those who were aware of their own involvement in the problem and actively promoted the child's autonomous development, (2) those who permitted their children to return to school because they had formed a dependent relationship with the caseworker, and (3) those who resisted treatment, were suspicious, tended to obstruct the child's development, and had limited contact with the clinic. Parents in the third group were immature, phobic, dependent, helpless, and sometimes psychotic; required continuous care; and did poorly if transferred to another worker.

If an entire family has problems involving separation and individuation, problems of separation, including school phobias, tend to affect more than one child in the family. In these families, ambivalence about closeness may lead to fear of a close therapeutic relationship; thus family therapy is often more productive than individual treatment.

Although removing the school phobia is important, it is not enough. The underlying anxiety is likely to continue when the child returns to school and it may interfere with learning. Furthermore, other symptoms, including somatic ones, are likely to increase. In other words, because neglect of the real problem may hinder the child's growth and development, work on that problem must continue.

Other Phobias

School phobias are similar to other phobias in the sense that the anxiety-producing conflict is repressed and unconsciously projected onto another object, usually the parent who is involved in the conflict, and then displaced onto another external object that is less affectively involved. The case of Little Hans, whose oedipal fears were displaced onto a horse, provides an early view of this phenomenon (S. Freud, 1909a). The common fear of snakes among prepubertal urban girls is a good example of how an external object can be used to limit, focus, and control anxiety. City girls can fear and avoid these wriggly phallic symbols with great ease. But many phobias are not this benign. School phobias are one good example of this.

Transient phobias are common in childhood. Young children can be afraid of many things: animals (domesticated and wild), storms, lightning, fire, deep water, doctors and dentists, the dark, being alone, ghosts, witches, policemen, boogie-men, and other culturally induced fears. The young child's egocentric and magical thinking contribute to the ease with which external objects become involved in developmental conflict. During latency, however, the conflict should be solved and the decline of magical thinking should diminish these fears. Berecz (1969) noted that fears related to sexual impulses and conflicts increase during latency.

Phobias first appear between the ages of 1½ and 3, the period when children are toilet trained and are struggling with separation and individuation. Because magical thinking is normal at this age, control of elimination is equated with other impulses as well as control of mother and other external objects and situations.

All phobias are attempts to control anxiety, but the causes of the anxiety vary. Colm (1970) suggested that phobias are a defense against rage about the danger of desertion or punishment by parents; the danger impels frustration of aggressive impulses and rage at the parent's inability to help with controls. In addition, she believed that phobias are related to parental fears and anxieties. Ordinarily, when parents criticize or are concerned about a child's behavior, they expect the child to change it, and this usually happens. If parental concern is an expression of intense anxiety, the problem becomes fearful. When parents are ambivalent, children become confused. Some will respond with overconformity and compulsive compliance; others will resist and become defiant; still others will withdraw from interpersonal contact or develop a phobia. Generally, the phobic object is a symbolic substitute that masks the child's rage, but it also provides clues about what the child perceives as the danger. The tenacity of the phobia will be directly related to the intensity of the rage.

Anger directed toward parents is dangerous for children because they are afraid that their murderous wishes will be realized. As a result, control is essential. Thus permissive, indulgent play in the treatment situation not only is not helpful, it can be extremely threatening because it signifies loss of control and repetition of the parent's inability to help, especially when parental overpermissiveness contributes to the problem. The worker's communications must be clear, unambiguous, and related to helping the child experience reasonable, appropriate limits. Although children will test the worker by resisting, refusing to cooperate, and provoking anger, the worker must not retaliate with real anger. The worker must clearly explain the child's provocative behaviors and help the child understand how these behaviors are repeated at home, school, and other areas of life.

Children initially will express their anger symbolically through drawings and games. Only when they feel less threatened will they express it directly to the worker. Although they may act angry because the worker does not behave the way their parents do, they will feel safer and thus feel less need to punish themselves. It is not necessary —indeed it is contraindicated—to bring anger at parents to the surface. Young children are too dependent on their parents, and older children too are still dependent and also identify with their parents. It is better if young children play out their anger or express it safely to the worker; older children may be able to understand some generalizations about how many children feel. The important point for children to learn is that anger does not kill.

Phobias rarely occur in isolation; a variety of other behaviors may accompany them. Illness is sometimes substituted if the phobia does not externalize the problem to a sufficient degree. What are sometimes called psychosomatic problems often camouflage severe phobias as well as a variety of other childhood disturbances. Body, mind, and spirit, the biopsychosocial aspects of living, are related at all ages, but never as much as in childhood.

Chapter 8

MIND AND BODY

Physical behavior is a child's way of communicating. Children react by acting. Traditionally, behaviors that deviate from the expectable have been divided into three types: (1) habit disorders, or disturbances of physiological functions, (2) conduct disorders, or disturbances of socialization, and (3) psychosomatic disorders, a group of somatic illnesses that have psychosocial roots and are symbolic expressions of conflict. All are a child's way of expressing conflict, fear, and anger.

These disorders rarely affect only the child or only the people in the child's environment; they have a dual result: the child is punished but also punishes others. Almost all of children's problem behaviors can be placed in one of these three categories: inhibited learning; certain speech, sleep, eating, and elimination problems; compulsive masturbation; tics; and violent and aggressive activities such as stealing, fire-setting, and hurting others or oneself. The troubled child will exhibit different combinations of these behaviors.

The Psychosomatic Concept

The biopsychosocial viewpoint, though not exclusive to social work, is emphasized by the profession, which views the person as organized on several levels—physiological, psychological, and interpersonal—each of which represents different but related systems. This is an approach to a totality of integrated transactions among many systems— somatic, psychic, social, and cultural—in both health and illness and one that accepts the relationship between emotional and physiological responses.

Under stress, children will resort to a variety of coping devices in an effort to maintain their equilibrium. The mechanism they choose will depend on heredity, constitution, development, experiences, and the responses of others, especially the family (Group for the Advancement of Psychiatry, 1973).

Traditionally, the term psychosomatic implied the existence of physical symptoms that lacked a discernible organic cause. These symptoms were viewed as conversion phenomena: symbolic expressions of conflict that resulted in a specific physiological disturbance. This made it easy to interpret each patient's life history and situation to fit the scheme (Stein, 1972).

The physiological response to stress is the same, whether the stress is physical or emotional. Multiple factors affect the mind-body relationship throughout life, and no bodily function is immune to being used to reflect emotional needs and stress (F. Deutsch, 1953). In infancy all responses are somatic; however, as physical maturation and psychological development progress, responses become differentiated, more specific, and increasingly conscious and thus are subject to verbalization and reason. Many psychosomatic illnesses of infancy and childhood indicate developmental disorders and failures in the process of developing more differentiated responses to stress (Dowling, 1973).

Far too many children suffer emotional injuries that interfere with normal development. And far too often, parents and other caretakers fail to recognize this—as does society, which does not provide resources to ensure environments that will meet children's needs and protect their rights. For example, many children in foster care have a wide range of physical, psychological, and social disorders because they did not receive the right care at the right time. Most of these children receive too little too late, as illustrated in the following case:

> *Jane*, the youngest of eight children, was the result of her young mother's relationship with a man who was not her husband. Because of Jane's frequent illnesses, her mother placed her in a children's shelter when she was 9 months old. Within three months, Jane was hospitalized for 26 days with diarrhea and then released to a convalescent home to recuperate. A few months later (at age 1½), the child was placed in her first foster home. A month later, the foster mother was hospitalized for two weeks and left Jane in the care of strangers. At about this time, an eye examination showed that Jane was legally blind. Toilet training was also initiated, but she was resistant.
>
> When Jane was 3, the foster parents were so close to separating that Jane was removed from their home. Several months after the second placement, Jane began refusing to eat unless forced and then vomited after meals. She also developed asthma.
>
> When Jane was 5, the agency decided to move Jane again because the foster mother was a rigid, obsessive person who was cold and distant to children and overly concerned about cleanliness and obedience. In the third foster home, she continued to have difficulties with eating and vomiting, began to vomit in her sleep without waking up, and refused to talk for long periods.
>
> When Jane started school a few months later, a second eye examination indicated that her vision had greatly improved. However, it was not until the following school year that the local agency for the blind reclassified her as not legally blind, stating that in their opinion "poor vision was not a primary disturbance for Jane," i.e., her problems were

emotional. At that point, the agency initiated a series of psychological, psychiatric, and neurological tests to see what could be done for Jane. While the agency waited for the test results, Jane was put back into kindergarten because she was now vomiting in school. The results of the psychiatric examination were as follows: "Jane is a mentally defective child with severe anxiety of a diffuse variety (not phobia). . . . Involvement of the respiratory system and stomach, resulting from increase in emotional stress. [She is] frightened, inhibited, orally centered, with dependency needs, anxiety and controlled aggression." Jane had temper tantrums and nightmares, was stubborn, and had a voracious appetite. When the foster parents decided they did not want to put up with her problems any longer, Jane was moved for the fourth time.

At age 11 Jane was placed in a CRMD class; at age 15, she became pregnant. Because her foster parents would not let her stay with them during her pregnancy or bring the baby home, she moved to a fifth foster home after delivery. By the time Jane was 22, she had two children; both had been in foster care since birth.

From the beginning, Jane's reactions to loss showed attempts to cope, failure, and then regression. Whenever there seemed to be some hope, she experienced another trauma, another loss. Her symptoms failed to communicate her desperate need—or was it that no one listened? The failure of her caretakers to deal with her initial loss and subsequent losses resulted in a deformed personality, an impoverished ego, apathy, and depression.

Children who feel overwhelmed by events beyond their control often choose somatic symptoms because they believe that through some magical process, illness will keep them at home close to mother. These disorders resemble phobias: i.e., they represent attempts to control both the child and others (Sperling, 1975). Young children especially will use body language to express their conflicts and feelings. This is particularly true in families that have difficulty recognizing and verbalizing intense feelings. Children's methods of communicating and reacting to health and illness are developed early in life.

Transitory psychophysiological ailments such as stomach aches can occur in any child, particularly in times of stress. Physiological reactions to prolonged stress are a different matter, however. The type of illness that will appear seems to depend on individual susceptibility, the family's response and expectations, and the models of identification that are available. If the stress is not alleviated, the physiological reactions may result in irreparable damage.

Although the personality is far more structured in latency than in infancy and conflict tends to be internalized, physiological responses to stress during latency are not unusual. The range of symptoms is wide, and some symptoms are transient while others are severe and long-lasting. Dermatitis, infections, muscular aches and pains, recurrent abdominal pain, headaches, vomiting, and even disturbance of growth may occur. These symptoms tend to be closely correlated with emotional stress and reflect a family history of similar symptoms. Unless one asks "When did this begin? What happens as a result?" the child will be subjected to too many useless physical examinations. Although a medical examination is the first step, one must also understand the child's situation.

If the stress involves a severe loss, somatic reactions are natural. But children who have not suffered such a loss also exhibit somatic symptoms. If parents are overindulgent, overprotective, and encourage infantile behavior, the child's symptoms are an expression of the struggle between dependence and independence and are designed to control the parents. If the parents are tense and compulsive and, in an effort to deny their own separation anxiety, force the child to become independent too soon, the symptoms express the child's dependency needs, which may be masked by pseudomaturity. How severely children will react to parental failure to meet their early need to be dependent and their later need to be independent will depend on when the pathological interaction between child and parent begins, how long it continues, and its intensity (Mahler, Pine, & Bergman, 1975).

The earliest indications of disturbance in the mother-child relationship will appear in the vital areas of eating, sleeping, elimination, and respiration. Mothers who try to maintain control over their children in these areas tend to have similar problems and preoccupations involving separation and reunion and unconsciously reward the child's illness and dependence and discourage health and independence.

The similarity between the dynamics of somatic disturbances and phobias indicates that somatic illnesses disguise severe phobias in both child and mother and the early traumatic experiences of both (Sperling, 1970). Between the ages of 2 and 3, separation-individuation is a normal developmental process. But some mothers resist this development, withdrawing when their children try to be independent and rewarding dependency in subtle ways. These women do not express their feelings overtly nor are they even conscious of them. Children, however, are more responsive to their parents' latent feelings and needs than to parents' overt behavior.

Fathers are implicated when they collaborate with the mother in continuing the unhealthy symbiosis between mother and child instead of serving as an external source of difference and support in the child's development (Abelin, 1971). Some fathers also use their children for their own needs by being seductive, overstimulating, or competing with the child for the mother's attention.

Parents of children with psychophysiological disorders overprotect and over-react to minor stress or trauma. But it is the psychodynamics of the entire family that perpetuates the child's difficulties; by focusing on the child's symptoms, the family can defend against having to focus on individual and interactive problems (Tichener, Riskin, & Emerson, 1971).

Latency-age children who are overprotected are as poorly equipped as underprotected children for the normative tasks of school and socialization. The reactions of teachers and peers and the child's own desire to be like others will create pressures to become independent. Thus extremely dependent children often feel ashamed, inadequate, and inferior and suffer chronic conflict and anxiety about their desire to be independent and their unconscious fear that their mothers will retaliate or reject them. The underlying rage that results only produces more anxiety (Millar, 1971).

If children are very young or are in early latency, they can often be helped simply by treating the parents. By understanding the parents, their needs, and the family dynamics, the worker can help them meet their own and the child's needs more appropriately. But if children are in middle or late latency and their symptoms are severe, they too will need therapeutic intervention. Medical treatment will also be necessary to prevent irreversible physical damage and to ease the symptoms.

Although many psychophysiological illnesses depend on susceptibility, others have no apparent anatomical or physiological basis: i.e., the physical complaints are not substantiated by physical or laboratory findings. Some psychosomatic illnesses resemble conversion reactions—misuse of a part of the body or a bodily function to decrease stress and to communicate symbolically a conflict that cannot be verbalized. The onset or exacerbation of the condition usually coincides with an emotionally significant event: in other words, the symptom is emotionally derived and serves an unconscious need (Loof, 1970; Rock, 1971). If symptoms such as headaches and stomachaches or those that affect muscles, speech, vision, or hearing persist *when organic causes have been ruled out,* the cause is probably emotional. The children will seem strangely unconcerned about their difficulties. Furthermore, this lack of anxiety will be most apparent when parents and the physician focus on the illness (Rock, 1971; Humphrey, Knipstein & Bumpass, 1975). Although the symptom protects the child from anxiety, it is also rewarding because the child gains attention and the power to control and make demands on the parents. If the symptom is the focus of treatment, the disability tends to be perpetuated because, again, the child perceives it as rewarding.

> *Frances T,* age 11½, was referred by the clinic that had been evaluating her hearing difficulties. Exhaustive testing had produced such inconsistent results that the examiner concluded that Frances's problem was emotional, not physiological.
>
> Frances was taller than average for her age and extremely thin. Although her verbal ability was excellent, she was timid in the initial stages of treatment. It was many months before she could understand this new relationship and its potential for her.
>
> Gradually, Frances talked about being different from her classmates and her sister, Melinda, who was three years older. Kids either avoided her or made fun of her. Once a boy emptied a box of garbage on her head, but she could not retaliate. She thought her problem was that her mother made her wear orthopedic shoes. They were ugly, and so was she. What Frances wanted most was to be pretty.
>
> When Frances began to feel more comfortable about sharing her feelings with the worker, she was able to talk about her anger at other children and her jealousy of those who did well. She felt that she was smarter than Melinda, who was beautiful but mean. From her viewpoint, Melinda received all the attention in the family. The pictures Frances drew showed her confusion and concern about her body and her sexuality. Indeed, her sexual preoccupations were extreme, even for a prepubertal child.
>
> Mr. and Mrs. T were articulate, well educated, and intellectual. Mrs. T., however, had a long history of physical preoccupations and difficulties. Her parents had doted on

and overprotected her. When her mother died, Mrs. T was 16; her father then insisted that she sleep in his bed. Although Mrs. T had married early, she was still dependent on her father. Mr. T, like Frances, was tall and thin, and he could talk for hours. When he came for an interview, he often asked the worker to double his time because he had so much to say. He was a twin and had never felt adequately appreciated.

Both parents were concerned about Frances, primarily because she was not doing as well in school as she should. It soon became clear that each girl was expected to fulfill a certain role: Melinda was stupid but beautiful and feminine; Frances was smart like her father but was not living up to her potential.

Family life was extremely important to the Ts. Aunts, uncles, grandparents, cousins, all were in constant interaction. Within the household, there was openness and sharing: doors were not closed, bodies were not covered, and Mr. T's erotic and pornographic books were available to be read and misunderstood by the children.

Frances was overstimulated, undereducated, and filled with frightening fantasies. She was preoccupied with the differences between males and females and their sexual activities. Although these interests are not unusual for a girl her age, her lack of appropriate social outlets and the family dynamics indicated pathology and interfered with her development.

As some of her ideas were explored and clarified, Frances began to giggle about what went on in her parents' bedroom. If they were out, she would lie down on their bed and imagine all kinds of things. The room she shared with Melinda was adjacent to her parents' room. When the worker suggested that she could hear all sorts of things in that room, Frances looked innocent. When the worker insisted that she knew Frances was smart and saw a lot, heard a lot, and knew a lot, Frances admitted that she often lay awake, listening to what went on between her mother and father.

Because Frances actually did hear too much, she needed to have a hearing deficiency. Now it was possible to talk about the symptom that had brought her to treatment, and she was relieved that she no longer had to have a hearing deficiency. She admitted that at first she had pretended she couldn't hear in the school tests, just for a joke. Then she was given all kinds of tests. At first, all the attention was fun, but after a while it was tiresome and frightening. She was glad the game was over.

From Frances's conscious viewpoint, her symptom was only a joke, but her sexual confusion, feelings of inadequacy, and the family interactions were the unconscious stimuli for her choice of symptom and its continuation. With intervention in the family's interactions and appropriate communications with Frances, as well as the development of a more objective, supporting relationship, Frances was able to make friends, attend to her school work, and spend less time being sick. In adolescence, she blossomed into an extraordinarily beautiful young woman. This, combined with her dramatic manner, flair in dressing, and good intellectual capacities brought her the public and family attention she craved.

HYPOCHONDRIASIS

Children usually do not take care of their bodies or observe the rules of health and hygiene until well into adolescence. It is more customary for this to be a parental responsibility (A. Freud, 1952). Yet many children complain consistently about colds, headaches, and stomachaches and worry about being ill. This is not uncommon among children who have been orphaned, institutionalized, or neglected early in life. They must worry about themselves and care for their bodies as if they were their own mothers.

As mentioned earlier, some children use physical complaints to control their parents, gain attention, or escape from tasks, especially school. These children are genuinely concerned and worried about body functions. Often there is a conflict between opposing desires; to be well but also to be sick. Unconsciously, illness—although equated with helplessness and passivity—also means pampering, love, and attention. Mother may seem attentive and caring only when the child is sick or seem to give an ill brother or sister all her attention. Some mothers who are rejecting and guilty compensate for this by being overly concerned about the child's health. Pathological interest in health and illness is often taught in this way or is modeled on other family members who are hypochondriacal. Parental overprotection or underprotection, in combination with the family dynamics, environment, and the child's inadequate knowledge of the body, can produce a hypochondriacal child (Koupernik, 1973). The choice of illness and part of the body that will be affected will reflect individual conflicts, including fears and fantasies about the body related to aggressive and sexual preoccupations within the framework of family dynamics.

Tics

Tics are muscular disorders: the rapid contraction of a group or groups of muscles that occurs inappropriately at irregular intervals. Eye-blinking, facial grimaces, twitching of the mouth, and a variety of gestures can be used symbolically as the physiological accompaniment to an affect. The tic will be accompanied by unconscious fantasies about the movement (Mahler, 1949).

Tics are not uncommon among young children. Some are transitory symptoms of tension related to what children perceive as an overwhelming experience and are appropriate to the specific event. The event may be acute fright, which normally causes violent muscular responses such as crying, temper tantrums, and running away, or physically aggressive reactions. If children inhibit these responses because they fear parental disapproval, conflict will result. Consequently, a partial motor response continues, permitting some release of tension. The tic defends the child against remembering both the experience and the prohibited wish and helps isolate the affect and fear. Later, the same involuntary movement may appear whenever the child is afraid or anxious (Gerard, 1947).

Tics can express a variety of fears: e.g., the dark, injury, separation, animals, or unconscious, prohibited wishes. Frequently, children with tics are subjected to high standards of performance as well as demands that they behave in nonaggressive, nonphysical ways at an age when they must be aggressively motile. When the underlying fears are clarified for these children and they learn how to deal with anxiety more constructively, the tics disappear. But the environment must also be modified so that they will be less fearful about expressive behaviors.

EATING DISORDERS

It is not surprising that children often express emotional distress through behavior related to eating. Eating is the earliest function that involves interaction with another person. Although the infant has hunger pangs, these are initially undifferentiated from other body sensations. Whether the child's hunger will be alleviated depends on the mother's cooperation and the interactions between the two that occur in this area will influence the child's eating patterns throughout life (Bruch, 1970). Because the earliest period of life is dominated by orality, many other needs become associated with feelings related to eating and being fed.

Some eating disorders are triggered by momentary upsets and disappear as quickly as they came. This occurs more commonly in young children and in those who have few emotional outlets. By the time a child reaches latency, one would expect a different means of communication. But in some families, mealtime is a battle. Food, as the symbol and foundation of other needs and other giving, can be used to play out parts of the family dynamics: positive and negative, pleasant and unpleasant. Family eating habits and attitudes about food play an important role in developing healthy or unhealthy eating patterns in children.

Eating problems never exist in isolation; they are always accompanied by other difficulties. When parents complain or express worry about their children, eating difficulties are rarely their primary concern. This is true, even when children suffer from gross disturbances such as obesity or anorexia nervosa, both of which require medical and therapeutic intervention (Tolstrup, 1970).

Obesity

Many latency-age children are overweight or fat but are not obese. Obesity refers to the accumulation of an excessive amount of fat, but this is difficult to measure. Obesity is most clearly determined by weight. Children whose weight is 10 percent above the norm are overweight; when this percentage is considerably higher, they are probably obese.

Because obese children often become obese adults, they will have problems in the future as well as the present. Accumulation of adipose cells in early childhood tends to be unchanged by dietary manipulation and can lead to a variety of health problems. Obesity may lead to acceleration of height as well as weight, an earlier onset of puberty, and musculoskeletal difficulties, especially in the lower extremities: e.g., knock-knees or weak, flat, or outwardly rotated feet (Stimbert & Coffee, 1972). Because of their abnormally large, awkward bodies, obese children are often picked on, laughed at, and isolated from other children. Despite the stereotype, obesity is not synonymous with jolliness; the majority of obese children have serious personality problems. They tend to be clingy, dependent, inactive, feel insecure and helpless, and are unable to cope adequately with many situations.

Ethnicity, culture, and class affect eating habits. In

some cultures, fat is equated with good health and good adjustment, and to eat a large amount of food is to be well mannered. This viewpoint contributes to the prime cause of obesity in children: the child simply eats more than the body needs.

A variety of somatic malfunctions have been blamed for childhood obesity. Hypothyroidism is rarely the cause, and even when it does exist, the individual tends to be pudgy rather than obese. Neurologic, enzymatic, and other hormonal causes are also rare, and again, the result is pudginess, not obesity. Obesity can also be a symptom of some illnesses, but these illnesses also interfere with other growth processes, involving stature and sexual or intellectual development (Stimbert & Coffee, 1972).

Although obesity tends to run in families, the genetic process is unknown. In most cases, parents covertly or overtly encourage a child to overeat and be inactive and resist suggestions that the child's intake of food should be restricted. Mother-child interactions during infancy are usually an important aspect of the problem. The parents of an obese child frequently expect the child to compensate for their own frustrations and unfulfilled ambitions. This increases the child's frustration and food intake: it is as if the child does not feel big enough to handle what is expected and tries to become bigger. Obese children are overprotected as well as overfed, and the mothers have erroneous, preconceived ideas about what children need based on their own unfulfilled needs.

How is it possible for so vital a function as eating to become so contaminated? Bruch (1975) asked herself this question and concluded that the precondition for all serious eating abnormalities is the failure to learn to distinguish between hunger and other sensations and feelings during infancy. In other words, because parental responses to the infant's cues are inadequate and indiscriminate, these children never learn to experience the pleasure of fulfillment, express their needs successfully, or correctly interpret the cues and messages of others. Neglect as much as indiscriminate feeding contributes to a child's confusion. A self-preoccupied, narcissistic mother will interpret all the child's activities from her own viewpoint; for her, the eating child is loving and loved and the noneating one is criticizing her.

> *Mary S*, an obese but pretty 31-year-old woman, entered group therapy because she wanted to lose weight and other methods she had tried—dieting, diet clubs, and individual psychotherapy—had failed. The group refused to discuss how she could lose weight and asked her why she ate more food than she needed.
>
> At first, Mary said she really didn't eat very much but admitted going on food binges, especially when something upset her. Telling the story of her life, she talked about her mother's coldness, perfection, and beauty and about her own inadequacy, loneliness, difference, and lack of someone to talk to. Once she described a visit home, where an old family friend had given her a gift she neither needed nor wanted. She had not only carried the gift back but had kept it. Another member of the group snorted and said: "When my mother-in-law gives me something I don't want, which is often, I say thank you and then throw it away in the first litter can I find." Mary then commented wistfully: "I've always wanted to have someone know what I want and to give it to me, but whatever someone gives me, I have to take." She was actually saying that she wished her needs had been understood and differentiated for her when she was an infant. Because Mary had never learned to differentiate her own needs, she was controlled by the needs of others and always wanted someone to know, without being told, what she wanted. So she "ate" whatever someone else gave her.

Anorexia

Anorexia is the opposite of obesity, and many of the dynamics are the same. Anorexic children do not eat—sometimes to the point where their lives are threatened. Here too, food is a central organizer. Like obese children, anorexic children are unable to differentiate between hunger and other needs. In both conditions, life gravitates around and depends on others, separation-individuation is incomplete, and the individual is controlled by the needs of others.

Anorexia nervosa is more common among girls than boys and usually occurs during prepuberty or puberty. Ostensibly because of society's norms concerning beauty, a girl will consciously and relentlessly pursue the ideal of thinness. She fears obesity, mistrusts and is confused by her body's signals, feels inferior and ineffective, sets perfectionistic goals for herself, fears growing up, and is hyperactive. Thus caloric output exceeds caloric input. In addition, she may have delusional ideas about food and parts of her body. Like obesity, anorexia is never an isolated symptom (Wiener, 1976).

Growing up is a problem for these children. In fact, malnourishment retards their growth and usually leads to retardation or cessation of menstruation. Sexual fears contaminate all their impulses; some perceive eating and gaining weight as symbolic pregnancy (Kissel & Arkins, 1973). By denying a basic need, anorexic children also punish themselves for their anger at parents. Unlike obese children, they are engaged with parents in an open battle over food and tend to be indiscriminately negative. Until the eating abnormality emerges, however, many of them hide behind a facade of compliance, proper behavior, and achievement.

Tolstrup (1970) stated that pathological ideas about the body, fantasies about its ugliness, and hypochondriacal notions accompany this eating disturbance. Although anorexic children do not eat, they are preoccupied with food, have few pleasures or hopes, and feel unloved and unloving. They are also inaccessible to logical argument: no matter how thin they are, they insist they are too fat and are indifferent to others' expressions of concern and to their own needs. Their avoidance of food is similar to a phobia (Galdston, 1974; Kissel & Arkins, 1973).

Here too, the family is involved in the development and perpetuation of this problem. Although the parents worry about being thin, food is of great concern. Mothers stress that thinness is beauty and are always dieting. Although they usually overidentify with the child, they may not notice that the child is refusing food and losing weight until the child is seriously ill (Shafu, Salguero, & Finch, 1975). The family dynamics tend to stress the denial of pleasure, and achievement and perfection are family goals. Thus therapy must focus on family structure and functioning because change will not occur until the parents' needs are met. As illustrated in the following case, parents of children with eating problems have similar problems themselves (Selvini-Palazzoli, 1970; Liebman, Minuchin, & Baker, 1974):

> Jenny D, age 12, was a lanky, verbal, intelligent girl who complained constantly, bossed her two brothers around, and was isolated from her peers. She had frequent colds and temperatures, which kept her home from school. She was referred for treatment by her pediatrician because of her complaints, preoccupations with her body, and poor eating habits.
>
> Mr. and Mrs. D had been legally separated the previous year and a divorce was imminent. Mr. D had initiated the separation because he no longer wanted to live with so disturbed a wife. Mrs. D was in treatment for depression and somatic complaints and preoccupations.
>
> Jenny was the oldest of three children. During each pregnancy, Mrs. D had been severely depressed. Although Jenny had been a planned child, both parents had wanted a boy. Mrs. D's pregnancies had been uneventful, but because she had not wanted to get fat, she had induced vomiting—to the point where her obstetrician had become concerned.

From the beginning, Jenny had eating problems. She could not keep milk down for the first four or five months, had skin rashes, and was difficult to toilet train.

After separating from her husband, Mrs. D went back to work and found Jenny's constant illnesses difficult to manage. Yet she was always upset when Jenny ran a temperature. Jenny had had difficulties leaving her mother since nursery school. Mrs. D commented that it had been harder for her to have Jenny leave than it had been for Jenny.

Mrs. D's parents helped the family financially, visited often, and gave advice. Mrs. D was as dependent on them as Jenny was on her. Mrs. D's mother reportedly told Jenny frightening stories: e.g., about a girl scout who was murdered while delivering cookies to someone's house. Ostensibly she did this so that Jenny would learn to be careful. Although Mr. and Mrs. D were legally separated and living apart, Mr. D often came to the house, bringing his laundry and visiting. Because the parents were obviously not separated emotionally and because each was in individual treatment with a different therapist, Jenny's social worker saw them together to discuss their roles and make plans for Jenny. Jenny was seen individually and with her parents, and several times her grandparents were included. When Mr. and Mrs. D were able to understand their children's confusion about the separation, family interviews were held to clarify the situation and give the children the opportunity to air their views. Plans were made to send Jenny to camp for the summer. Mrs. D wanted to be free of the children for a while, and it seemed to be a good way to get Jenny to be more active, make friends, and divorce herself from her mother's problems. Jenny, however, had all kinds of conditions that had to be met before she would agree to go to camp—one was that she could come home after a week if it didn't work out.

Jenny wrote six letters to her mother during the first week. Two are presented here:

> *Day 1.* "I hate it!! Please, don't tell me I should stick it out and it's only adjustment, because I tried, I really tried, but it's tearing me apart!!! Get me out now!!! I'm spending my whole time crying! I want to leave before four days is up!!! I'm the only 1 in the whole camp who

cried. Write back soon and everyday." *Day 3.* "Please have either you or dad bring up Wooly if you're going to make me suffer and stay here. When are you coming up and how often? Incidentally, I haven't eaten anything only water and 1 glass of milk, since I got here. From now on I will do this on purpose if you make me stay. Don't think I can't. Either you bring me home or I'll have to come home after recuperating in a hospital; I've only found 1 nice girl I like. If you plan on making me stay bring my photo albums. I don't care if I get hungry, I won't eat. There's only one counselor I like, I wrote a great deal of this with tears in my eyes. There isn't one girl who has cried so much, I'm so damn homesick!! Please take me home."

The fourth letter announced that she was staying up late and waking up at 2 A.M. to make herself sicker.

Jenny's use of eating and illness was overt at this point, but she continued to use it to control her mother. Although she was conscious of this, she was unaware of the tremendous hostility and rage that her behavior revealed. Unconsciously, she had been using these methods to punish and to be punished. Mrs. D understood this, but had to speak to the worker before she was able to call Jenny and tell her calmly that she had agreed to stay one week and could come home after that if she wanted to. She made this call after the fourth letter.

The fifth and sixth letters were quieter. Jenny had had a nightmare; she thought up a speech to the kids if she left camp. People were getting fed up with her and she was trying. She did not write on the seventh day. Her mother received the following letter after the weekend.

"Please remember to bring up the stuff all carefully hidden. I mean Wooly. I traded Lois for this one piece of stationary. I finally wrote Grandma, grandpa and the boys. Also Dad has been up and we're going to correspond by tape.

We've had 2 socials and I met a guy name Ed at the second one. He was really very nice and good-looking too! I can't wait for the next social. Next week we're going on a trip. Can't wait to see ya."

Disorders Of Elimination

Elimination of the body's waste products is another vital function that concerns many children and parents to an unusual degree. Problems involve where, how, and when this natural process will occur. Although infants void automatically, maturation of sphincter muscles and an increasing awareness of societal requirements for cleanliness are involved in voluntary control of elimination.

Although the age at which children are expected to achieve control varies in different societies, 6 or 7 is the upper limit. By then, all children are expected to adhere to their culture's requirements. It is reasonable for society to insist that children learn to control these processes; even mature dogs and cats do not sully their living spaces. It is adaptive and healthy to eliminate properly; it is a distortion when society denies or abhors these necessary functions.

The contents of the diaper do not disturb the child until they disturb the parents; children discover the pleasure and stimulation involved in the elimination and retention of urine and feces when they are extremely young. They experience additional pleasure during the wiping and fondling that accompanies the cleaning process. This assists the early discovery of pleasure in genital, urethral, and anal sensations. Children frequently (and normally) discover that feces have a remarkable consistency and can be spread, touched, and even eaten. At the same time, they usually discover the social injunction to destroy these marvelous products.

By the second year of life, mother is differentiated from the self; she is an important giving and sometimes frustrating object in the child's life. She is frustrating because, among other things, she insists that the child deposit waste products in a specific place. In the child's view, feces are part of the body and become the equivalent of gifts, but the child may be ambivalent about meeting the demands of

toilet training. In most western cultures, this struggle during the "anal" period coincides with the child's increased
awareness of the distinction between the words "you" and
"me" and "yes" and "no."

Because children have idiosyncratic explanations for
all bodily functions, the stool has a different meaning for
them than it has for most adults. For example, it may symbolize a penis, a baby, a gift, or a weapon (Prugh, Wermer
& Lord, 1956). Using Piaget's concept of animism, Anthony (1972) suggested that for children younger than 7,
everything that moves is alive; therefore, feces are alive
inside the body but not outside. Until they reach age 9,
children believe that everything that moves by itself is alive;
therefore, feces that control themselves are alive, but feces
the child controls are not. By age 10 or 11, children usually
have a clearer understanding of biological concepts. Since
parents rarely share or understand these childish views, it
is not surprising that control of elimination is an area with
the potential for serious conflict.

Complaints about the child's functioning cover a continuum ranging from mild concern and occasional dysfunction or regression to severe malfunctions such as enuresis,
encopresis (soiling), and pathological constipation. The
dynamics are similar to those encountered in the area of
eating; the basic issue is who will control the function, the
child or the parent. By the time children enter latency,
elimination should be under voluntary control.

Although some methods of toilet training are considered unwise, there is no unequivocal one-to-one relationships between specific practices and disturbances in the
area of elimination (Prugh, Wermer, & Lord, 1956; Anthony, 1972; Baird, 1974; Gerard, 1957). This is similar to
the statement that *no single* child-rearing practice causes
any disturbance. Children who have problems in the area
of elimination tend to have a variety of associated problems. Among the biopsychosocial factors involved in these

difficulties, the environment is most critical. The common variable is the parent-child relationship, which involves the dynamics of the entire family (Prugh, Wermer, & Lord, 1956). In this area too, the child's symptom is the family's symptom.

Enuresis

Enuresis, the most common problem of elimination, is defined as chronic and repetitive voiding of urine, usually during sleep, by children who have no organic disturbances and normally should be toilet trained. Nocturnal wetting is more common than day-time wetting, but some children are "dribblers" and always have damp underpants. Some children continue to wet during the day after night wetting stops; however, most children only wet at night (Greenberg & Stephans, 1977).

More boys than girls are enuretic, and institutionalized children of both sexes have a considerably higher incidence than do noninstitutionalized children. No more than 7 percent of the child population older than 7 is enuretic, and spontaneous remission commonly occurs during adolescence. The term primary enuresis means that the child has never been dry; secondary enuresis means that the condition is transitory or began after the child was toilet trained. This regression usually follows a traumatic event and seldom occurs every night. Many enuretic children will not wet when visiting or sleeping away from home or when other changes occur in the environment, but changes such as foster home placement will cause regression in some children. Organic and genetic factors, reactions to toilet training, and environmental and emotional factors are offered as explanations of this condition.

Organic causes tend to be rare. Esman (1977) believes that a constitutional, maturational lag is involved in primary enuresis and bases his conclusions on data obtained during studies on the neurophysiology of sleep. Although it is not uncommon for parents of enuretic children to have been enuretic themselves, many researchers question the validity of genetic predisposition. What seem to be inherited are parental attitudes (Sperling, 1974). True enuresis is unconscious, but so is a parent's tacit permission for it, and children are not misled by overt parental concern, rewards or punishment, or being awakened at night.

Aggression seems to be an unconscious component of enuresis because the mother must wake up to change the child's sheets and there are secondary gains from the attention the child receives. Yet most latency-age children are ashamed of being enuretic; do not want others, especially peers, to know about it; and tend to deny and externalize the problem. If the enuresis is a family secret, the parents will join in the denial.

Disorders of elimination commonly are linked with a variety of other problems. Some contributing factors are sibling rivalry, inconsistent toilet training, and parental problems. If parents were enuretic in childhood, they often do not view enuresis as a problem although they may resent the inconvenience. The inconsistency of some parents may be an unconscious compensation for the severe training they received as children. Sometimes children are over-stimulated when they share the parental bedroom, or they are rewarded after wetting by being placed in the warm, dry, cozy parental bed. Furthermore, being cleaned and handled by the parent can be erotically gratifying and may satisfy an exhibitionistic wish. And for some children, enuresis is a substitute for masturbation.

According to Gerard (1957), enuretic boys and girls have different dispositions: the boys seem passive, retiring, and self-deprecating whereas the girls are aggressive, active and competitive. Both tend to have nocturnal fears. Yet Wax and Haddox (1974) have stated that enuresis is the most persistent disorder accompanying aggressive and violent behavior in adolescent boys, particularly fire-setting and cruelty to animals.

A variety of etiologies and personality constellations are found among enuretic children. Benjamin et al. (1971) suggested that children whose bed-wetting persists are insecure because they feel they have been abandoned or fear they will be; some will view their parents' reaction to the bed-wetting as a reassurance against abandonment. Although this fear of abandonment is most critical between the ages of 2½ and 5, the enuresis may continue if children have not worked through their earlier anxieties.

Encopresis

Encopresis occurs only one-tenth as often as enuresis, but it is far more serious and suggests a defect in impulse control. The encopretic child frequently is also enuretic (Shane, 1967). Either the child is unable to control defecation or deliberately defecates into a receptacle not intended for the purpose. As in enuresis, the condition is called either primary or secondary, depending on whether it is long-standing and chronic or is transitory and occurs after toilet training.

Anthony (1972) suggests that there are three types of encopresis: continuous, discontinuous, and pathological retention. The continuous type occurs in disorganized, messy families; the child simply has not been toilet trained. The discontinuous type occurs in families that are rigid, compulsive, overcontrolled, and inhibited. The soiling becomes a dirty secret—a mutual source of shame and anxiety for child and parents. These families tend to view all activities as either good or bad, clean or dirty. All members are preoccupied with dirt, although they disguise this preoccupation as an interest in cleanliness. Children who suffer the third type are pathologically constipated, often in response to severe toilet training and intense struggles with the parent. Eventually, leakage and "involuntary" soiling occur. If the disorder continues for too long, physiological changes take place in the large intestine and rectum (Warson et al., 1956).

A constellation of parental practices seems to contribute to encopresis: maternal insensitivity or rejection, paternal lack of interest, maternal depression and so forth. Some parents assume responsibility for their children's elimination rather than teach the children to control themselves. Then the focus of attention involves struggles over control, and the child becomes the family symptom-bearer: the child attempts to control by withholding the stool and the parents attempt to control by removing it. Maintaining the symptom is mutually advantageous: the child gains attention and the parents can avoid examining their own relationship (Hoag et al., 1971).

Baird (1974) suggests that families of encopretic children have four characteristics in common: withholding, infantilism, denial of anger, and faulty communication. As illustrated in the following case, anger is a predominant emotion, it is severely repressed, denied, and ignored, despite the hostile intent of the child's soiling and the family's reaction to it.

> *Tomaso*, 11 years old, was referred by his mother, who had difficulty with both of her sons, but especially Tomaso, who had temper tantrums and swore at her. His school work was poor because he daydreamed and refused to do anything that required effort. He wet his bed almost every night and soiled frequently. He also had trouble sleeping, sucked his thumb, and complained of frequent headaches. Although Tomaso's 13-year-old brother also was defiant and angry, the mother was more concerned about Tomaso because he was more like her. She had wet her bed until she was a teen-ager, had difficulty sleeping, and suffered from headaches.
>
> The boys' father had lived with the mother intermittently and been abusive. The two had never married and had

separated after Tomaso was born. The father did, however, visit the boys a few times every year. After the separation the mother lived with her parents most of the time. She had a continuing relationship with a younger man, which broke up when Tomaso was 8. It was then that Tomaso began to soil himself regularly, except for a period of five months when his mother was in treatment. At the time of referral, a 37-year-old recovered drug addict lived with the family and contributed to their support, but this man did not have a good relationship with the children.

Tomaso's birth had been normal and there were no difficulties during pregnancy. His mother had intended to place Tomaso immediately after he was born because one child was all she could handle, but she changed her mind. He ate well, walked when he was 12 months old, and began talking shortly after his second birthday. He was toilet trained by a baby-sitter when he was 1½, but his mother did not know how the sitter had accomplished this. Although Tomaso learned to stay dry during the day, he was always enuretic at night. His mother punished him until he was 7 or 8 and then gave up. When Tomaso began to soil himself regularly, she had him evaluated at a clinic, which recommended placement. But she felt guilty and could not follow this recommendation.

The mother seemed to be a chronically depressed woman, involved with herself and unable to give her children the emotional support and consistency they needed. She constantly berated herself as a bad mother; she could not make the boys clean up their room unless she yelled at or hit them. Although she expressed conflicting feelings about Tomaso, calling him dumb, crazy, wishing he would live with his father, she overprotected him and encouraged his infantile behavior in many ways.

Tomaso denied soiling, even when his mother confronted him with his dirty underwear. He responded by accusing her of picking on him. Once, when the worker asked him why he thought he was coming to clinic, he pointed at his mother through the closed door to the waiting room, saying "That's the problem." When his mother called him dumb or crazy, he would lose his temper. He also felt that she treated him like a baby. It took a long while before Tomaso could talk about his habits and problems; on one occasion, he said he still sucked his thumb because his mother let him have a pacifier for too long. Tomaso spoke for many children whose parents are ambivalent, overprotect them, treat them like infants, and do not teach them how to care for themselves.

SLEEP DISORDERS

Sleep is another vital human function. Newborn infants sleep most of the time and wake up at irregular intervals. As children develop, their patterns of sleep and wakefulness are influenced by individual constitution, neurophysiological maturation, and their mothers' characteristic responses to their emotional and biological needs (Nagera, 1966b). It is natural to fall asleep when one is tired if there are no disturbing stimuli in the environment, but cultural and social customs tend to interfere with the self-regulation of infancy, especially when individual sleep patterns do not coincide with the norm.

When children are older and sleep at regular, more limited times, parents may disapprove of their idiosyncratic methods of falling asleep, which usually are autoerotic: e.g., thumb-sucking or masturbation. Many cultural groups acknowledge the universal need for close, warm contact, even during sleep, by seeing to it that children never sleep alone in a bed or room (A. Freud, 1965). Hygienically oriented modern groups, however, tend to frown on these practices and stress the child's need for privacy.

Disturbances of sleep are the first reliable signs of emotional conflict in children (Sperling, 1971). Transitory sleep disturbances are common in the second year of life, when going to sleep means coping with separation from mother. If autoerotic activities are curtailed, young children may become extremely anxious. Darkness, loneliness, and childish fantasies may contribute to periods of wakefulness and demands for a parent's presence through the preschool years (A. Freud, 1968b). Most of these difficulties disappear as development progresses, however.

Latency-age children are expected to be sufficiently self-regulated to satisfy their individual requirements for sleep within the context of cultural patterns. Therefore, sleep disturbances tend to disappear in latency, and problems are expressed in other ways. Latency-age children may develop ceremonies such as reading in bed, playing with a toy, or listening to music to help them fall asleep (Nagera, 1966b). (Many adults use similar devices as well as the ritual of preparing for bed to achieve the necessary degree of relaxation). Yet sleep disturbances can continue into latency. A few latency-age children will walk into the parental bedroom or demand company at night as younger children do, but nightmares, sleepwalking, and presleep ceremonies and delays are more common (Patterson & Pruitt, 1977).

Nightmares or night terrors caused by anxiety about repressed impulses and wishes are the most common problems of sleep during latency (Sperling, 1971). Children of all ages will have nightmares after an acute trauma such as surgery, an accident, a death in the family, or the birth of a sibling. The dream will repeat the trauma and sleep will be fitful; feeling helpless and terrified, a child may cry out, wake up in a state of anxiety, and need to cling to and be reassured by parents.

Recurrent nightmares usually represent forbidden and dangerous impulses that arise during the day. When children feel, even in sleep, that these impulses might be carried out in reality, their sleep will be interrupted. In the extreme form of night terror, children have difficulty reorienting themselves to reality and are difficult to awaken and comfort. The panic and fear they experience is almost psychotic. Unlike other nightmares, this type of dream will not be remembered. This disturbance is often accompanied by sleepwalking, which in a way permits the somatic discharge of anxiety that is usually related to sadistic, aggressive, and sexual impulses. It also contains a self-destructive element since it exposes the child to danger.

Persistent sleep disturbances and nightmares indicate that children are struggling with overwhelming anxiety; usually they will exhibit other symptoms such as phobias and psychophysiological illness. Some of the anxiety may be related to fear for a parent's safety, fear of separation and rejection, or fear of aggressive wishes. The problem may reflect parental problems more than the child's. For example, some parents unconsciously encourage a child's sleep disturbance because it interferes with their sex life or use their differences about the child's sleep patterns as an outlet for marital discord (Nagera, 1966b).

Often children are overstimulated by sleeping in their parents' bedroom and even in their bed. Some parents encourage this because it prevents sexual activity or gratifies their exhibitionistic tendencies. One mother reported that in childhood, family vacations meant that she slept in her parents' bedroom. When she heard her parents having intercourse, she yelled "Stop it! Stop it!" yet this did not stop their activity or the custom.

Sleeping customs vary in different cultures and homes (A. Freud, 1965; Kaplan & Poznanski, 1974). Many families cannot afford the amount of space that permits privacy yet manage somehow to protect their children from activities that are difficult to understand. When the child has a sleep problem and it is related to an unconscious parental need, educating the parents will not cure the problem; if forbidden to engage in one activity, they can easily substitute another, equally undesirable one that serves the same purpose. On the other hand, when children wake up complaining of a variety of ailments that have no organic cause, they may be attempting to separate their parents and prevent intercourse. Thus although sleep disturbances can arise from the child's conflicts, they are abetted by the family dynamics.

DISORDERS OF SELF-PRESERVATION

Infants and young children must depend on their parents to protect them from physical danger. Infants scratch and even bite themselves until they learn to distinguish the source of the pain. As experience permits a better orientation to reality and as cause and effect become more comprehensible, children understand other dangers and can avoid them (A. Freud, 1963). Latency-age children are expected to assume more and more responsibility for their own safety as their physical and cognitive skills develop.

It is natural to avoid pain and try to be safe and secure. Yet even this basic function can be distorted. For example, some children have repeated accidents or deliberately injure themselves by pulling their hair out, scratching or cutting themselves severely, refusing to eat, or attempting suicide. Other acts, such as running away, are tantamount to seeking injury because of the dangers to which the children expose themselves (Foster, 1962).

Often, children who do not protect themselves have not been protected and cherished. They may be victims of parental aggression or feel rejected and unwanted. They may direct aggression against themselves if prevented from expressing it verbally against others or if they feel guilty about their hostile wishes.

If parents do not want or feel ambivalent about a child, the child may incorporate the parents' views. Parental ambivalence can be expressed through oversolicitous warnings or anticipations of danger, which encourage preoccupation with the body as well as fear. Children also learn that injuries bring attention and physical contact, which are especially desirable for children whose mothers avoid body contact.

Suicide

Some children will threaten to kill themselves in an effort to elicit love and attention. Any trivial situation can be the precipitating factor if a child believes that a suicide attempt will make everything better. Although suicide is rare among children younger than 10, many accidents and other medical emergencies are suspected of being unconscious suicide attempts (Bender & Schilder, 1937).

Children may threaten to kill themselves when they want to influence, manipulate, or punish their parents (Glaser, 1971). Suicidal gestures are more serious, but their intent is similar; the problem is that children may not understand the danger to which their actions expose them. Similarly, children may resort to impulsive acts if they do not understand that death is final, have childish feelings of omnipotence and magical return, or believe in the reversibility of death (Aleksandrowicz, 1975).

In prepuberty, the incidence of suicide increases. Mattsson, Seese, and Hawkins (1969) found a high percentage of suicidal behavior among prepubertal children referred to a child psychiatric emergency clinic. The most common cause was acute conflict between child and parents. Sometimes unrealistic expectations cause feelings of inadequacy, worthlessness, and helplessness—all of which are aspects of depression.

Accidents

Hazardous behavior and unreasonable risks are also forms of suicidal behavior. Accidents are the leading cause of death among American children from birth to age 15. Children who are accident prone usually have a history of psychosomatic illness and physical complaints (Plionis, 1977). Frequent accidents also occur among children who live under constant stress, are institutionalized, or are in foster care (Malone, 1967). These accidents can be viewed as desperate cries for attention. Accidents and injuries are forms of self-punishment in children who tend to be impulsive and express their emotions and conflicts in physical action. They are filled with rage toward the mother but also need and love her. Never having learned that it is possible to love and hate the same person, never having fused love and aggression sufficiently, they lack the resources to express their despair appropriately. They seem to feel that they are responsible for their bad lives and must punish themselves over and over again (Frankl, 1963).

Self-Mutilation

Healthy narcissism, caring appropriately for oneself, is the result of being cared for and loved. Young children usually direct their anger and frustration at their mothers. If their expressions of anger are punished, they may turn the anger against themselves. Head-banging, hair-pulling, and biting and scratching of different parts of the body are expressions of autoaggression in very young children (Buxbaum, 1970).

Self-mutilation during latency is a form of suicide. Children this age turn their anger and aggression against themselves as if punishing themselves for a desire to hurt others (Lester, 1972). The despair of these children is deeper than in those who are accident prone. Some will literally tear their hair out, which is not only self- punishment but a sign of despair and mourning. Children who are isolated, neglected, and lonely may need to hold on to themselves when others fail them. Buxbaum (1960) suggests that these children prove they exist by making themselves feel, even if that feeling is pain. In other forms of self-mutilation, children will pick viciously at scabs or deliberately cut themselves.

The various forms of self-injury have multiple causes. Self-inflicted injuries may be more common among children whose parents communicate physically or are abusive. If parents are emotionally unavailable, their children may injure themselves to get attention as well as inflict suffering on the parents. Often these behaviors create emergencies, and the child—the family symptom-carrier, is brought to the attention of the health care or welfare system. By shifting its responsibility onto institutions, the family also gets the attention it needs (Plionis, 1977).

Children who hurt themselves are difficult to engage in a relationship because they cannot trust. If they can learn to feel cared for and to trust enough, they may stop destroying themselves, but whenever they are disappointed again or feel deserted, they can easily revert to self-destructive behavior. This often happens when social workers leave their agencies or when foster children are moved from one foster home to another. No explanations can protect these children because they have not learned to love themselves through a caring relationship in infancy nor have they had a sustained, dependable, corrective, and caring relationship later with an important adult.

DISORDERS OF COMMUNICATION

Although latency-age children express many feelings through motor activity, development of verbal expressiveness is a significant and essential task during this period. Speech assists thinking, communication, ego integration, and development and stimulates growth of the ego's controlling function. The capacity for language is biologically innate in humans, but speech will not emerge and take form unless it is taught and rewarded. McLaughlin (1974) described an ancient experiment conducted by Frederick II, who intended to discover what language children would speak if left to their own devices. Would it be Hebrew, Greek, Latin, Arabic, or the language of their parents? Although the children were physically cared for, no one spoke or sang to them. Apparently, all the children died. This is similar to Spitz's studies (1946) of babies who died because they lacked the opportunity to interact with others. Other reports of children who grow up in the wild and have no contact with humans indicate speech does not develop without human contact (Lane, 1976).

Infants begin their communications by crying. The responses of significant others who meet the needs expressed by these cries, who play with words with children, who name objects and take pleasure in children's attempts to speak encourage the desire to speak.

Children understand speech before they talk. Later, their initial sounds are accepted and translated into Mama and Dada. Still later, they learn and repeat the names of persons and objects, encouraged by the pleasure of their parents and the pleasure of learning to get what they want by asking for it. This early language is concrete. The ability to use language to convey feelings develops slowly, in step with maturation and cognitive growth and through interaction with others who verbalize abstract feelings.

Pain and fear tend to be the first feelings a child verbalizes. Because sadness, excitement, happiness, and anger are more complex concepts, parents usually verbalize these for the child as they interpret the meaning of the child's physical behavior. If these emotions are not verbalized for children, they may never become part of the communication repertoire (Katan, 1961).

Disturbances of body functions and physical acting out may result when children's verbalizations are inadequate to communicate their needs, wishes, and fears. Verbalization helps to delay action and provides time for making judgments and experimenting mentally with possible actions. If this is not learned, actions will predominate. But vocabulary alone is not sufficient; words can be used to defend against feelings. When words do not actually mean what they seem to mean, children become confused, caught in a double-bind.

Since speech begins with object relationships and continues to function in this manner, it will reflect interactive and intrapsychic processes. Thought processes, normal and abnormal; conflict and pathology; mother-child conflicts; and family dynamics are reflected in children's speech patterns (Kolansky, 1967).

Disorders and impairments such as delayed development of speech and language, problems of articulation, and stuttering or stammering affect approximately 7 percent of the population. Because many of these disorders are influenced by maturation, it is not surprising that the greatest amount of improvement occurs during the first and second grades (Connor et al., 1975). Children whose speech problems persist often have other disturbances as well. Many theories have been advanced to explain language disorders: e.g., neurological, emotional, cultural, or environmental deprivation and severe psychopathology. But whatever the cause, speech disturbances interfere with a child's learning, socialization, and self-image.

Stuttering

Stuttering is a common disorder that frequently appears as children begin to speak (between the ages of 2 and 4). It may be the result of delayed maturation, emotional crises, struggles over control, or parental demands. If it is not overstressed, it usually disappears. Some children begin to stutter when they enter school; in these cases, the problem is related to tension, fear, and separation anxiety. If the stuttering continues, it usually reflects tension, blocking, or withholding, and other psychological disorders (Hirsch, 1972). The degree of stuttering varies and sometimes occurs in relation to a specific topic, person, or situation.

Stuttering often reflects parent-child conflicts and the child's ambivalence, guilt, and aggression. It is more common among males than females, tends to run in families, and may reflect the high value a family places on speech.

Research on families of children who stutter indicates that the parents tend to be critical and overprotective (Bloch & Goodstein, 1972). Essentially, stutterers withhold: at first their speech is blocked and is then released, either slowly and with difficulty or in an explosive torrent. The process is similar to the pathological withholding of feces, and the problem varies in degree, as do anal problems. Inhibition of speech is aggressive, controlling, and self-punitive. The listener suffers while the speaker struggles with words; the speaker suffers the consequences of having difficulty communicating, being criticized, or being the butt of jokes.

Mutism

Some children will speak only at home or to specific persons such as parents, siblings, and a few peers; in school they will be silent. Social workers frequently encounter children who will not speak during interviews although they are seen regularly for long periods. These children may communicate through gestures or facial expressions, or answer yes or no in response to questions. In general, they are resistant and angry or fearful and timid. When this voluntary withholding of speech occurs during contact with others outside the family, particularly in school, it tends to be an elective mutism, that is, one part of an overall social adaptation and an attempt to manipulate the environment.

Traumatic experiences while learning to talk, such as overly critical reactions to initial efforts to speak, may make children insecure about expressing themselves verbally. Such children come from homes where there are severe marital difficulties and family secrets. By not speaking, they not only prevent themselves from telling these secrets but protect themselves and others from their hostile impulses. Often the family encourages infantile behavior in the child and traps the child in a family system that excludes outsiders. Usually elective mutism is accompanied by other symptoms such as school phobias and speech difficulties (Halpern, Hammond, & Cohen, 1971).

The therapist who works with these silent children feels frustrated because he or she knows how important it is for them to talk. Although the therapist must talk, a child's silence and other nonverbal communications must be accepted as real. If the therapist tries too hard to make a child talk, it will exacerbate the already-existing problem of overvaluing the magic of words (Chethik, 1973; Kaplan & Escoll, 1973).

In extreme cases, children will stop talking altogether, usually in response to acute external stress. True aphasia is usually accompanied by organic abnormalities, seizures, lack of attentiveness, and behavioral problems. When these symptoms do not exist, mutism probably represents emotional withdrawal (Humphrey, Knipstein, & Bumpass, 1975).

In severe psychotic regressions, loss of speech or speech that is bizarre and unintelligible is a symptom of withdrawal from object relations. The tone, expressiveness, and quality of speech of all children are related to the nature of relations with others, whether feared, desired, or impaired.

It is apparent that symptomology in childhood and the totality of individual children's behaviors are closely related to their interpersonal situations, past and present. Unless the environment is examined, a study of the child will yield only a list of symptoms, none of which will make sense. A study of symptoms alone will not determine the appropriate intervention.

IV

TREATMENT

Chapter 9

BEGINNINGS

Social workers come in contact with families and troubled children in a wide variety of settings and encounter a wide variety of parental attitudes. Some parents consciously recognize that their child has a problem while others will deny it. Some believe that they have contributed to the problem, but do not understand how and want to do better. Others refuse to accept responsibility and blame the child, another person, or another system, such as the school. If the child is the family scapegoat, he will be perceived as having few, if any, good qualities. Some parents request assistance with a disturbing symptom but want the worker to leave the family interactions and underlying pathology alone. Others are actually requesting help for themselves.

Parents will also have a series of expectations about the treatment process and about the professional ranging from informed, sophisticated knowledge to idiosyncratic, uninformed ideas. These expectations will be influenced by their education, previous experiences, and the attitudes of their culture about receiving help from social workers or "psychological" experts. Of necessity, they will be apprehensive at the beginning.

Children approach treatment with different goals and expectations. They too may want external circumstances to be changed, but do not wish to change themselves. Or they may view themselves as bad and in need of punishment and want to change but feel it is impossible. Some may be convinced that their lives will never improve. Although their expectations are somewhat dependent on parental attitudes and previous experiences, they will have highly personal sets of ideas about the aim, meaning, and function of the treatment process, including conscious and unconscious fantasies about the purpose of treatment and the person who conducts the treatment (Blos, 1970).

A beginning goal of treatment is to increase the understanding of all participants: adults, child, and professionals. This means examining what is wrong, why, and what can be done—a process that continues until termination. To facilitate this process, it is essential to clarify the participants' expectations as well as what the treatment relationship has to offer. More important than the realities is an empathic understanding of the clients' human struggles, concern for their pain, and the offer of hope for the future (Ripple, 1964). This hope must be in tune with the clients' hopes because understanding is only achieved with their collaboration.

When children are the focus of concern, an understanding of the interactive nature of their needs and those of others in the environment is essential. The perceptions of parents, foster parents, referral source, medical authority, and school all contribute to an understanding of how the child's life is played out. But parents are the most important aspect of the child's environment (A. Freud, 1965).

First Contact

The client's first contact often consists of a telephone call requesting an appointment. In an outreach program, however, the worker may telephone the client to arrange an office or home visit. When clients request help, it is important to respond quickly so that they will feel that their needs, problems, and sense of urgency are respected. Although the entire family may come to the first interview, whether requested to or not, the worker should always interview the parents first.

Frequently, the client's first unrehearsed statements are likely to be the most complete and reliable. The tension of the first meeting, the urgency of the need, and an atmosphere of interest and exploration may stimulate clients to make significant connections between events and feelings. At times, they seem to have insights into the difficulty, but these may be momentary. Later, they may defend against knowing consciously what they know unconsciously.

It is difficult for anyone to relate a problem to his or her own deficiencies, whether the problem is economic, marital, or involves a child. Thus the worker should begin with the client's view of the problem, saving confrontation and disagreement for a later time, when the unpleasant impact is softened by relationship and trust. This process is illustrated in the following initial interview:

> *Tom B* was referred to the social worker by the school nurse because of his underachievement and unmanageability in school. Mrs. B made the appointment, and she, her husband, and Tom, age 12, arrived for it. Two other children lived at home: Simon, 25, a premed student, and Betty, 18, a high school senior. Theodore, a married son, 22, lived in his own home. Mr. B's 60-year-old crippled sister had lived with the family for seven years. Mr. B., 50, was unemployed and disabled; Mrs. B., 47, was a housewife. They had been married for twenty-nine years. The parents were inter-

viewed together first, Tom was then seen alone, and finally all three were interviewed together. Mr. B., a huge, athletic-looking man, wore a leg brace and walked painfully with a cane; Mrs. B. was handsome but looked tired. They complained that Tom was uncooperative, never obeyed, lied, stole at home, and performed poorly in school. When asked what they believed was wrong, Mrs. B said that Tom had been a straight A student until the fourth grade, when his father was hospitalized after being severely injured by a hit-and-run driver. For the first three months, he had been in intensive care, and Tom had not been allowed to see him. Mr. B. didn't know what to make of this; what bothered him was that Tom hated to lose when they played games and always had to have the last word; Tom did help him get around, however.

According to Mrs. B, Tom had been an easy child—until the fourth grade. At the time of her husband's accident, her mother was dying of cancer, and Mrs. B had been away from home twice for a month to take care of her. The family had tried to avoid talking about Mr. B's condition in front of Tom, but Mrs. B thought he probably knew. When his grandmother died that summer, Tom, who always had intense feelings about death and injury, was extremely upset.

The other children had never given their parents any trouble. The family lived on disability insurance, which was not very much. Mr. B had been a milkman and was in too much pain to be retrained for another job. Both parents described their marriage as uneventful, satisfying, and normal but seemed tense when they talked about it.

Tom, sturdily built and pleasant looking, was shabby and untidy. He was articulate when seen alone. He said his trouble began in the fourth grade "because of a bad kid I was with then." Although his school work had fallen down, he never failed. It just got harder. He knew that what he did got him into a lot of trouble, but he kept doing it over again and didn't know why. He spoke most about his father, who taught him chess when he was in the hospital but always won. Tom said he slept in the same room with his father to help him, except when he was so sick that Tom couldn't stand it. His mother slept in a room by herself. He got along fine with his brothers but fought with his sister and her boyfriend. His oldest brother was engaged, and when he left home, Tom would be his father's only buddy.

When Mr. and Mrs. B came in for the family interview, Tom found a place for his father to sit. When Mr. B asked Tom why he behaved so badly, Tom looked nervous and looked pleadingly at the worker. Mrs. B also asked Tom this question, adding that he seemed to feel he was under-privileged and was always complaining. She asked Tom to count all the clothes and games he had. Neither parent seemed to listen to Tom, who didn't say much anyway.

Seeing Tom and his parents together at the end of the interview was important for two reasons. First, it was possible to make joint plans during the first contact. Second, Tom probably was less threatened than he would have been if the worker had seen his parents alone after talking with him.

Many problems surfaced during this initial contact: Mr. B's accident and subsequent disability, simmering marital tensions, inappropriate tasks assigned to the youngest child, a mother who was under great strain, and a child whose behavior and poor school work seemed related to family problems. If crisis intervention had occurred at the time of Mr. B's accident, the entire family would have been better off.

The worker knew that realistic problems, familial tensions, and the family dynamics needed to be investigated in addition to Tom's difficulties. At this point, Tom seemed to accept the idea that he was bad and that he was somehow responsible for his father's illness. Yet part of him was angry about this. Was this his conflict?

Accepting the parents' concern about Tom as legitimate, the worker explained what needed to be done in the future. First, she would obtain the school report, which included the results of tests administered by the school psychologist, and a medical report from the family physician. Second, she would need to see each parent separately to get a clearer picture of their individual ideas about the problem. (All three agreed to this plan.)

FAMILY DIAGNOSTIC INTERVIEWS

The initial interview just described was inadequate for the following reasons. Two adult, apparently capable children and an aunt, who presumably played a significant role in

Tom's life, also lived in the household, and a married son was still involved with the family. To comprehend the family dynamics and locate untapped resources within the family, the worker needed to meet with the entire family. For example, in an attempt to avoid burdening the hard-working older children, did Mr. and Mrs. B withold information from them or at least avoid asking them for help?

Seeing the entire family together and noting the relationships among the different members (e.g., who reinforced whom and who was aligned with whom) is a significant part of the diagnostic process. Several sessions with the entire family might help the worker appraise the dynamics of Tom's symptoms and behavior within the family matrix. But as Sherman (1974) has pointed out, the family must participate in choosing which family members will be included and when. Thus one might suggest to the B's that it would be useful if the older children could join them in helping the worker understand Tom. While discussing the pros and cons, the parents, child, and worker would learn something. If the older children actually participated in a family session, the worker could hear their opinions, observe how the family interacts, and with carefully timed questions, help the family to marshall support for Tom and his parents as a beginning step in treatment.

Parents as Collaborators

The reasons why a family and a child are having difficulty may seem apparent to an outsider, especially a professional. Sometimes the reasons are so obvious that one cannot believe the family does not know. For example, Mrs. B apparently realized that Tom was disturbed about his father's illness, but Mr. B defended against this fact. In addition, she seemed to be speaking through Tom about her own problems: the simultaneous demands of a critically ill husband and a dying mother and the serious financial, social, and sexual changes that had occurred after her husband's accident. An outsider might have noted that the discrepancy in ages between Tom and his siblings placed Tom in a special category. Did his parents feel closer to him than to his siblings? Why was Tom the one who cared for his father? Why not his older brother or sister or his mother? Yet the problem the parents complained about involved Tom's behavior. If the worker investigated with them why such well-meaning, responsible parents are having these problems with their son, they would feel understood and become collaborators in studying and understanding their child and themselves.

Unless parents collaborate in treatment, little can be done to help the child. However, the worker should not expect them to begin investigating their own contribution to the difficulties immediately. In the beginning, parental willingness to cooperate in examining the child's difficulty is significant. The worker in this sense and in this case would be supportive and use the intelligence, thinking, and caring that already exist.

Foster parents need to become collaborators; living with the child, they not only experience but often contribute to the child's difficulties. However, the worker can ask for their professional collaboration, one worker with another. From their past experiences and their interest in the child, they may learn new ways of helping the child by cooperating in this way. When they are not asked to collaborate, foster parents often feel they have been attacked, judged, and found wanting. This will not help the child. Foster parents, after all, are people. Some are rigid, righteous, and view themselves as saviors of poor neglected children, and find it more difficult to tolerate failure than do natural parents.

Some parents come to the first interview armed with a ready-made solution to the problem. For instance, they may insist that the worker tell the child what to do, interfere with school, or even arrange placement. In these cases, the worker must help the parents realize that although they believe that this solution is necessary and are perhaps correct, both the problem and the solution must be clarified so that they can rethink their conclusions or understand the problem better. Respect for their ideas, combined with the process of thinking rather than acting immediately, may help them modify their ideas. Acting quickly, as some have done in the past, will only help to perpetuate impulsive behavior.

Some parents are so discouraged, depressed, and harried that they cannot see the point of coming to the agency. They will, however, allow their children to come so that someone else will take over the burden. In these cases, the worker should see the children as long as the parents will send them. By working with a child who needs help, the worker may eventually reach the parents (Feldman, 1958; Riese, 1962).

If the worker tells the parents too soon that they are the ones who need help or gives them advice before they are ready for it, they may feel criticized and attacked, become angry and frightened, and then leave, taking their child with them. But if the worker asks them to help by supplying information about the child and even by complaining, they will feel they are being asked to collaborate. Many parents say: "I have to live with this twenty-four hours a day; you see the kid once a week." After all, they are right. By acknowledging that their job is far more difficult and that they know more about the child than the worker does, the worker can enlist their cooperation. If the worker shares the results of tests or other evaluations with them and asks their opinion, they will be even more cooperative.

Some parents come to the agency only because they have been forced to do so by some outside authority. This is often the case in neglect and abuse situations. The worker must recognize this reality and try to assist them with this pressure by respecting their belief that they have done all that they can, and acknowledging how difficult their situation must be.

Other parents recognize that their own problems are contributing to the child's problems and will accept treatment for themselves. Some will use their child's difficulties as a way of obtaining help for themselves; others may feel guilty and ineffective. In these cases, the worker should focus on the strengths and positive aspects of the family and the child as well as their problems (Hallowitz & Cutter, 1958). This will help the parents view treatment as a constructive force, whereas criticism alone or a focus on pathology will be destructive and depressing.

Children As Collaborators

Children too are clients. Thus they have the right to participate in the plans that are made for them, even though their dependence on adults necessitates doing things they may not want to do. Coming to see a social worker may be one of those things. Children do not like to come to a strange place and be questioned by a strange authority. Therefore, one begins by recognizing that they were brought to the agency and then asks them to describe the problem.

Because Tom was old enough and his parents apparently had communicated adequately with him, Tom had some understanding of his problem. In addition, because of his intelligence and verbal ability, he was able to express his discomfort relatively clearly. But some children Tom's age are frightened and mute, either because their parents have used the impending interview as a threat or because the children are so isolated from and afraid of people that their fantasies are terrifying.

One should talk openly with children about their parents' complaints in simple but general terms. This is not a breach of confidence since it is about the child and the fact that it will be done has been clarified with the parents. Children can respond to a general complaint such as trouble at school because it allows for their interpretation. Complaints about lying or stealing are too specific and thus are more difficult to talk about during an initial interview with a stranger. For example, during the interview with Tom, the worker might note that his parents seem to feel he is having problems in school and at home. This would permit Tom to present his own views. She could also ask for Tom's opinions about how this came to be, what would make things better, and how she could help. In this way, she would be asking him to collaborate in planning for the future.

Of course, children's expectations must be discussed and clarified. The worker should also clarify the difference between a social worker and other authorities such as teachers and doctors. When children are seen in the office, they will note the presence of toys. Young children and those who are relatively unafraid may begin to play with the toys spontaneously. But gentleness, care, and creative approaches may be necessary to "warm up," frightened youngsters.

The Contract

The first contact with parents and child must conclude with a contract—an agreement about future contacts or a decision that no more needs to be done. The agreement may be only a tenative, time-limited one in which to study the situation together. Many agencies have a formal intake period, at the end of which there will be planning about future work. Parents and child should also be informed of agency procedures and policies concerning fees, assignment to other workers, and the like.

A period of exploration is useful even when intake is

not formalized. This establishes an atmosphere of freedom of choice and acknowledges the need for study and reflection with the client's cooperation. However, clients who view their situation as an emergency may find that waiting for something to be done too frustrating. In Tom's case, Tom and his parents talked with the worker about their current concerns, and she told them that she would study his test results and contact the school. This made all three feel that something was being done.

Goals must be clarified, in a general way, as part of the intial contract. Obviously, Tom's parents would want to know that the goal would be to improve Tom's behavior. This is a reasonable and acceptable goal. Tom might want his parents to stop picking on him or let him sleep alone.

BIOPSYCHOSOCIAL DIAGNOSIS

With all clients, the diagnostic process begins during the first contact, but it is not separate from treatment. The study that is part of the process is also part of treatment and the first contact is the beginning of treatment (Hollis, 1964: Perlman, 1957). In studying, the worker treats and clients learn the value of thinking through, thinking back, and thinking out with another person. This is the essence of treatment. In the long run, treatment is education.

Diagnosis begins with beginnings and formally ends with endings. It is a process of inquiry, understanding, and predictions based on contingencies. A series of hypotheses examined in the light of an individual's total functioning produces other hypotheses, which are confirmed or negated during the course of treatment. As in all educational experiences, the processes of growth and reflection should be well established when treatment ends and continue throughout life. In other words, clients learn in good treatment to teach themselves. Thinking professionals also reflect back on processes of treatment before and after endings; by thinking through in this way, they often learn new possibilities and ways of working that can be tested and explored with new clients.

If diagnosis is never ending with adults, how much more a continuing process there is with children. Children are not finished products, they are in the process of development. With proper understanding, the forces of life can be enlisted to facilitate this ongoing developmental process. The worker's main focus should be on making available to the child the natural push toward mastery, competence, effectiveness, and industry that will replace inferiority (Erikson, 1963). Treatment that accomplishes this is successful.

The biopsychosocial diagnostic process focuses on health even more than on disability. It is a comprehensive approach to a child's life experience and includes an understanding of the situation, the person, and the person's reactions to current as well as past experience (Hamilton, 1963). The process should lead to a treatment plan that involves child and family.

The diagnostic process is usually formalized by a professional statement that makes available for objective scrutiny the evidence leading to inferences that influence the treatment approach. This formulation should contain a brief summary of the available facts about the child's and family's present and past history and functioning and note the areas that need future examination. The dynamic diagnostic formulation represents the professional's interpretation and evaluation of the facts, including the forces that play an active role in the client's current functioning. The genetic diagnosis is an attempt to interpret the etiology of the current problem. The clinical diagnosis categorizes a group of related phenomena into standard formulations to facilitate record-keeping and provide a short-hand method of communication.

The Facts

The information required for diagnostic formulations about children is obtained from their histories, school and medical reports, and the results of a variety of tests, including psychiatric examinations.

Historical information about children and families usually is obtained from parents, who may not understand the relevance of specific information such as at what age a child walked, talked, or was toilet trained or how the child reacted to school, the parents' disciplinary methods, and so forth. Parents may wonder what age 1 has to do with age 12, but this can be explained as trying to understand with them how the child was before the trouble started, how the child developed, and what might have contributed to the difficulties. Sometimes parents cannot remember or will say that the child's development was normal; they may say that, compared with siblings or other children, the child was advanced or slow. These general statements are not facts; they represent the parents' point of view.

The validity of retrospective information tends to be poor with respect to factual matters (Sears, Rau, & Alpert, 1965). Significant distortions in parental recall are related to how specific and objective the questions are and how much time has elapsed. Answers to questions about concrete behavior tend to be more consistent with the facts (Thomas et al., 1963). Winnicott (1971) believes that there is no value in histories obtained from anyone but children because although children will be incorrect about details such as how old they were when an important event occurred, they know, even if unconsciously, the significant and essential facts. In addition, what they may have viewed as a deprivation may not have been noticed by the parents. (It was Tom who confirmed his mother's impression that his father's accident upset him, and he also brought other aspects of current and past problems to light.)

Despite errors, obtaining a history from parents is part of the process of understanding with them how problems developed. Often in telling about the child's life and their own experiences, they will make important connections. For example, Mrs. B noted that several crises had occurred in the family at the same time. Although Tom did not mention all of them during his initial interview, he did talk about the most important and still current problem—his father's illness. By knowing about the concurrent events, the professional would understand his future communications concerning these areas.

Sometimes a history suggests that a conflict appropriate to an earlier developmental stage is still active. For example, the B family related that the crippled aunt joined the family when Tom was 5; at this age, injuries to one's own or another's body activate unconscious fears of castration. Was this related to Mrs. B's statement that Tom always had intense feelings about death and injury? The worker would keep this hypothesis in mind for later study or in case Tom referred to this fear later in an indirect, unconscious way.

School reports contain a combination of facts and opinions. Facts are the grades received from teachers and from the series of standardized tests usually given to all children. Teachers' grades include subjective opinions about a child's performance and behavior as compared with classmates. Consequently, grades can be influenced by whether the teacher likes the child. Achievement tests indicate how the child performed at a particular time in relation to norms based on grade and age. Because many variables can contaminate the testing process, test results provide only a comparative and general idea of what a child learned. They do not establish with certainty what the child knows (See the case of Kate, Chapter 7).

Psychological and intelligence tests are often used as a source of information about the child and may provide an added perspective. But these tests too often are treated as objective rather than conditional (Bachrach, 1974). Becuase psychological tests are often summarized and include the psychologist's interpretations of the child's productions, they are diagnostic statements rather than fact.

It is important for social workers to be aware of the controversy that intelligence tests have caused over the years. Intelligence testing was developed at the turn of the century, when there was a reemergence of interest in the Mendelian laws of inheritance. Originated by Binet, who did not believe that IQ was a fixed quantity, intelligence tests were adopted in America by Terman and others, who believed that they would be useful for diagnosing previously undetected borderline deficiencies. The results of these early tests revealed that IQs of 70 and 80 were common among American Indians, Mexican-Americans, and blacks. These judgments had serious social consequences: e.g., some groups demanded sterilization laws, believing that immorality, crime, poverty, prostitution, epilepsy, and even excessive masturbation were transmitted through the genes of individuals with low IQs.

In 1912 intelligence tests administered at Ellis Island indicated that more than 75 percent of the immigrants from Poland, Russia, and southern Europe were feebleminded. Further corroboration was obtained in 1917 when mass testing of army recruits "proved" that many blacks and members of Slavic and Latin ethnic groups were feebleminded. As a result, immigration quotas based on national origin were instituted in 1921, formalized in 1924 by the Johnson-Lodge Immigration Act, and continue to the present day (Kamin, 1974; Lubove, 1965). Social workers now had an explanation for immorality, degeneracy, poverty, and other problems that had formerly been attributed to individual character. Although Jane Addams and Edith Abbot spoke out against the quota system (Cohen, 1958), many charity organizations and social workers participated in anti-immigration movements. Mary Richmond accepted the new understanding of problem behavior and the value of scientific testing, but her firm belief in investigation and evidence helped her to caution that although tests were valuable if properly administered and interpreted, an equally important method of evaluating individual capacity was to determine how a person performed at home, at work or school, and in human relations and understand character tendencies and personal traits. In her opinion, personal habits established by social training had the most to do with success and failure. The most difficult social questions concerned whether deviant behavior was caused by innate deficiencies or an unfavorable environment (Richmond, 1922).

For more than 30 years, there has been increasing disillusionment with the validity of intelligence tests as predictors of future behavior and as determinants of innate intelligence. They are now viewed as reflecting a series of environmental variables and are perceived as man-made rather than God-given. They also are criticized for neglecting the process of learning, which includes interaction with the environment (Voyat, 1970). The validity of a wide variety of so-called objective and projective tests was seriously questioned in 1947 when graduate students in psychology from universities across the United States were given a series of tests and evaluations by experts who predicted the students' future success as clinical psychologists. No relationship could be found, however, between actual professional accomplishment and predictions based on the tests because too many variables contributed to both academic and professional success (Gottesfeld, 1966).

The problem of validity is important today because black, Mexican-American, Puerto Rican, and American Indian children generally obtain lower scores on traditional intelligence tests than do white middle-class children. Generally speaking, all "culturally disadvantaged" children, including lower class white children, perform less well on these tests (Kagan, 1969).

It is important to realize that intelligence tests are imperfect instruments, imperfectly understood. Although they allow general predictions about future academic performance and some estimate of what has been learned, they cannot predict performance in all areas of life (Hobbs, 1975; M. Deutsch, 1969). What they actually test is the ability to supply correct answers; they cannot be used to assess reasoning and creativity (De Vries, 1974).

Test performance is affected by variables such as socioeconomic conditions, cultural context, type of community (rural versus urban), experience in test-taking, motivation, bilingualism, and the prejudices of the examiner (Padilla & Ruiz, 1973). Nutrition and home environment also contribute to the facilitation or retardation of many cognitive and verbal abilities.

When Thomas et al. (1971) studied the effects of how tests were administered and the impact of the examiner's behavior on the scores of a group of children, they found that scores improved when the examiner encouraged active participation, verbalization, and repeated effort on the children's part. When the examiner was matter-of-fact, the children's scores were lower but better correlated with their actual academic achievement, possibly because this approach is similar to the methods of instruction used in teaching.

Anxiety about the tests can also contaminate the results. Thus if testing is a part of an agency's intake process, the results may be affected because the child has not had sufficient time to establish a relationship with the worker or adjust to the therapeutic process. Often, no one talks with children about their reactions and fantasies concerning the testing or about the purpose and results of the tests. Although tests may help clarify serious emotional, intellectual, and even organic deficits, they will be more valuable if administered when children want to find out why they have problems.

Another procedure that is used routinely during the intake process is the psychiatric examination. As a result, children are asked to talk with another adult stranger. Older children may joke about the "shrink," but underneath they may wonder why they need a "mental" examination. Presumably, these examinations are used to ascertain the degree of disturbance, apply a clinical label, and satisfy legal requirements for medical supervision. Often treatment plans carried out by the social worker are prescribed by the psychiatrist.

It is doubtful whether anything but a hypothesis is justified after one interview in a strange setting. In reality, the social worker's observations and biopsychosocial summary guide the psychiatrist's interview and conclusions. In this sense, the psychiatric examination is a valuable form of consultation when the consultant has had experience with and is knowledgeable about children. In situations that involve extreme pathology or the possibility of severe organic deficits, medical evaluations are needed to determine the best treatment plan. Generally speaking, consulting with an experienced child therapist is helpful for the professional; however, children should not be seen routinely. If a psychiatric opinion is necessary, the child should understand why and be prepared for the interview.

The rights of child and parents may be violated if information obtained from these tests is revealed carelessly to a variety of sources. Although professional practice requires signed consent from parents for release of information, parents usually comply without understanding the problems inherent in the procedure. Information released to others must be specific to the purpose for which it will be used. For example, if the school wants to know the results of children's tests or facts about their lives, the information should only indicate the need for specific educational interventions and be phrased as positively and generally as possible. This is essential because the right to privacy is not always respected, evaluations trigger expectations and tracking, and too many negative statements about children become part of a permanent record that haunts them as adults. Protection of confidentiality is an important social work value, but workers seldom ask children how they feel about the release of information concerning them. This failure to use children's special knowledge and feelings about what is done to and for them is an abrogation of their rights.

Children usually have regular physical examinations unless they are improperly cared for. Thus facts concerning health, illness and the results of a recent physical examination are an important part of a diagnostic formulation because a variety of undetected physical problems can contribute to a child's problems.

Children's current activities outside of school and relationships with adults within and outside the home and with siblings and other older and younger children, all help to develop a picture of flesh-and-blood youngsters in real life current encounters. Positive, age-expectable attributes should be viewed in the context of their particular milieu and culture to help in understanding how they adapt and cope.

Parental ways of coping and adapting are also important aspects of a child's life, and an understanding of their past and present functioning will help put parents in perspective. In telling about themselves, parents often begin to understand the aspects of their past that influence their present. Sometimes a series of marital and familial problems have been simmering for years, and the child's behavior may be symptomatic of the boiling point. In some cases, however, dysfunctional or "pathological" parental behavior is responsive to a child's problems rather than causative. For example, some severely disturbed or retarded children have innate intellectual and verbal deficiencies, gross disturbances of perceptual processing, and a variety of neurological dysfunctions (Whittaker, 1976).

Diagnostic Formulation

Direct observation of children includes their appearance, dress, responses, attitudes, and affects and supplements the facts and reports of others. But because observers are also actors, their conscious and unconscious reactions may reveal the subtle, unconscious nuances of a problem (Hartmann, 1964) Workers often struggle with these reactions, which may be personal and subjective and require study and clarification. When this is done, they may understand how the child induces these reactions in others.

The diagnostic formulation is an attempt to explain and interpret a child's multifaceted behavior within a variety of contexts. It begins with a base of expectable developmental norms and is modified by individualized differences. It is motivated by the philosophy that areas of strength can be used in treatment and the possibility that some symptoms indicate the existence of ego strengths which could, with appropriate intervention, be channeled into more productive behaviors.

First, accumulated information about the family realities is evaluated to determine strengths that are evidenced in stability, values, cooperation, caring, and coping. Second, stresses and problems are identified. The history often reveals that events of special significance occurred at certain developmental stages; by cross-referencing the chronology of these events with the child's age at the time, possible traumas can be located. Of special importance are separations from mother or father; maternal depression; emotional disturbance in a parent or other family member; neglect or abuse; hospitalization or traumatic medical manipulation; illness or operations; and the deaths or illnesses of important others (Nagera, 1966a).

Ego functioning is studied by examining the child's achievements, thinking processes, intelligence, and ability to tolerate anxiety and frustration in the context of activities that are appropriate at the child's age. Physical development, coordination, and capacities as well as general health are also important. To understand the balance between progressive and regressive tendencies, areas of difficulty must be identified and positives and negatives must be weighed.

The presenting problems, their timing, how they affect the child's functioning, and their possible meaning need clarification. The variety of symptoms may clarify the nature of the child's anxiety, which may be fear of annihilation, loss of object, loss of love, or fear of criticism and punishment. These anxieties are related to the external world. Children whose problems involve the superego and conflict about impulses may feel guilty or believe they are bad.

Aspects of the past may be involved in children's current problems. Some problems may bring secondary gains such as attention, hurting others, or hurting oneself. Some behaviors seem to be reactions to the child's situation; others are the result of internalized conflict. In the latter case, changing reality may not affect the child's anxiety.

Normal emotional upheavals that are realistically related to the situation and the child's developmental phase and those that are transitory must be distinguished from emotional disturbances expressed by unmanageable anger, fears, grief and mourning, or a disproportionate need for love. The child's feelings in situations of frustration, deprivation, danger, pain, and loss must also be understood because they will be expressed through efforts to maintain control and difficulties in sleeping, eating, working, and playing. When a child's functioning is retarded, emotional factors are either the cause or the effect of this retardation (Murphy, 1963).

Diagnostic thinking can be facilitated by considering

the preciptating, predisposing, and perpetuating elements within the child-in-situation configuration. The precipitating factors are the stimuli that trigger the problem, encompassing the nature and degree of the impact of actual events at a particular developmental stage with consequent conscious or unconscious perceptions or misperceptions. The predisposing factors that influence the child's reactions are preexisting elements such as constitution, heredity, endowment, previous events, personality, family patterns, and parent-child relationships. The perpetuating factors are those within the child and situation that coalesce to foster continuation of difficulties.

Clinical Diagnosis

The clinical diagnosis or classification is another way of systematizing and organizing the facts and observations. Classification schemes are summaries represented by the verbal shorthand of labels, which suggest certain general themes. Unless accompanied by a dynamic diagnostic formulation, these labels do not explain enough to guide interventions (Prugh, Engel, & Morse, 1975). Categories alone may overemphasize manifest symptomology and neglect the underlying causation and individuality (A. Freud, 1965).

Labels do not communicate pain, weakness, and discomfort. Furthermore, they tend to highlight disease and illness rather than the potential for social and personal well-being. They have often encouraged discrimination against certain individuals, especially the poor and members of minority groups. At times, the main purpose of categorizing children seems to be the protection of society. The result has been lowered expectations among labeled children, stigmatizing, tracking, self-fulfilling prophecy, and social and political implications that follow children through life (Hobbs, 1975).

Social workers tend to be reluctant about applying and using clinical labels. By deferring to psychiatric opinion, however, they often permit others to assume the responsibility for diagnosing, labeling, and determining the treatment their clients will receive. Since clients *are* labeled, social workers must understand the systems of categorization and their implications (Perlman, 1957; Hollis, 1964; Hamilton, 1963). Social work can contribute to the appropriate use of categorization by highlighting the relationship between the person and the situation to maximize opportunities for support of clients' needs, rights, and access to social facilities. Nowhere is this more necessary than in the study and diagnosis of children because children are dependent on the emotional and physical environment. Their emotional needs are related not only to instinctual drives but to the satisfactions and frustrations of their environment (Kanner, 1970). Later development is influenced for better or worse by environmental circumstances.

Classification is necessary to estimate the prevalence of problems so that programs can be developed, funding can be obtained, and the setting for preferred clinical intervention can be established. But the label, as part of the initial diagnostic phase, is only one step in a clinical process that will involve new observations, new hypotheses, and refinement of diagnostic thinking until treatment is no longer needed. This is particularly important when working with children because they change continually.

Categorizations that are applicable to adults are inadequate for children because some conditions are peculiar to childhood. Some currently used diagnoses are determined by statistical or legal requirements but do not inform treatment. Newly devised and exploratory classification schemes of childhood disorders emphasize developmental status and recognize that similar behaviors are significant in different ways at different ages. Healthy reactions and normal variations are also important diagnoses (Group For the Advancement of Psychiatry, 1966).

In an effort to establish some uniformity in the diagnostic labeling of children and to enable cross-cultural international testing and study, the World Health Organization (WHO) (Rutter et al., 1969) developed a triaxial classification of disorders observed in children ages 3 to 12. The child is categorized according to (1) clinical psychiatric syndrome, (2) level of intellectual functioning, and (3) associated etiological factors, physical and environmental. A social work diagnostic formulation always includes an evaluation of etiological factors and intellectual functioning. Although the revised psychiatric syndromes suggested by WHO have some utility for social work, some are too specific yet lack clarity and others can be subsumed under more general categories. The larger categories related to problems at different stages of development include the following:

1. *Normal variation or healthy responses.* Variations of personality within the expectable range; transient disorders or emotional upsets and behaviors common to the child's developmental age. In general, the child's development progresses relatively smoothly and functioning is stage-appropriate in many areas.

2. *Adaptation reaction or reactive disorders.* Reactions to overt environmental circumstances tend to be circumscribed and specific to the situation. They usually are reversible, usually but not always last for a short time, and do not distort the development of the basic personality to a significant degree.

3. *Neurosis.* Marked emotional disorder without loss of contact with reality and a history of relatively normal development. A disproportionate degree of anxiety is common and based on unconscious internalized conflicts over sexual and aggressive impulses, with a genesis in preschool

years during the period of individuation, early sexual identification, or social integration. Regression, disturbances in
behavior, hyperactivity, and a variety of symptoms such as
obsessions, compulsions, phobias, hypochondriasis, and
conversion reactions may exist.

4. *Personality disorders.* Relatively fixed abnormalities
of personality of behavior and relationships, which are in-
grained in the personality structure. Defenses tend to be
rigid, and there will be less anxiety about one's own behavior than is normal.

5. *Psychotic disorders.* Marked, often bizarre deviations
from expectable behavior accompanied by distorted ego
functioning and development. Severe and continued im-
pairment in emotional relationships with persons and in
thought, affect, perception, individuation, object relations,
and reality testing. Development is markedly uneven.
Severe psychopathology in children necessitates careful
physical and neurological evaluation as well as evaluation
of areas of strength to facilitate decisions concerning educational approaches that will enhance functioning (Piggott,
1975).

6. *Borderline personality.* A category that may not be
separated from psychosis in some categories or from personality disorders (Group For the Advancement of Psychiatry, 1966). However, it is widely used to define children
who are "felt" not to be psychotic but are severely disturbed. Pine (1974) suggests that borderline personality
and psychosis are overlapping diagnoses, that they exist on
a continuum ranging from relatively mild to severe disorganization. Although the ego functioning, object relations,
and reality testing of borderline children are better than
those of psychotic children, developmental arrest or aberrant development exists. Their ego limitations, awareness
of reality, ability to test reality, and the nature of their
object relations fluctuate: are sometimes better, sometimes
worse. Anxiety can escalate to panic rather than be de-

fended against as in the neuroses. Borderline children tend to split objects into good and bad, have difficulty seeing the separateness of others, and become anxious about control and loss of identity.

The case of Tom B illustrates the difficulty of determining the clinical diagnosis during the initial contact. Adaptive reaction seems to be the most meaningful category because his behavior changed in reaction to severe crises and, despite much acting out, he had many ego strengths. However, the extent to which the family difficulties activated Tom's earlier neurotic problems and the degree to which his development was impaired by prolonged stress and his accelerating conduct disorders would require study. In this case, the total diagnostic formulation suggests that intervening in the family system and working with Tom to clarify his underlying anxiety and apparent guilt would be the first priorities.

From Diagnosis To Treatment

A differential diagnosis should lead to a differential intervention that encompasses a range of growth-promoting procedures to enhance the child's present and future, assist in reversing debilitating destructive trends, and increase the constructive forces in the environment.

The clinical diagnosis, as part of the formulation, may suggest some guidelines. Thus if the diagnosis points to neurosis, planning would focus on how to correct and alleviate the underlying fantasies and anxiety of a child who has many ego strengths. If the diagnosis is personality disorder, which indicates trauma during the period of separation-individuation, the emphasis would be the development of corrective object relations and issues of autonomy and control. A diagnosis of borderline personality would require a well-structured treatment situation, a reality orientation, a constant and reliable treatment relationship, and assistance to the child in developing the ability to fuse aspects of the good and bad in objects. A diagnosis of schizophrenia or psychosis might result in institutionalization if the disturbance is extremely severe and appropriate supports are unavailable in the home. Clinical treatment would emphasize a constant relationship, development of basic trust, and separation-individuation of self from others. Because of the child's extremely weak ego boundaries, the treatment would not be diffuse, lack structure, or elicit fantasies; the focus would be on strengthening ego boundaries and functioning and reality testing.

Goals

The total diagnostic formulation is goal oriented. The understandings that emerge from the process of study and evaluation should contribute to short-term, specific goals and long-term goals concerning developmental processes. These goals should be reasonable: not so high that they are unattainable but not so low that the child's potential is underrated.

The target and timing of interventions must be related to the needs and realities of the child and family. The clinical conclusion may suggest that it is appropriate to deal with the parents alone or that intensive involvement of the child, parents, other family members, and the community is indicated.

The family and the child are as much a part of treatment planning as they are of the study and diagnostic process. Although the professional's orientation is different from that of clients, treatment cannot occur without their willing and active participation. Often, enabling their cooperation is a reasonable beginning goal.

Parents will want to know what the worker thinks is

wrong and, if the child has been tested, what the findings are. Clinical diagnoses are of doubtful value in these discussions and may cause overwhelming anxiety and misunderstandings. Sharing of conclusions related to parental and child concerns is part of the total process. Thus in Tom's case, one might recognize that Mrs. B was wise to wonder whether her husband's illness and all the demands that were made on her caused Tom's disturbance. Examining with both parents how things could be improved at home would lead to discussions about children's anxieties in these situations and possible ways of easing them.

Reaching an agreement with clients about the general problem is a beginning step in the clinical process and is essential for setting and achieving goals. A research study of family social agencies concluded that serious disagreement between counselor and client about the definition of the problem, the kind of help needed, and the appropriate treatment approach was significantly related to clients' perceptions of unfavorable outcome (Beck & Jones, 1973).

Treatment planning includes setting both short- and long-term goals and deciding how to achieve them. Ideally, modality, nature of services, time limitations, and selection of personnel should be related to goals and the diagnostic assessment. Agencies may not have the resources to provide the preferred service or treatment. In these cases, clients are usually referred to other resources, but they often do not follow through on these referrals. Sometimes it may be necessary to compromise if this is not contraindicated by the needs of the case. When clients must be referred elsewhere, active help in making the transfer may encourage them to follow up on the referral.

Because personality growth or restructuring, reversal of regression, release of developmental energy, major shifts in family balance, or improved interpersonal interactions are rather general goals, they are appropriately viewed as long-term. The way to achieve them is to set a series of shorter more concrete goals; when one is reached, another is set, then another. This would permit ongoing assessment and necessary changes in direction, method, or approach. Each specific goal would be related to the larger goal. In Tom's case, a series of steps related to the stresses at home would lead to an understanding of his confusion, fears, and ambivalence. As the causes of his problems were addressed, his conduct and school performance would gradually improve.

Types of Treatment

Treatment planning includes consideration of who will be seen and in what combination. Starting one way should not preclude change when other needs emerge or treatment has progressed to a point that allows a change in focus or process. How people can best be helped should suggest the preferred method. Individual treatment of the child and each parent, conjoint interviews with parents, family therapy, and group therapy of various kinds are possible choices, singly or in combination. The choice depends on an understanding of the client's true need and its relationship to the total family dynamics.

A basic foundation for any treatment modality is a sound knowledge of human needs and individual dynamics. In addition, each modality demands specialized skills and methods, which can be learned only through training, study, and practice. Work with children demands specific knowledge, an understanding of children, and the ability to communicate and work with them, regardless of the modality employed.

Group therapy. Social workers, especially caseworkers, tend to believe that the individual case approach is the preferred one. But some children are inaccessible to individual treatment because they fear closeness and are unwilling or unable to communicate in the one-to-one interview. Thus group activity that caters to the special problems these children present may be desirable initially (Lieberman & Taylor, 1965; Ganter, Yeakel, & Polansky, 1967). For similar reasons, this also may be indicated as a first approach for some parents.

Yet group psychotherapy cannot be applied universally either to children or adults. Often it is an inadequate substitute for the individual therapy required by children and adults who have deep-seated neuroses or severe personality pathology (Rosenthal, 1956). In some cases, the combined use of group and individual treatment is valuable.

Although group treatment for latency-age children seems to be the natural choice because peers and peer-group activities are important during this stage, a treatment group is different from groups that are normally a part of a child's life-style. Group treatment begins with a diagnostic approach to individual, troubled children and becomes the treatment of choice when it seems the best way to meet their needs and foster their development. When children are placed in groups that focus on superficial behavioral change, the therapist replicates the demanding, angry, adult world that may have contributed to their difficulties. Other types of groups demand discussion and insight or cooperation and sharing from children who lack the ability to comply (Frank, 1976). Thus some may be antitherapeutic or even dangerous.

All social workers involved in group treatment of children must meet the following criteria: they must be familiar with developmental norms, understand the emotions of children, appreciate the dynamic uniqueness of the individual, and be able to select for group membership children who have the capacity to assimilate multiple relationships and endure the frustrations of a group setting (Rosenthal, 1977).

Activity group therapy is useful for children who need

help in increasing their self-esteem; in dealing with authority, sibling rivalry, issues of cooperation, and social fears;
and in satisfying their social hunger. These children may be
socially fearful, constricted, and withdrawn; others may not
be as well controlled. But for children who are unable to
control their impulses, have a severely defective sense of
reality, or cannot tolerate even minimal social contact, the
classic form of activity group therapy is contraindicated
because its permissive atmosphere encourages a limited
form of regression (Maclennan, 1977). Children who defend themselves by externalizing their unacceptable impulses tend to be uncooperative and disruptive if placed in
insight-oriented discussion groups; those with serious ego
defects may become worse if placed in unstructured groups
that do not protect them from their own impulses or the
aggression of peers (Slavson & Schiffer, 1975; Schamess,
1976). In addition, too wide an age or developmental span
creates too much diffusion because the members will have
different concerns, tasks, and needs. For similar reasons,
latency-age children usually do better in a group where all
members are of the same gender.

There are many group models, addressed selectively
to the needs of children with specific problems. These
groups differ in structure, setting, process, and therapist's
role. Thus modified groups have been developed for
psychotic latency-age children who have many social deprivations (Scheidlinger, 1960). Activity interview groups are
helpful for preadolescents. A form of interpretive group
psychotherapy may be useful for neurotic or behavioral
difficulties that are treatable and responsive to verbalization (Slavson & Schiffer, 1975; Sugar, 1974). Duo therapy,
in which two unrelated children are seen together on an
ongoing basis, may help children form a stable, deep relationship with one child and serve as a basis for other peer
relations, thus benefiting children who are unsuitable for
larger groups (Fuller, 1977; Mitchell, 1976).

Choosing a group for parents requires an equally careful diagnosis. Adults who need control, fear confrontation, are severely disturbed, paranoid or suicidal, or are only capable of narcissistic gratification are usually not good candidates for group therapy (Kaydis et al., 1974; Yalom, 1970). Groups for parents vary widely in focus and therapeutic intensity. Guidance groups that focus on the child may be acceptable to parents who are too threatened to face their own involvement or have weak defenses and great anxiety. These groups initially provide distance from personal pathology, avoid confrontation, and are sufficiently structured to be protective. When they continue for a significant period, the development of group relationships can support and foster growth, the strength to address the question of "How come?" and encourage a beginning study of self. In any case, the interactions and successes within the group often enable parents to deal better with their children's problems.

Family therapy. Family therapy is both an orientation and a method. As an orientation, it can coexist with many other approaches (Wynne, 1971). As a method, it implies that two or more family members meet together with a therapist. Like any other approach, family therapy is not the treatment of choice in all cases.

The capacities of latency-age children may contraindicate family therapy. Children younger than 10, and even older, may not understand the experience or the conversation; they may explain some communications to themselves in their own age-appropriate way, which may lead to distortions that they are unable to verbalize. Their natural restlessness and physical activity may be disruptive to a treatment that emphasizes talking. Just as often, they will be peripheral to the discussions, their confusions may not be clarified or understood, and their symbolic communications may not be integrated into the process (Guttman, 1975). There may be discussions about parental interactions and sexual activities that are inappropriate for them to hear (Sherman, 1974). Although children know some of these things anyway, as is often claimed, it is better to clarify their confusions and fantasies and help their parents appreciate the value of privacy. Too often, children are treated in family therapy as miniature adults and their developmental needs are neglected (McDermott & Char, 1974).

Generally speaking, family therapy emphasizes interpersonal interactions and communications, and this aspect of family life often contributes to a child's difficulties. There are children whose disturbances are not only the result of family pathology or whose degree of internalization or developmental arrest is so great that treatment within the family group alone will not provide appropriate attention to their needs.

The diagnostic assessment must suggest that family therapy will help the child with its problem. A first priority is a family system that is workable: i.e., it has some stability, affectional ties, and significant relationships (Sherman, 1966). Some family members may be so psychologically unavailable that their interaction with the child may only intensify the child's deprivation. Serious intrapsychic problems of either child or parent, or a destructive motivation based on an unconscious need to encourage and perpetuate the child's difficulties may subject the child to undue stress. The cultural beliefs of some families may be contrary to the democratic processes that are inherent in family therapy. Demanding that children be allowed to speak up when this is unacceptable in the culture may violate the family's rights and needs and certainly will not help the child (Offer & Vanderstoep, 1974; McDermott & Char, 1974). Extremely dependent children may need separation from their families or the symbolic feeding that is inherent in individual treatment (Hallowitz, 1966).

A systems approach or a transactional multipersonal

understanding can augment knowledge of individual functioning, but it does not replace it (Group for the Advancement of Psychiatry, 1970). The family is the child's natural
environment and as such assists the worker in understanding the child and in discovering what causes and perpetuates the child's difficulties. Family therapy may be the
treatment of choice in situations where the child is not the
problem but the family cannot see its own difficulties. It
also can be an effective way of dealing with a sudden crisis
or trauma that is shared equally by all family members.
Finally, it can be a useful supplement to individual treatment.

Duration of Treatment

All treatment involves a commitment of time by agency,
worker and client. Limited resources make it difficult for
agencies to offer unlimited services, yet some clients are
reluctant to enter treatment because they believe it never
ends. With them, the fact that time is limited can be used
dynamically to focus and direct treatment (Mann, 1973).

When clients express reluctance to become involved,
it is sometimes appropriate to suggest a trial period during
which they can decide whether they want treatment. Allow-
ing them to set the limits can be helpful if they need to feel
they are in control. Their feelings in this area can be studied with them in relation to the treatment arrangements as
well as other aspects of life. In other planned approaches
to the use of time, the agency sets the limits. Crisis intervention and brief therapy are time-limited treatment plans
by definition.

Crisis intervention is a method of actively influencing
the psychosocial functioning of individuals during periods
of disequilibrium. Its aim is to alleviate the immediate impact of a critical event and to mobilize the latent psychological capacities and social resources of those directly affected

(Parad, 1971). In addition, it can be a preventive measure for dealing with anticipated critical events or events that have already occurred and have precipitated maladaptive adjustments (Golan, 1974).

Intervention with children before traumatic events such as hospitalization and operations may help them understand and cope better. If these events occur and children have not been prepared, then it is necessary to speak clearly and honestly about the realities of their situation when they are ready. It is not pathological for latency-age children to be reluctant to discuss their fears; thus one does not confront them with facts too soon. Because children must be able to trust and relate before they can hear, premature interpretations will only make them more anxious (Wolff, 1969). When they are ready, they will be able to use the willingness to be honest with them to master upsetting fears and face painful realities (Stein, 1970). When children express their feelings in play or other symbolic communications, they provide adults with an opportunity to understand their concerns and, when appropriate, to clarify their misconceptions and anxieties. Today many hospital pediatric wards use social workers and children's groups to help children play out—if possible, talk out—shared fears about illness and hospitalization.

Mobilizing parents for a crisis that involves children is the most basic kind of support; the younger the child, the more important this is. But the most serious crisis for dependent children is the separation from parents because of death, illness, or an inability or unwillingness to care for them. In these situations, the child needs the sustained help of some other interested and involved adult.

Separation from significant others, particularly parents, is a loss that must be mourned, regardless of the cause. If death is the cause, the normal tasks of bereavement are compounded by the difficulty children have in comprehending death and by the new stresses in their daily life. Separation becomes a continuous stress that interferes with development and causes problems in adulthood if it is not worked through as soon as possible (Jacobson, 1965). Crisis intervention in these situations can be preventive but the amount of time it will require will depend on the child's previous experiences and strengths. When parents are divorced, preventive work should begin before the divorce to prepare children and continue afterward to provide them with continuity and support (Wallerstein & Kelly, 1976).

When a child is placed, the actual separation is only a symptom of longstanding problems. Brief intervention will not deal adequately with a deep-seated pathological history of deprivation and disturbance. The severely deprived child with widespread psychological and environmental dysfunction and inconsistent and emotionally unsupportive relationships is not a candidate for any kind of time-limited therapy—all of which have built-in expectations of desertion (Proskauer, 1971).

Time-limited therapy with a child requires a stable, supportive family. When there is severe family instability or marital disharmony or a history of crises, this type of treatment is contraindicated. These families often have too many major problems in too many areas for one problem to be the major focus. Because crisis intervention depends on the client's motivation and ego strengths, it is contraindicated for individuals who are members of multiproblem families, have been diagnosed as borderline personalities or as having a character disorder, or have marginal lives and are chronically unable to cope. The aim of crisis intervention is to restore individuals to their previous level of functioning as quickly as possible. When that level is the cause of the crisis, nothing is achieved. Such parents and their children need a broad spectrum of services ranging from concrete to insightful and a long-term, dependable, consistent relationship with one worker (La Vietes, 1974). Someone to "come home to," a worker in the agency, may be a family's first experience with consistency and dependability.

Brief therapy is planned intervention of limited duration, varying from a few weeks or stated number of visits to several months with the date of termination set at the beginning. It is an appropriate treatment for children when a specific, dominant problem must be resolved to permit healthy growth and functioning. For others with multiple problems, each of which seems as crucial as the other, brief intervention may be the worker's or agency's way of denying and resisting demands on their resources. Perhaps the reason why social workers view many working-class and lower class clients as able to tolerate only short contacts is that these clients want fuller, more intensive, and personal relationships than either the therapist or agency is willing to offer (Miller & Mishler, 1964).

Some clients cannot tolerate lengthy contacts, usually because in the past caring has meant being hurt. But there is a difference between a client's leaving a worker and a worker leaving the client. The latter is desertion. Clients who leave and then return, leave and return again—one hopes to the same worker—may be testing whether the relationship is like earlier ones. The testing may be to see whether someone finally cares enough to look for them and take them back. These clients leave and look back, very much as young children do during the process of separation and individuation from the parent. Unfortunately, families that need permanence the most are often handed down from one trainee to another; i.e., each academic year, they are asked to "relate" within a professional situation that duplicates the inconsistency and impermanence of their lives.

To latency-age children, a contact that spans the school year may not seem so artificial because much of their time is organized by school time. When workers or students know they will be leaving at a particular time, their clients, whether children or adults, are entitled to know this in advance. When this relationship ends, clients who wish to continue because they realize that more needs to be accomplished have the right to be provided with the service they need, this time with a worker who stays.

Concrete Services

Planned brief service of any nature requires great skill, the ability to make an assessment during the first contact, and to differentiate those for whom brief service is inappropriate. Concrete services—too often the stepchild of clinical services—demand equally great skill. There is deep psychological significance in the proper use of financial assistance, help with contacts with bureaucracies, home visits, help with school work, assistance in obtaining clothing or decent living quarters—all the traditional and remarkably diverse social work services.

Doing things with people and sometimes even for them, if decided on diagnostically, is a way of understanding and communicating with the language of action— the language of people who live by impulse, do not trust words, and are still at the preverbal level of development although they speak. In families where crisis is a way of life, concentrating on any specific problem of immediate urgency, reaching out and helping parents do things, may bring order out of chaos and enable the development of trust and the beginnings of hope that will motivate and enable treatment (Young, 1966). For all clients, but especially children, simple supportive activities at times may be worth a million interpretations.

Teamwork

Workers need support too, and this should be a part of treatment planning. This support can be provided by supervision or consultation with peers not only for learning and discussion but also for help when the demands of working with difficult clients are overwhelming, a situation seems hopeless, or a child is involved in unusually desperate circumstances.

Sometimes more than one worker will be assigned to one family or even an individual, who may be seen in both group and individual treatment. This co-worker relationship is similar in many ways to the formal co-therapy that often exists in group leadership. Norlin and Ho (1974) suggest assigning two workers, preferably a man and a woman, in a co-worker relationship so that dysfunctional families have a therapeutic model to emulate. The workers can demonstrate how to disagree agreeably, check and balance one another, and increase the range of transference objects. But to work together successfully, they must respect each other and share common theoretical beliefs. If they are competitive, families can manipulate and repeat with them the divisiveness of their lives. If they cooperate with each other and understand their transferential, symbolic meaning to the family as a whole and as individual clients, they can provide a corrective and therapeutic experience. Whenever more than one person is involved with an individual client or a family, a form of co-therapy is involved whether one worker sees the parents and the other the child, or a team works with the family, or two workers see one client. Equality, respect, and communication are as important as they are in more formalized co-therapy relationships (Johnson, 1953). Often, one family member will react to workers who treat other members, although the client does not know the workers personally. These reactions tend to be transferential and can be used therapeutically.

On occasion, it is unadvisable for several workers to be involved with one family. Young children do not think it is strange when the worker they see also sees their parents, and their parents may feel more comfortable about the arrangement. This makes it possible for the worker to note similarities in behavior and to know what has happened to the child day by day and how the family is doing.

In other cases, parents or children need to have someone only for themselves, and thus more than one worker will be involved. In all cases, the parent should meet the child's worker before work with the child begins. Avenues of communication must be open, transmitted through the parent's worker or through telephone calls when necessary.

Evaluations, diagnostic formulations, and treatment arrangements are functional. They must not only contribute to understanding and improve communication but at the same time be modified and deepened during the life of any treatment situation.

Chapter 10

COMMUNICATION

Communication—the essence of treatment—is both verbal and nonverbal, manifest and latent. Affects and attitudes are reflected in the focus of the communication, the choice of words and the language of gestures and facial expressions. Clients enter treatment as they are, communicating as they can and in their customary ways. This is appropriate because, by doing so, they bring themselves. It is the professional's responsibility to communicate appropriately in response to their needs.

COMMUNICATING WITH PARENTS

Parents who view themselves as clients differ from adults who view their children as clients. Because the child's problems are the focus of attention, parents will talk initially about the child's difficulties. As they talk, their rejection, anger, and neglect, unreasonable expectations, ignorance, and poor child-rearing practices will be evident. Recognizing that these contaminate the child's environment and affect development, professionals may become impatient with parents who are so negative. The good professional, however, will not say anything that reveals these feelings because most clients will sense the negative judgments and feel unaccepted and misunderstood.

Resistance

No parent consciously wishes to be unsuccessful or enjoys the social condemnation that occurs when others believe they are bad parents. All parents understand that the twig does not fall far from the tree, whether they admit it or not. Even clients who have been forced to come to the worker by some external authority and seem angry and disinterested are afraid of being judged (Argelander, 1976). Some parents will loudly deny playing any part in their child's problems and blame the child or someone else, and those who express the belief that nothing will help may resent it if another person succeeds where they have failed. Although the worker may view obedient clients who talk about guilt, ask for advice, or talk in psychological terms as more caring because the language they use or the information they request is familiar and appropriate for a parent who has problems with a child, these clients may be more like than unlike the overtly rejecting parent. This may be only one more opportunity to avoid spontaneous emotional expression or to deny negative feelings (Bruch, 1948).

Underneath these expressions are fears of parental inadequacy and of change. Because they know only established patterns, discomfort with themselves and their children may not be enough to enable these parents to use suggestions for different behavior. Their conflict with the child or the child's difficulties often have unconscious roots in the past. In some cases, the child's symptoms maintain the family's precarious homeostasis (A. Freud, 1965).

Parents are both children and parents. They have to cope with their own internalized parents, who may have disappointed them, and with their knowledge that they are the child in their child. Thus their disappointment with the child may be disappointment with themselves. They may relate to the worker with childish expectations that were appropriate in an early stage of development, expecting the idealized perfect parent but simultaneously expecting to be disappointed as they were in the past (Feldman, 1975). Their expectations concerning their child's behavior may mimic the unrealistic expectations they assumed that others had of them as children. Thus disappointment and rage —whether at the agency, the child, or themselves—will reflect their own unconscious struggles.

Parents who are willing to talk about their problems, ask for advice, and when they receive it, follow it, are often described as cooperative and nonresistant. Those who do not follow advice, are resistant to change, and have negative attitudes toward the individual who gives the advice are described as uncooperative. Yet in the broader sense, cooperation implies that clients feel free to be themselves and can express their attitudes and feelings openly. The cooperative, nonresistant worker accepts parents as they are, including their resistance to change and negative feelings. Thus parental resistance may be the offshoot of countertransference on the part of therapists who introduce barriers against understanding and hearing parents' emotions and needs (Allen, 1934).

When workers identify with children, they see the parents from a child's eyes. These may be the eyes of their child-clients or their own eyes and their own view of the idealized parent. The goals these workers select will be leveled at changing specific behaviors and attitudes. They may be too zealous about obtaining the parents' histories and establishing the part that parents have played in their children's difficulties. These workers will become correctors rather than clarifiers, and their clients will be doomed to resist the therapeutic objectives they have projected onto the case.

Workers who align themselves with children against parents increase the gap between parents and children and reduce children's opportunities within their families. One cannot treat children successfully if one does not respect their parents. When clients are accepted as they are, even when they are parents; when one begins where the parents are and permits them to reveal their situations and opinions without pushing them toward another viewpoint; parents will not need to resist learning how to help their children.

When parents are allowed to scold instead of being scolded, to express their negative feelings about their children and the worker, they have less need to be negative about themselves and their children. When they learn that they can be respected and accepted although they are not always perfect, they will teach this naturally to their children.

The histories of many parents contain traumas, losses, inconsistencies, frustrations of needs, premature requirements for maturity, and inadequate nurturing. Their feelings of helplessness and rage may be bottled up, defended against through denial and repression, or acted out in life and in treatment. When these parents are allowed to keep their defenses until they no longer need them, they will give them up voluntarily. And they will no longer need them when they can recall and spontaneously feel their own deprivations and experience a new and safer relationship with an important object (Love & Mayer, 1959; Nagelberg & Spotnitz, 1958).

Listening

The nature of parents' communications will reveal the essence of their problems as people and as parents. But only when workers listen and observe and then reflect objectively and professionally about these perceptions will they find the empathy that will facilitate treatment. In a study of child welfare services to children in their own homes, Sherman et al. (1973) found that the emotional support evidenced in caring, reassurance, and understanding, although necessary, was not the only condition for successful service. Other conditions included the positive effect of longer service and the frequency of contacts within a specific period.

Parents who are listened to feel they are given to because many have never had the undivided attention of someone who listens carefully to what they say regardless of how they say it. Parents' own childhood struggles are sometimes reawakened when their children have social and developmental difficulties. Consequently, they are often talking about themselves when they talk about their children, although they are unaware of it. They are not ready to ask for help for themselves, they can do so only through their children (Feldman, 1958). When encouraged to talk about their children, they will provide clues to their own needs. In this sense, children become a metaphor, bridging the gap between their parents' current thoughts and feelings and unconscious early experiences. In other words, parents can safely express archaic and primitive affects and thoughts by displacing them onto their children.

If parents are confronted too directly with their own difficulties before they are ready to speak of them, or if they are brought to an adult level before they are ready, they must resist and defend (Chapman, 1977). When a worker listens to parents describe the difficulties their children create for them and encourages them to express their feelings, parents begin to understand their own difficulties. Being understood in relation to their needs provides a corrective experience that enables them to grow. After talking about their children, they can begin to talk about themselves and learn more about the reasons for their own behavior and difficulties. In the final stages of treatment, these parents may talk about their children again, but at that point they will be adult parents who want to know how to guide and help their children better.

By listening to many parents with the intention of understanding, a worker learns that parents have different attitudes, needs, and problems. All parents who talk about their children are not talking about themselves. Some are concerned about their children in adult, parental ways. These parents may be overwhelmed because a family member is seriously ill, a child is chronically disabled, or the family is having critical financial problems. All too aware of their parental responsibilities and at a loss because the situation is beyond their control, these parents are worried about their inability to provide their children with the comfort and protection they wish to provide. They too need to recognize and accept their grief, air frustration about their helplessness, and come to terms with their inability to provide all that they want to provide. They need a place to cry and a person to understand and to help as much and sometimes as concretely as possible. Because they will not be alone in their struggle, they will be stronger for themselves and their children. By making peace with their own humanness and forgiving themselves, they will accept what they have to give and thus will receive more from their children.

Playing with Parents

Some parents talk about themselves from the beginning, but not because they want to learn about themselves. These parents are so deprived and developmentally disturbed that they can be involved only with themselves. Needy and narcissistic, their feelings and thoughts revolve around their own needs, yet they have never learned how to ask properly for what they want. Because their basic needs were never met, they never learned to trust or feel secure. Their children are shadows: unreal and demanding objects. These parents must be fed before they can feed their children (Frailberg, Adelson & Shapiro, 1975).

Words are not enough for these parents. They often view their children as rivals and feel even more needy when others provide for their children. Because they never experienced proper nurturing, there are many things they simply cannot understand. As children, they were never cared for, never had toys, never played happily, never went to camp, never had a proper education, were never allowed to be children. Providing all these things for their children will not help unless something is provided for them. The usefulness of this approach is illustrated in the following case:

> The S family consists of Mrs. S, age 31, and eight children, ages 14, 11, 10, 8, 7, 6, 5, and 2. The two oldest had different fathers; the next two had another father, and the four youngest had another. Several years earlier, one father had requested placement for the children. At the time, he had stabbed Mrs. S, necessitating her hospitalization, stating that he was angry because she neglected the children.
>
> Mrs. S was an alcoholic and habitually used barbiturates (often to the point of overdose). The home was chaotic, dirty, and infested with roaches, and the children were physically neglected and frequently left alone. But when Mrs. S returned from the hospital, casework service stopped.
>
> Four years before, the oldest son, then 10, was found wandering in the street at night. Evaluated as severely disturbed, he was placed with his paternal grandmother. Although Mrs. S did not like this, she agreed because she felt she could not care for him. One-and-a-half years later, the second son, then 8, fell during a school trip, and a medical examination revealed scars from repeated beatings. While

placement was being considered, he became suicidal and was sent to a residential treatment facility.

With homemaker service and casework support, Mrs. S was able to accompany the worker and her children to a clinic, welfare center, or school appointment and occasionally meet some of the children's medical needs. However, she continued to drink and at times was afraid that she would hurt the children.

When play therapy was suggested for three of her children, Mrs. S agreed because she hoped it would prevent placement of her remaining children. The plan was that she would bring the children for their therapy and spend part of this time with her own caseworker. She kept two appointements and then cancelled the next three.

During a home visit, the worker said that although Mrs. S's excuses for not keeping her appointments had been reasonable, she felt that Mrs. S had some feelings about the play therapy. Mrs. S began to cry and blurted out: "Why should the children have all the bright new toys?" The worker acknowledged her feelings of neglect, gave her cake and soda, and permitted her to sit in the staff lounge and watch TV while she waited for the children. With this tangible attention, Mrs. S's attendance improved.

Mrs. S's deprivation was not limited to material things. Her developmental immaturity arose from a more serious lack of object constancy in her early years. Mrs. S's mother had been the kind of mother Mrs. S became, and Mrs. S had been the kind of child her children were.

Parents who lacked adequate parenting in childhood are childish in their relations with people and are depressed, hopeless, and helpless about life. Rather than ask them to regurgitate their problems, the worker must demonstrate that someone recognizes their wish that things were better by reaching out to them, helping them with real problems, and visiting them (Enzer & Stackhouse, 1968).

But things are not enough. Although these parents need closeness and caring, they distrust people and closeness. Thus they will test the worker's sincerity by competing with their children. These parents may be borderline personalities with deficiencies that stem from trauma in early life. Fixated at a preverbal stage of development, they do not trust words. They are, however, sensitive to behavioral cues, hidden thoughts, and rejection. Consequently, the worker must be equally sensitive to behavioral cues and help these clients verbalize and think about their perceptions. Often their feelings about workers, agencies, and other authorities are correct, and their perceptions must be validated so that they can begin to trust their own feelings as a preliminary to trusting others.

When these clients learn to trust the worker enough to establish a relationship, they may idealize the worker, beginning anew the unfinished process of their childhood. Initially, they may identify by improving their appearance, copying the worker's hair-style, mannerisms, and the like. When their depression lifts, they may experiment by disagreeing with the worker and become negative and complain in a way that resembles the child who must move away from its mother. This is an attempt to establish difference and distance. If the worker remains constant, understanding, and resists the urge to retaliate against these frustrating unreasonable demands, these clients will gradually achieve greater mastery over themselves and their environment (Lackie, 1975). They will also be better able to be parents to their children, having been helped to be children in a better, more growth-producing way.

Other parents who have had adequate parenting have been economically deprived, which limited their toys, interfered with their schooling, or forced them to become financially independent too soon. Some have lived at a marginal income level all their lives. These parents may do one of two things: overindulge their children because they want the children to have everything they never had or teach their children responsibility and spartan living to justify their own experiences. They may not understand what playing has to do with their children's problem or believe their children play too much anyway.

These parents need someone who will understand their need to play and teach them how. There are many ways that a worker can demonstrate this. If children go to camp, their parents can also go, with financial assistance if necessary. Many Ys and community centers that offer camp programs for children have similar programs for adults. In addition, the worker can encourage parents' need for a social life alone together as well as with their children. If necessary, the worker can play with parents. For example, one father noted wistfully that he had never learned to play chess (his son was learning to play the game). His worker offered to teach him, and the father was soon playing chess at home with his son.

Sometimes, children want a parent to be present during a session. There are many reasons for this. They may want to show the parent that the worker is much nicer than the parent or, just as likely, teach the parent how to play with them. Sometimes children will ask the parent to play a game and, as they play, competitive interaction will occur. All these communications further the treatment process.

Giving Advice

Parents who observe how the worker treats and plays with their child may try to imitate the worker's behavior. More often, however, they come into treatment expecting the worker to tell them what to do and even ask for this type of advice. If the worker takes their requests literally and gives them advice without considering their needs or the source of the difficulty, the advice may hurt rather than help. Many parents view advice as criticism and either will not follow it or will follow it in a way that defeats treatment (Feldman, 1958). This often happens when workers, learning about seductive sleeping or dressing arrangements, advise a parent to change those arrangements. They then discover to their chagrin that the type of change the parents made has simply intensifed the seductive activities.

Sometimes requests for advice are a method of challenging the worker to produce a perfect solution or of proving the worker wrong. When parents accept advice too quickly and without question before a significant treatment relationship has been established, they will learn nothing because they are following the worker's advice by rote. More often, however, they will distort the instructions to meet their own needs and in the end make the situation worse.

Ewalt and Kutz (1976) found that parents usually wanted advice about the primary problems and advice that would provide a direct solution. But parents who felt that the worker had supported their own ideas and actions used the advice more appropriately than did parents who felt that the advice ran counter to their own needs or ideas. The ability to use advice appropriately was also correlated with the duration of treatment; the longer the time, the greater the parents' ability to use the worker's advice. In another study, Davis (1975) concluded that the effectiveness of advice seemed to depend largely on the client-worker relationship and the blend of techniques the worker used.

When parents are ignorant about a topic, their requests for information and advice are reasonable, and advice may be useful to them. Generally speaking, it is best to explore possible alternatives, including what they have tried, what they believe may work, and why. This teaches them that there is more than one way of doing things and that making choices is difficult. As part of this process, workers may have to share their own uncertainties and lack of knowledge—and thus demonstrate that one can feel comfortable with human limitations.

Parental requests for advice often express a wish for magical solutions and can easily intensify a worker's wish to be a magically powerful influence and thus save the child by manipulating parental behavior and creating the perfect environment. These feelings are derivatives of infantile omnipotence: some workers will respond with excessive regard for their own advice and influence; others will defend against these feelings by refusing to offer advice or use their influence (R. Miller, 1977). Because clients come from many different cultural backgrounds and have many different life-styles, social workers who give advice in the context of their own life-styles promote a superficial mimicry. Advice that is appropriate to a client's life-style can only be determined in conjunction with the client.

The best advice emerges when decision-making is shared. This demonstrates to parents an understanding of the difficulties involved in being a parent, helps them develop and use their ego capacities to reason and evaluate before acting, and in turn supports reflection and reduces impulsive behavior. During emergencies, the worker may have to accelerate this process so that parents will be able to cope and act when action is necessary—again demonstrating ways of handling crisis and stress.

In the long run, work with parents approximates work with any client. One goal is to improve the parent's functioning in relation to the child. But the greatest progress occurs when the parent's functioning and feelings improve. This then enables appropriate interactions with the child.

Although the necessity of being aware of parental needs seems to complicate the child's treatment, it is more difficult to work with a child whose parents are unavailable. This is often the case when parents of children in foster care are not a vital part of the children's growth and therapeutic experience. The process is slower and more problematic because the children constantly experience a sense of loss and feel unhappy and incomplete. It is difficult for these children to establish relationships with others because they cannot intergrate their negative and loving feelings toward their parents. As a result, they deny the rejection that is often implicit in placement and retain an idealized image of the parents. This tends to make them feel unfaithful if they trust another. Furthermore, because they are deprived in reality, their caution about depending on another adult is realistic (Rose, 1949).

The environment of children in foster care needs as much attention as that of children who live with their natural parents. The interaction between foster parents and children may resemble those the children previously experienced more than is wished: i.e., the environment may not meet their needs. Placing the children in another foster home may not improve matters because their sense of rejection often increases. The foster parents' responsibility for the children and their expectations concerning their involvement with the child's psychological problems differ from those of natural parents, and it is easier for them to hold the child responsible for the difficulties.

Foster parents are asked to provide a therapeutic milieu twenty-four hours a day. This formidable task is complicated by the comings and goings of a variety of therapeutic personnel and the natural parents. Foster parents must be part of a cooperative effort to unify the child's milieu and the interactions of the various participants. If they are not included, therapy with the child will be of little avail.

COMMUNICATING WITH CHILDREN

Therapeutic work with children differs from therapy with adults in several ways. First, the distance between child and therapist is greater than the distance between adult and therapist. Second, children communicate differently than adults do and tend to do it through actions rather than words. Third, the language and level of children's communications are similar in some ways to those of infantile, regressed adult clients who have weak egos and child-like defenses and whose thinking is confused.

Young children are close to infantile conflicts and un-realistic and magical thinking; words have different mean-ings for them, and their use of words is often idiosyncratic. Past, present, and future are easily condensed, but the present is most important to them. It is during the latency period that thinking and communication become more log-ical and ordered and that an awareness of cause and effect develops. It is appropriate for latency-age children to de-fend against their anxiety through projection, denial, dis-placement, and repression. But these defenses make therapy difficult. Furthermore, 6- to 8-year-olds cannot sit still during interviews and tend to regard interpretations of their behavior as criticism. They also can misconstrue a therapist's understanding or permissive attitude as seduc-tive and as permission to do forbidden things. It does not take much for them to engage in wishful thinking or to employ primary process thinking, both of which interfere with reality testing and the development of logical thought, which are appropriate to their age.

Older latency-age children are better able to evaluate reality, integrate contradictions, and abide by rules. But they also have strong defenses that shield them from their painful feelings as well as criticism. Children older than 11 who can better distinguish among behaviors and have ac-cess to their painful feelings also have more elaborate de-fenses (Williams, 1972). Far too many children have experienced too many losses and have suffered too much. To defend against their pain, they try not to feel. But the therapist's job is to keep their capacity to feel alive, to contact their suffering and to develop the trust that will enable these children to communicate and be understood (C. Winnicot, 1964). Because latency-age children cannot communicate in a forthright manner, it is the adult's responsibility to understand their indirect communications; establish the relationship through friendliness, understanding, and constancy; and provide an experience that is free of fear, anxiety, and uncertainty (Buxbaum, 1954).

The aim of therapy is to locate developmental weaknesses and help restore functioning and initiate growth. Normally, latency-age children cope with impulses and the demands of conscience and society by developing numerous coping mechanisms. Mastery and achievement are interfered with, however, when their ego defenses are too weak. When their defenses are too rigid, their efficiency is limited and learning and exploration are inhibited. Therefore, in work with latency-age children, therapeutic goals focus on the development of flexible defenses and more reasonable demands from the superego (Buxbaum, 1951).

There is an educational goal as well. Because children often misunderstand daily events and become frightened by their thoughts and feelings, their confusion about these events must be clarified. Yet children cannot report accurately or supply the missing historical links required. Similarly, they may react to an earlier trauma or loss that they do not consciously remember. Therefore, the history, information about day-to-day living, and, when possible, clarification must be obtained from the adults with whom they live.

The Worker's Problems

Entry into a child's world and proximity to a child's highly charged emotions, narcissism, and unconscious processes can threaten the worker's repressed feelings. Children are sensitive to nonverbal behavior, nuances, and feeling tones, and they easily discern anxiety and tension. They also know how to seduce, cajole, provoke, and upset adults and will employ these talents whenever they need to test the environment and adults.

Severely disturbed children may express their sexual impulses in regressed, infantile, messy ways; expose their bodies; and seek inappropriate body contact (Yandell, 1973). It takes considerable knowledge, self-awareness, and skill to provide the control and closeness these children seek and need without feeling anxious, tense, or angry. Psychotic children will sense these emotions, even when the worker does not express them, and be convinced of their own destructive powers.

Therapeutic work with children requires the ability to be both child and adult simultaneously—to feel as the child does while retaining the judgment, understanding, and observational powers of an adult. Olden (1953) suggested that child therapists need some infantile traits; some passivity, which permits patience; some remnants of belief in magic; and a comfortable sense of themselves as adults.

When therapists regress to a child's level and then behave with the child as they wished and still wish to be treated, pseudoempathy is the result. When their actions are based on their own narcissistic needs, their judgment will be faulty. They may confuse what they wanted as children with what the child-client needs from its parents. They may foster the primary process rather than help the child develop and sublimate through a relationship that supports growth.

A therapist's inability to tolerate the child's regressive behavior may be rationalized into concern for future consequences if the child does not act more grown up. Yet demands for reasonable behavior before the child is ready may be viewed as moralistic and aggressive and as repeating the world outside of therapy (Bornstein, 1948). When a child is not permitted to be a child, natural development is impeded. There is a time to be a child: a time to play at mastery and a time to develop mastery.

Sometimes a therapist's capacity to empathize with a child depends on whether that child is loveable. Yet loveable children sometimes need to risk being unloveable, and unpleasant children need to learn why others do not like them. Children do not need to be loved by their therapist, and therapeutic empathy is not dependent on love for the client. Loving can contaminate understanding and appropriate intervention.

Finding the midpoint between overindulgence and extreme frustration that most children need can be as difficult for therapists as it is for parents. Although it helps when the client loves and trusts the therapist, many children mistrust others, especially adults, and do not relate easily because no one taught them that it was worthwhile to do so. They see others in the light of what they can get, but they never expect to get anything. Because they suffer from unmet needs, therapy must provide a corrective relationship that will stimulate development which goes beyond the satisfaction of needs by first meeting their needs (Neubauer, 1970; Alpert, 1959).

Children's Resistance

As outlined in an earlier chapter, children tend to report concretely, if at all, because they resist strong feelings. At the same time, they may react strongly. Children lack insight into their need for therapeutic help and view problems as external to themselves. They displace dangerous impulses onto external events, things, and people and expect their workers to improve the environment without having to do anything themselves. And if they feel guilty, they tend to provoke the punishment they believe they deserve (Bornstein, 1948; A. Freud, 1965).

Because children are frightened about treatment and find it difficult to understand, they will express anxiety in their habitual way. Even those who have had a therapeutic experience with another therapist and have learned it is not frightening will be cautious about and test a new therapist.

Children who have been passed from one worker to another are difficult to engage in a therapeutic relationship. Some will talk and play easily and seem cooperative. Yet their extreme extroversion and the frequency with which they change activities may mask a superficial friendliness. Because most will relate to the therapist as they do to their parents and other important people, how they relate will demonstrate the depth of their relationships.

Many workers find that silence is the most difficult resistance to tolerate. As mentioned in Chapter 8, some children are completely mute; others will only respond in monosyllables to questions. Because it is frustrating, a child's silence can provoke anger or a struggle to get the child to speak (Kaplan & Escoll, 1973; Chethik, 1973).

Silence represents a variety of conflicts and problems. It can simultaneously be a defense and a gratification. Stubborn children and those struggling with problems involving separation and autonomy may withhold speech. Suspicious children who have lost the courage to test out new situations must keep to themselves to feel safe (C. Winnicott, 1964). Children who are afraid they will be destroyed may try to control the situation by feigning indifference and refusing to cooperate. Depressed children cannot believe that anything or anyone, including themselves, is good. Severely disturbed children may withdraw to insulate themselves from strong environmental and emotional pressures and to protect against feeling. Because they equate doing with dangerous, destructive things, they do nothing (Nagleberg, Spotnitz, & Feldman, 1953).

Some children use words to avoid communicating and relating. Although they are loquacious, intelligent, and verbally proficient, they look unhappy and serious and lack humor and spontaneity. They tend to overvalue talk and achieve control through words that isolate and deny affective content. They are perpetually involved in a power struggle and in the issue of autonomy (Adams, 1973).

When confronted with this kind of child, a worker may become bored and withdraw emotionally.

Even more overtly oppositional are children who refuse to cooperate about anything, break appointments, and in general resist suggestions, clarifications, or interpretations (Gilpin, 1976). Some are hostile, provocative, and disruptive; others will attack the worker physically. How difficult they will be to treat may depend on the worker's ability to understand and cope with this overt, seemingly angry resistance. Some of these children are incapable of maintaining control over their impulses: others still have some fight in them and may have some hope left.

Listening to Children

Because displacement is a common defense among children, it is easy to understand them if one is willing to listen to what they actually say. When they talk about an animal, another child, or a storybook character, the character will be speaking for them and for the important events in their lives. The character's feelings will be their feelings. At times this is so transparent that it is difficult to believe that children are unconscious of it. At other times, even the character's emotions are disguised. Children also use jokes to disguise their fears and anxieties and transform painful experiences into pleasurable ones. In therapy, the themes of jokes tend to deal with knowing or not knowing, triumph, superiority, competition, rejection, and aggression —and either the child or adults may be the target. Jokes permit children to play with words, incongruities, exaggerations, and minimizations (Orfandis, 1972). Distortions of well-known jokes can reveal important conflicts and anxieties. Jokes can ease tension and disguise forbidden impulses sufficiently to permit the child to talk about them indirectly. Children who can joke with or tell riddles to their workers tend to have good rapport with them, feel

comfortable enough to be children, and use age-appropriate communication (Yorukoglu, 1974).

When workers listen quietly and attentively to a child,
they are communicating that the child is important and that
they have set aside time for the child to use as needed.
Children need to be listened to rather than talked at; most
of them have already experienced enough of the latter. All
children will respond to someone who is interested enough
to listen. The following case illustrates the complexities
involved in listening to children:

> *Kenneth M*, age 8, was brought for treatment because he was
> having difficulty with his schoolwork and with peers, moved
> slowly, was oppositional, and whined constantly at home.
> Mr. and Mrs. M's quarrels about how to handle Kenneth
> reflected their own marital difficulties; Mrs. M was particu-
> larly upset with Kenneth.
>
> Kenneth was an only child, and his parents were mar-
> ried for many years before he was born. Because he was not
> walking at age 2, Mrs. M. took him to a neurologist, who
> diagnosed Kenneth as suffering from a congenital neuro-
> muscular disease that did not have a degenerative course.
> Thus physical activity would be difficult for Kenneth and he
> would be slower than normal. Although the physician sug-
> gested that Kenneth had inherited this condition from his
> father, Mr. M had never been diagnosed as having this diffi-
> culty.
>
> Kenneth was a small, thin boy with an awkward, floppy
> walk and slurred but intelligible speech. When the worker
> told Kenneth during the first interview that he could do
> anything he wanted to do, the boy replied: "Then I am the
> boss here, not you. We have a playroom at school, but it's
> for twenty-five boys, but this one is all mine." When the
> worker told him about the time limit, Kenneth wanted to
> know whether the worker went home after the appointment
> and whether he saw any other children.
>
> Kenneth said that because he was boss, he would make
> the rules for all the games they would play and planned what
> they would do this time and the next. He knew he was com-
> ing to talk, but when the worker asked him what they should
> be talking about, Kenneth didn't know and asked what time

it was. When the worker suggested that it was hard for Kenneth to talk, the boy said the worker had only four minutes left to talk.

Kenneth began playing darts but did not have the strength to throw the darts even a few inches. When the worker commented that it must be difficult to play with other children because he was not as strong, Kenneth did not respond. But when the worker asked how much he knew about his illness, Kenneth said: "Don't tell me now. Wait till next week."

In subsequent sessions, Kenneth chose the games and designed new rules that favored him. When the worker said that winning seemed very important to him, Kenneth said he did not want to talk, he wanted to play. When the worker asked him about his family, he was able to say that he liked his father better than his mother. He then mimicked Mrs. M in a loud voice: "Kenneth, do this; Kenneth do that. Make your bed. Kenneth don't yell." The worker commented that it seemed as if his mother yelled a lot at him and that he didn't like it. Kenneth said: "Let's stop talking and just play. No more talking. We just play in this room."

Kenneth tried to stay after his appointment was over and always manipulated games so that they favored him. After several months, his school work and relations with peers improved. However, Mrs. M reported that Kenneth had defecated in three different rooms one day, leaving the feces so she would find them. The day before, Kenneth had been angry with her, said he hated her, and hoped she would go to the hospital and die. Mrs. M. had told him he made her angry because he made other children laugh at him because he was different. Kenneth had then thrown dishes on the floor and had gone to his room. This was not the first time he had soiled.

During the next interview, the worker mentioned the incident (Kenneth knew that the worker had talked with his mother) and suggested that Kenneth must have been very angry at someone. Kenneth said he was angry at the worker for canceling their appointment the previous week. "I thought that you thought I was not important. Don't ever cancel." When asked about his soiling, Kenneth said he didn't remember anything. He didn't want to talk about it; it was too embarrassing. If he made a mistake while playing,

he would say "Bad Kenny, clumsy Kenny." The worker suggested that sometimes people who made mistakes felt they
were worthless. At first, Kenneth was silent; then he mentioned that a man was coming to his school to talk about
handicapped kids. When the worker said that it must be hard
to be a handicapped boy, Kenneth said nothing. After a few
minutes, however, he said: "You don't understand me."
When the worker commented that he was trying to understand but was finding it hard, Kenneth responded: "It's not
hard, just listen."

During the next session, Kenneth began playing with
the marble game. The worker asked him how the talk at
school had gone. "It was an important talk about handicapped kids. All the parents were going to be there and
going to talk about me. My mother said it was important to
go and I agreed. *She* should know how to work with handicapped kids." The worker commented that it was hard to be
a handicapped child and hard to be a mother of that child,
and Kenneth nodded. But when the worker said that it was
hard to be different from other children, Kenneth did not
respond. When asked whether the doctor had ever explained his problem, Kenneth said he had not. The worker
then explained it to him simply. After this, Kenneth began
playing with the marble game, changing the marbles so that
he would win. When the worker said that Kenneth needed
to change the rules so he would not lose, Kenneth had a
small smile on his face. The worker then stated that he
realized things were difficult for Kenneth and that sometimes people needed extra help. Kenneth replied: "Let's
play, not talk."

Although it was necessary in this case to clarify with
Kenneth his differences and the problems that would arise,
the worker was too intent on this goal from the beginning
and did not permit the process to unfold by listening so
that he would understand Kenneth's feelings and situation
without preconceptions. If he had explored what Kenneth
meant by the term handicapped children and how Kenneth
believed they could be helped, he would have understood
better what needed to be clarified. Furthermore, by trying

to elicit Kenneth's feelings too soon and too directly, and by encouraging the boy to express his hostility toward his mother, he removed controls instead of strengthening them. Yet this worker empathized with Kenneth and was interested in him; if anything he cared too much, and Kenneth realized it.

Talking with Children

All children need contact with patient adults who not only permit them to play out their problems but help them to talk. Playing helps discharge tensions, and the nature of the communication that occurs during play lends itself to clarification and interpretation (Lamont, 1958). However, the interpretations must be appropriate for the child and timed properly. Interpretations are not for the worker's benefit, nor are they always correct. When children are confronted with dogmatic interpretations, they have only two alternatives: accept the interpretations and feel coerced or reject them (D.W. Winnicott, 1971). When interpretations are too close to unconscious material, children equate them with mind reading, and because they tend to believe that adults can read their minds anyway, they become frightened.

Interpretation is a process of deducing what a client actually means and then pointing it out (Fenichel, 1945). Ekstein and Wallerstein (1966) separate the process into two steps: clarification and interpretation. Clarification consists of helping clients verbalize by restating their statements in a more precise form. Only after this preparation can the worker interpret hidden meanings and unconscious connections that transcend the clinical data and the client's methods of defense. But these interpretations must be rigorously attuned to the client's individual needs and be expressed in the client's language. The best interpretations deal with what occurs between worker and client and reflect the history between them, including the outside events that the client brings in for discussion. The most accurate and useful interpretations are those that clients arrive at themselves.

A simple and effective rule is to respect clients' defenses: if they use them, they need them. When children talk about current situations, it is necessary to talk with them until their feelings are understood. Then it is appropriate to address the affects and feelings revealed by what they say. But rather than directly address how a child feels, the worker should use the subject and language that the child uses. The characters in stories the child tells, the characters that appear during play, or what the child says about peers or friends will provide the clues. For example, a child may talk about a stupid boy in class who is always laughed at by the other children. When the therapist asks what the boy does that makes others laugh and recognizes how unhappy that boy must be, the child will feel understood. The worker might ask the child what would help the boy do things correctly so that others would not laugh. Much can be learned in this way. Then, feeling safe, the child will sometimes emerge from the play and say that he feels like that boy.

It is extremely important to learn the child's language. Families often have special names for bodily functions, especially those involving elimination or injuries. Knowing these words and using them assists in communication. Very young or disturbed children tend to use symbolic language and may not be able to talk clearly even about other children. In these cases, a therapist can deliberately use these symbols to establish communication on the child's level. Symbolic language is primary process language, which the worker can manipulate but should not translate. The replies, rooted in reality, deal with meanings beyond the verbalizations, but at a safe distance, indicating that the worker understands the affect, fear, sense of danger, and weakness.

The workers communications must either indicate complete acceptance of children's fears concerning the topics discussed or consist of generalized statements about "some children." The worker must also promise and provide protection (Ekstein & Wallerstein, 1956). As children feel safer, their expressions usually become more realistic and mature.

Children sometimes ask workers personal questions about where they live, whether they are married, and so on. Although these questions express a view of the therapist as a person, they can also mean something else. Rather than answer quickly and factually, the worker should first determine why the child is interested and if possible, what fantasies are involved. For example, if a child asks whether the worker has children, it is necessary to explore why this information is important. The child actually may be asking: Can you care for me if you have other children? How do other parents behave? and so on. When the group of prepubertal girls described in Chapter 5 asked the worker how many children she had, they had wanted her children to be boys. The worker had replied that if she had children, she would have one boy for each of the girls. This answer addressed their emerging sexual interests. Many years later, when one of the group members returned to the worker for help with her adult problems, she recalled this incident. She then remarked that she did not believe the girls had really wanted to know whether the worker had children; they preferred to play with their fantasies. On occasion, factual answers are important. But this can only be determined by examining the reason for the child's question. If facts are important, the child will return to the subject again and again.

Children often ask workers if they also see other children. Perhaps they fantasize that they are the only child the worker sees or that the other children are of the opposite sex and therefore preferred. More important than facts are the feelings that underlie the question. In many instances, facts cut off exploration and understanding and do not advance the work.

It is incorrect to tell children that they can do anything they wish during the time they spend with the worker. Time restrictions are an ever present reality, and frequently children's physical activities must be limited because of the needs of others in the agency. Furthermore, children cannot be allowed to hurt themselves or the worker. Limits can be therapeutic if they are well-defined, are easy to distinguish, and are applied only to behavior rather than to attitudes or feelings (Bixler, 1964). Establishing these rules and gently enforcing them provides the control and protection that latency-age children need.

When anxious, some children become hyperactive and aggressive and attempt to hurt the worker or themselves. To prevent this, they must be physically restrained, if necessary, but as gently as possible (Szurek & Berlin, 1973). It is difficult for most persons to be objective when they have been kicked, and children become frightened when they actually hurt an adult because they are then without the supports they need. When a child must be restrained, the worker should explain how the curtailed action would have hurt the child and the worker. If the child wishes, the therapist can then explain how to express anger safely.

It is always crucially important to understand what aggression means to the child. Aggression includes hostile wishes toward others as well as the fear of being the victim. Children can panic at the prospect of annihilation. Even aggression acted out on a toy or doll convinces some children of their destructive potential. Therefore, the worker must determine how much adult participation, if any, will be therapeutic for a specific child. Aggression can connote a child's desire to punish or to be punished and indicate identification with either the aggressor or victim. In this sense, the child's affect before and after the aggressive event is significant (Haworth, 1964).

Some children fight the worker by breaking appointments, arriving late for them, opposing clarifications or requests, and so forth. When these reactions occur, the worker must recognize that the child may feel threatened by being controlled and help the child to achieve real control rather than fight aimlessly. By permitting this struggle for autonomy, the worker helps the child grow (Gilpin, 1976).

When children are silent, their silence must be respected. Some children need a person with whom they need not communicate and from whom they can withdraw (Fraiberg, 1962). Some withdraw to avoid expressing objectionalbe, crazy impulses or thinking or acting in destructive ways. When the worker meets a child's silence with silence and allows the child to regulate attempts at contact, the child's fragile defenses are protected. Silence is a form of insulation for extremely disturbed children. By not stimulating them, the worker maintains this insulation and these children maintain control and achieve independence from their frightening impulses. When children are less afraid, they learn to express their destructive impulses in fantasy and then in more appropriate direct ways (Spotnitz, Nagelberg, & Feldman, 1956).

Because words are abstract substitutes for physical behavior, they tend to be less meaningful to children than are actions. Language, after all, is only one aspect of behavior, and meaningful therapeutic work can occur when behavior is understood and translated into appropriate verbal or nonverbal behavior according to the child's needs (Smolen, 1959).

Children need to be physically active; they take pride in accomplishing physical feats that assist their coordination and promote control and mastery. Until they are about 10 years old, children easily express impulses, solve problems, and communicate through actions (Mittelman, 1957), and their use of motion tends to reflect their conflicts and concerns. Some movements will be exhibitionistic; others will be seductive. Awkwardness may reflect insecurity and conflict about control of impulses. Diminished activity may reveal depression, withdrawal, shyness, or anxiety. Children who are constricted in this way need sympathy, patience, and assistance in engaging in activity. Overactive, hyperkinetic behavior may be the consequence of overstimulation and sexual excitement and often has strong destructive components. Sometimes it is a reaction to early physical restriction because of illness. When the environment is overstimulating, it must be corrected. The therapeutic session must provide the control that these children need. When they are overactive because of early restraint, they need the opportunity to play out these restrictions in an acceptable way.

Peek-a-boo; I Hide, You Seek

Some children consciously play hide-and-seek, often repeatedly. Mittleman (1957) suggests that this activity represents a reversal of the anxious child who searches for its parents or turns a passive experience into an active one. It also can be a teasing, seductive game. In therapy, some children hide behind objects or wait outside the room, looking in at the worker. They have often lost a parent or have had inconsistent care, especially during the period of separation-individuation. Many foster children fall into this category. Their physical movements seem to play out a wish to be looked for and found—the opposite of the wish to look for and find the lost object.

This form of hide-and-seek is the latency-age child's version of the peek-a-boo game that babies enjoy (Bruner & Sherwood, 1976; Kleeman, 1967). It enables children to test the permanence of objects. During latency, the struggle with the missing object can be played out in many diverse ways through a variety of devices that provide distance or reversal. Sometimes children will throw a ball out of the room or to the therapist, who rolls it back—as if this will enable them to control coming and going and to master their impotence (Ekstein & Friedman, 1956). When therapists play these games with a child who needs them, they symbolically assure constancy and can verbalize the child's feelings about loss and recovery when appropriate. More than words, however, stability and attention to the meaning of separations such as vacations, cancelled appointments, transfers of workers, and termination of treatment provide opportunities for working through and understanding earlier losses.

Through shared experiences, worker and child can be together and yet remain separate. These experiences permit communication in many ways and on many levels; what the two experience together can be understood together. They create a mutual history that permits clarifications, interpretations, and corrective experiences to occur in the context of shared current events. The child's needs and the nature of the setting will influence the types of activities that worker and child will engage in. The two can walk, play ball, or even plant something and together watch it grow.

PLAYING WITH CHILDREN

Playing is a natural part of a child's life and development. Play actions are complex mental phenomena: they include the act, a fantasy, language, and aspects of reality testing (Ekstein & Friedman, 1966). Through play, children release tension, express forbidden impulses, and assign to dolls and other figures their own fears and fantasies.

Play and Therapy

In therapy, play can be a child's form of communication. With nonverbal children, it can be used to establish a working relationship. As a form of therapy, play enables children to experiment and plan. And it is, as Erikson (1963) pointed out, the most natural method of self-healing that childhood affords.

Playing in therapy permits children to verbalize conscious material and associated feelings safely and to act out unconscious conflicts and fantasies (A. Freud, 1966). They can communicate about past as well as current daily events. Play reflects anxieties that latency-age children are reluctant to share openly: e.g., they may be frightened because they realize that their parents are not omnipotent and thus cannot protect them from all danger, or they may fear that dangerous ogres, witches, and monsters exist (Gondor, 1964). Latency-age children have difficulty talking about these fears because on one level they know they are unrealistic.

When children play, their verbal expressions tend to become less logical, coherent, and rational, and displacement, repetitiveness, distortion, and exaggeration is evident. The central theme of the play will elucidate a child's problem.

Therapeutic play differs from the play of ordinary life because the therapist accepts a role in a make-believe game and takes the role seriously. The child often assigns the role, and the worker is willing to play out that role as the child expects. Yet the therapist always remains an adult. This kind of play is special, and children know instinctively that it can help them.

Play can be used diagnostically to understand children's perceptions of and relationship to themselves and others (Amster, 1943). For example, much can be learned from the materials children choose; the inhibitions, excitement, aggression, immaturity, and degree of regression they exhibit; and whether they elect to play alone or with the worker. But the accuracy of the diagnostic assessment will depend on the worker's knowledge of how children of the client's age, community, and culture usually play (Erikson, 1963). The content of the play will differ less from the norm than its structure, style, and cohesion, and objects will have different meanings for each child. When play becomes too real or too stimulating, children will stop, change the theme abruptly, or act out impulsively, even though they realize that they are only playing. This disruption, accompanied by words and visible affects, will be especially relevant to children's specific problems.

When playing therapeutically with children, workers must accept the fantasies and feelings that arise and explore them to understand rather than enforce society's labels and ideas. Criticism, reward, and approval have no place in therapeutic play (Moustakas, 1973). Workers must also be prepared to change their roles and activities as the child's needs dictate.

Play Equipment and Setting

Diagnostic understanding of the dynamics of a child's personality and therapeutic need will determine the therapist's words, actions, and the kinds of materials selected for the child. Although access to a wide variety of play equipment is valuable, no child should be presented with a large selection. Different children need different play materials.

Materials should be as simple as possible so that children can use their imagination. The basic equipment for play therapy would include a fixed or portable blackboard, a work surface, blocks, dolls that represent family members of different ages, animals, clay, a few dishes, crayons, paints, paper, a toy telephone, playing cards, and some games that have simple rules. Doll houses, for example, are unnecessary because children can create houses that express their own reality or fantasies. Furthermore, because doll houses are usually one-family houses, they are inappropriate for children who live in apartments. Although furniture such as beds, tables, and toilets can be used, they too are unnecessary since children can create these objects from blocks or clay.

Bulletin boards have no place in a room used by many children. Placing one child's work on the board intrudes on another child's interview. Instead, each child should have a special box, drawer, or closet in which to keep drawings, special toys, and so forth. Although children are curious about locked drawers and boxes, they can learn to respect the privacy and possessions of other children and appreciate the worker's respect for their own privacy and possessions. The worker can accept their curiosity and then explain that it will not be gratified.

Whenever possible, toys and other equipment should be unbreakable. Dolls and toy animals with limbs that can be torn off do not permit children to play out their aggressive wishes safely; some children will be convinced that they can destroy in reality. For children who are struggling to maintain control, structured games are often more helpful than unstructured materials such as finger paints. Children who have had or will have an operation may be helped by playing doctor or nurse, changing and assigning roles to suit their struggles. Darts should have rubber tips, but some children will avoid using them in any case.

Few agencies have the space or the money for a special playroom. An ordinary interviewing room can be used as long as the furniture can take a beating and the floors and walls can be washed. Having to worry about keeping a room in good condition is distracting and interferes with therapeutic decisions about how much freedom and restraint the child needs.

Some interviewing rooms contain equipment such as typewriters, dictaphones, and telephones. Children love to dictate radio programs and stories on a dictaphone or write stories on a typewriter. When working with destructive children, however, these items should be removed from the room.

Cheating at Games

Games governed by rules are an important part of life during latency. The rules provide the external controls that were previously imposed by parents, help develop skills, and provide an outlet for competitive strivings. Parchesi and checkers are favorites during early latency, while complex games such as chess and Monopoly become more popular in later stages of latency. Loomis (1957) suggested that the game of checkers is helpful to some children who are afraid of succeeding. The therapist symbolizes parental figures. Children may change the rules to lose because of a fear of winning or win by cheating because winning safely or on their own seems impossible. They can also use checkers and similar games to express resistance, create distance, or maintain silence to control therapy and the worker, or symbolically kill the worker. (In the heat of competition, a child may even say: "I'm going to kill you!")

Meeks (1970) discussed in detail the different meanings of cheating at games. Many children are referred to therapy because they cheat in school and do not observe rules and regulations. Despite their constant and obvious cheating, they often act as if the therapist does not know.

Some children cheat to deny the role of skill and affirm their belief in luck and magic, which are typical of the preschool child. Or they may do so as an expression of the invincibility of the oedipal child. When children cheat against themselves, changing the rules to help the worker, they may be afraid of winning. Sometimes cheating represents the struggle for independence and autonomy and against externally imposed rules. Children who have strong symbiotic ties to a parent whom they regard as omnipotent not only refuse to acknowledge rules but are not interested in learning how to play properly. Severely disturbed children will play in a scattered, disorderly way, making moves at random. Some children equate losing with total helplessness; the alternative is omnipotence, which can only be achieved by breaking the rules.

Because cheating involves strong emotions, the worker must understand its meaning before attempting to intervene. Children who are confronted prematurely may feel mistreated or else conform superficially. Because the therapeutic medium, not the game, is the focus, it is sometimes therapeutic when the therapist plays to win, but it is always therapeutic to play to understand.

Often children test a therapist's self-esteem in the face of losing as though trying to learn how to behave in this situation. The eventual aim is to increase children's acceptance of their actual capacities and limitations; this may have to wait until children view their therapists as noncritical and nonjudgmental. Meeks (1970) suggested that the time to explore cheating is when a child expresses guilt or asks why the worker permits cheating. Beiser (1970) believed that permitting a child to cheat supports feelings of omnipotence and that it is better to suggest that when the child changes the rules, the changes apply to the worker as well as the child.

Because cheating and rule-changing occur for so many diverse reasons, it is best to view these activities in the context of the child's developmental abilities and treat the problem in relation to its significance, symbolism, and communication. Some children do not understand that adults are more skillful simply because they are older and more knowledgeable. It is helpful for these children to realize that adults who know more can be more helpful than those who do not. Children's beliefs in their own capacities must be strengthened through the therapeutic relationship and the worker's empathy and help. Children need to know that by cheating, they cheat themselves out of learning the skills they need and that the worker is prepared to teach them those skills when they are ready

Fantasy Play

Make-believe and fantasy play enable latency-age children to express their guilt, fears, and forbidden thoughts indirectly and safely. Usually these feelings arise spontaneously during play; however, constricted children may need assistance in expressing these feelings. With paints or crayons, they can create pictures that communicate their concerns. Choice of color and freedom of expression and movement will convey the tone of their mood. Finger-painting provides a more direct cathartic tactile experience; it requires little technical skill and is a socially acceptable way of playing with mud or feces (Arlow & Kaydis, 1976). Play dough and clay offer a similar form of release.

D. W. Winnicott (1971) suggested using the "squiggle" technique to stimulate free communication. With eyes closed, the therapist draws a pencil line on paper, which the child then makes into something else. Then the child draws a line and the worker expands on it. The pictures enables fantasy, story telling, and interpretation. And because the game has no rules and requires no skill, anyone can play.

Gardner (1971) has developed the mutual story-telling technique to elicit children's inner thoughts and feelings through fantasy. The therapist asks the child to tell a story and then, using the child's own language, characters, settings, and initial situation, retells the story with a more appropriate resolution of the important conflict and suggests more alternatives. The initial story tells the child's difficulties, the meanings of which must be surmised. The new story must avoid deeply unconscious meanings and anxiety-provoking communications. When the child seems deeply interested or becomes anxious or hyperactive, the therapist knows that the child is hearing something important.

Puppets can be used to make up plays and stories, and they offer the worker and child similar opportunities to communicate. Stories recorded on tape or a dictaphone can be played back and talked about together.

Fantasy is not for every child, and is even prohibited for some. Obviously, psychotic and severely disturbed children do not need encouragement to indulge in make-believe because too often they already live in a frightening, imaginary world. They require the safety of control and order and need to be reassured about their fears.

No one technique is useful with all children or with any one child. Techniques of communicating must be geared to individual children's developmental needs and modes of communicating. Sometimes several techniques must be combined in new ways for a specific child.

Because pets are some children's only friends, they may need to participate in the therapy. One child brought his chicken and his turtle and together worker and child talked about how lonely his pets were without other chickens and turtles. Some inhibited children benefit by playing with water; with the intent of cleaning, they will joyfully make a mess. Some children need to be fed. Occasionally, a child will ask to bring a friend, a sibling, or a parent to the session. There can be no firm rule. When the worker understands the reason for the request, it is easy to decide what to do. Those who work with children must be flexible; tolerant of noise and messes; able to change as the child changes; and imaginative. Most important, however, they must value and respect children.

Chapter 11

LEAVING AND BEING LEFT

All human relationships involve a coming together, a being together, and a separation. It has been said many times and in many contexts that separation is an inevitable and universal life experience, starting with birth and culminating in death. Human development itself involves the gradual separation and individuation of the child from its mother. The fact that all things must end, then, is the prototype for the termination stage of therapeutic intervention. For it is by learning to deal with separations and endings that we begin to grow.

In all separations, someone leaves and someone is left. To leave and be left are different experiences and reflect different consequences, affects, and meanings. Some separations occur in the normal course of events and thus have the potential to enhance development. Others are abnormal and inappropriate and as such are potentially traumatic, critical events that necessitate therapeutic assistance to prevent developmental damage. In all separations other than death, both parties are potentially available for contact. However, the experience can be traumatic when the one who leaves simply abandons the other, as happens in some divorces or when children are separated from parents who do not remain in touch with them.

Therapeutic processes emulate life processes: both have growth-producing developmental models or growth-disturbing traumatic models. The variables of therapeutic process and procedures interact with the variables of client need and developmental state (not chronological age) and the nature and stage of the relationship.

BEING LEFT

Mahler, Pine, and Bergman (1975) speak of a developmental process during which children gradually differentiate themselves from symbiotic oneness with the mother by practicing leaving and coming back. When this practice assures them of the object's constancy, they internalize the object, which in turn permits them to differentiate from and be without the object. The mother-object remains constant, and the child looks back. Going to kindergarten is another milestone in separation; believing that mother is safe in the familiar home permits children to leave comfortably to enter a wider world. Even then, mothers take children to school, introduce them to the teacher, and help them to make a new beginning with others.

A new struggle concerning separation and individuation occurs again in adolescence. Blos (1967) called adolescence the second stage of individuation because, again, the child struggles to leave and struggles against leaving. The separation of adolescence permits a looking back and a different kind of coming back in maturity.

Despite these processes of coping with separation, the final separation of death and the loss of a loved one is never

easy. Pain, dejection, inhibition of activity, loss of the capacity to love again, proving the loved object no longer
exists, and recapitulating the past over and over again are
all part of the work of mourning, which takes time. Only
when mourning is completed is the ego free and uninhib-
ited again (Freud, 1917).

Occasionally, a worker dies during the course of a relationship. The need to help a client to work through this
kind of loss is usually understood. But clients are left in
many other ways. A worker may become ill, go on vacation,
or leave the agency at a time that is unfortunate for the
client. Or agency policies concerning length of treatment,
transfers, and intake may be unrealistic for some clients. In
too many of these situations, clients who have suffered
inappropriate losses in childhood experience new inappropriate losses during treatment. Some clients are always being left, in therapy as in life.

> Michael F, an obese 8-year-old, was an amorphous mass of
> energy and overwhelming anxiety, barreling down the halls,
> climbing on furniture, yelling, and provoking peers and
> adults. Yet he was intelligent and verbal; his learning prob-
> lems were secondary to his sexual role confusion and inabil-
> ity to control his impulses.
>
> Michael was an only child whose mother attempted sui-
> cide in the seventh month of pregnancy after learning that
> her husband was AWOL from the army. Despite this, Micha-
> el's early development was described as normal. Mrs. F re-
> turned to work when Michael was 5½ months old and left
> him with a variety of baby-sitters. He was hospitalized briefly
> at 18 months for a hernia operation. At 2½ he was found tied
> to a chair in a baby-sitter's home. When he was 4, his parents
> separated, and Mrs. F returned to her parents' home. She
> did not explain what had happened to his father. She re-
> ported that Michael had asked, "What did I do that Daddy
> had to go?" and that his hostile, uncontrolled behavior be-
> gan at that time.
>
> Mrs. F seemed to have a poor opinion of herself and
> expected Michael to make up for this as well as meet her

needs. Although harsh and punitive in some ways, she permitted him to sleep in bed with her and excused this by saying that he was afraid of being alone at night. She and her father often argued about how Michael should be brought up.

Michael seemed eager for treatment and never missed a session. But he would run, shout, climb on window ledges and furniture, yelling: "Ooh, this is high, right? Shit, bullshit. Oh, I'm scared. I can jump this far, right?" Then he would laugh hysterically. He carried on a monologue with himself and acted as if he did not hear anything the worker said. But several minutes later, he would comment that he felt fat, silly, and stupid, and no one liked him. He also made frequent sexual references that reflected confusion and an anal orientation. When the worker repeated these sexual references, Michael accused him of being a mind reader. He criticized his own drawings and clay figures, saying they were shit. He would ask the worker to make something, try to copy it, and finally give up, saying the worker's production was no good. He was constantly testing limits, even hitting the worker.

Michael began to try to extend sessions. He also would start a drawing, leaving it to be finished the following week. When he left, he would remain half in and half out of the room, knowing that once he left he could not return that day.

After the Christmas vacation, Michael initiated a game of hide-and-seek, playing out his fear of abandonment symbolically for several months. He continued to be aggressive toward the worker, but his peer relationships improved, and he was able to assert himself appropriately rather than provoke other children to attack him.

Michael was being seen in a school. When he was told that the worker planned to leave, he became even more angry. Each week he denied that the worker had told him about leaving and reacted with vituperous expressions of hatred when the worker mentioned it. During the next to last session, he could not speak but threw toys on the floor and kicked in the closet door. Returning to his classroom, he was loud and boisterous, almost asking to be punished. Then he began to cry and was able to tell his teacher how unhappy he was and why. But the following day, Michael again denied

that the worker was leaving, attacked him physically with a
pencil, and threatened to kill him. When he had to be restrained, his aggression accelerated. When he regained control of himself, he pushed the worker away and denied any
positive feelings.

The worker left when Michael was half in and half out
of treatment. The boy was still testing the constancy of this
new relationship against his earlier experiences when suddenly the worker left, as Mommy had gone to work and
Daddy had gone away. No one had died, yet no one was
available for him. It was not unrealistic for an 8-year-old
boy who had had these experiences to feel abandoned and
rejected again when his worker left. Although he expressed
his feelings as a much younger child would, it would have
been more pathological and would have indicated he had
lost all hope if he had not cared when his worker left.

Vacations and Illness

Christmas vacation was the first reminder to Michael that
this new relationship, which he hoped would be different
from the others, held the same dangers as the old. He
began to test whether the worker cared enough to look for
him. In the previous chapter, Kenneth scolded his worker
for canceling an appointment by saying "I thought that you
thought I was not important. Don't ever cancel."

Treatment does not have to be interrupted for an extended period to threaten an insecure person. Children are
confused about present and future time. Yet vacations and
illnesses are unavoidable components of any treatment relationship. They become shared experiences that worker
and child can talk about; it is easier to discuss current
happenings between worker and child than to probe for the
child's reactions to earlier trauma. When current events are
handled with attention to a growth-producing develop-

mental model, even absences can assist the therapeutic process.

It is important to inform clients about planned vacations well in advance. Clients, after all, are expected to keep their appointments, and workers should keep theirs. But the meaning to clients and the fantasies aroused must be explored. For some clients, an alternate session can be scheduled, if possible: short breaks during holiday seasons are often handled in this manner. Clients also are entitled to simple explanations of the worker's absence and a specific time for the next meeting.

Because young children think concretely, dates alone may not be enough. It is helpful to count the days on the calendar, marking the reunion date. Some children are certain that they will be forgotten, but may not say so. However, their histories should indicate whether they are likely to have this fear. Promising to send a postcard and then sending it provides a link and constancy. For some a transitional object may be reassuring: a favorite play toy or an unfinished project can be taken home and returned at the next session. This is a concrete way of helping children to feel more in control of the relationship.

When worker and child meet again, they should discuss what the child did on the day of the appointment and how the child felt. Many children will try to act as though they did not care, but by listening and watching, the worker will recognize that they did care.

It is best if the first absence is a brief one. Later, this shared experience and similar ones become the history of the therapeutic relationship. When preparing a child for a second absence, the child can be reminded of the previous leaving and return. If the child remains distrustful after testing the worker's constancy many times, it is appropriate to comment on why the child cannot believe that the worker will return when the worker always has. This may enable the child to remember all the people who did not return. The child who has experienced few real losses will trust relatively easily, whereas the child who has had many losses will need to experience again and again that return occurs.

Often an absence related to illness cannot be discussed in advance. If possible, the worker should call the child to explain the cancellation. If this is not possible, an agency representative should ask the parent or foster parent to explain the worker's illness. Despite these attempts to prove that the worker has not disappeared, the worker may find, upon returning, that the child is angry, resistant, and cautious. In protracted illnesses, a transitional agency representative should talk with the child about the worker and about being left or help the child play out his or her feelings. Telephone calls can maintain the contact if the worker is able to do this. A worker's death is a crisis situation, and the child must be reassigned immediately to another worker, informed of the death, and helped to work through this final separation.

The Worker Leaves the Agency

Because of staff turnover and student placements, premature terminations, although undesirable, are common. In these situations the child is left before it is therapeutically indicated. This new loss will reawaken previous losses, be a new rejection, and injure the child's self-esteem For some children the expectation of loss becomes a part of their character (Wallach, 1961).

In this final stage of the relationship, symptoms hat are similar to those that were observed at the beginning of treatment will appear, themes of loss, mourning, and grief will be expressed symbolically rather than directly. The worst effect is that being left ends any fantasies about being special.

It is the worker s therapeutic task to deal with these

emotions (Levinson, 1977). The more involved children have been with a worker, the more intense will be their reactions. Their way of defending against the pain of the loss will reflect old patterns of behaving, even though they have learned new ones. Denial, acting out, even leaving the worker first by breaking appointments may be attempts to master and control their feelings. Some children become seductive, good therapeutic clients and seriously misbehave at home or in school. Others will withdraw emotionally and their sadness will be obvious.

Therapists who leave a client prematurely tend to feel they are guilty of desertion. Their own feelings about separation and their own methods of dealing with these feelings may interfere with their ability to work with the child in this last stage of the relationship. As a result, they may delay telling the child, rationalizing each time that it was not the right time or that it was impossible to break into the child's communications.

Children need sufficient time to express their pain. When they are still in need of therapy, the agency should make every effort to provide them with a new worker, who will be introduced by the first worker. The child and the two workers should then meet together.

Workers who leave should not drop into oblivion. Whether children verbalize it or not, a normal question is: "Will you remember me?" Social workers do remember clients for many years, and children remember their workers into adulthood because the process of internalization keeps an important object with one forever. Forgetting is only a form of denial.

It is helpful if the child and the worker who has left can write letters to one another. If it seems unwise for the child to know where the former worker is, their correspondence can be forwarded through the agency or transmitted through the new worker. These contacts often help children make the transition to a new worker because trusting

is possible. It may be appropriate to give the child something to keep as a remembrance, and children often bring
something to their workers. A guiding principle is that
there is nothing therapeutic about a relationship that simply ends. It is as cruel an experience in therapeutic life as
it is in real life.

Some children are constantly assigned to students and
thus are perpetually left behind. Children who have a life-
time of similar experiences are not helped by having life's
inconstancies repeated in the therapeutic experience. No
client, child or adult, should lose a worker more than once;
every effort should be made to prevent this. When a worker
leaves, the client should be transferred to a worker whose
history with the agency indicates there is less possibility of
leaving.

Parents have feelings similar to their child's when a
worker leaves. Although they are usually better able to
understand explanations, they may be as emotionally upset. When parents and child share the same worker, both
suffer the loss if the worker leaves. Parents are often comforted to know that they are not alone in their struggles to
help their child with problems. Thus their own loss may be
compounded by the loss of help with their child. When
parents and child have different workers and only one
worker leaves, either the parent or the child may feel sin-
gled out for punishment.

Parents should not hear that a worker is leaving, is
going on vacation, or is ill from their children. The worker
should communicate with the parents directly. Making alternate plans with the worker validates their parental rights
and enables them to cooperate in the child's treatment.

Transfers

Transferred clients are displaced people, moved around
they know not where. Administrative decisions are not

comprehensible to children; it is difficult for them to understand transfers that occur after an intake evaluation or because of workload. Children who see a former worker and do not understand the reasons for the transfer may view it as punishment. In all cases, it is helpful if the first worker facilitates the transfer by introducing the new worker and participating in one or two joint sessions. This enables children to see that both workers care about them and also connects the new with the old.

Although it is natural for children to say that things were much better in the past, this may be difficult for a new worker to hear. However, if the worker can listen to and accept the wistfulness, mourning, anger, and fantasies, children will have less fear of abandonment as punishment. This acceptance also validates feelings that too often are ignored, denied, or criticized by other important adults in the child's life. Knowing that these reactions are usual and expectable, children are freer to feel, and this propels treatment forward.

LEAVING

Although leaving differs from being left, the processes are similar in some ways. Affects of loss accompany all separations, even those that are a consequence of growth. When a client leaves, the therapist is left behind; the child terminates instead of being terminated.

Planning a Termination

It is always difficult to decide that a client has completed all the work that should be done. The question of when a client has finished is compounded by the ever changing needs of the child. Even if latency-age children are doing well, how well will they do in adolescence? Everyone knows how difficult adolescence can be, and few parents are sufficiently prepared to provide consistent help during this stage of development.

It is a sad reality that social workers rarely are equipped to be parental substitutes, nor can they be insurance policies for the future. There is no perfectly finished case, no perfect person, in or out of therapy.

In addition to having specific goals for individual children, general goals for latency-age children concern improving the child's natural abilities to engage in appropriate developmental tasks. Van Dam, Heinicke, and Shane (1975) caution that the disappearance of symptoms is not a reliable sign. Termination should stem from a multiple view of the child's functioning, supplemented by the fact that the child is now too busy for therapy. For example, latency-age children should be involved with peers, school, and other appropriate activities; child-parent interactions should be stabilized and in the main be helpful rather than detrimental. If children are terminated at this point, it may help them to shift their attention to objects outside the family and find sublimatory outlets.

The Process of Leaving

Children should participate in planning their termination, but their ambivalence will bring back old symptoms, defenses against the pain of separation, and some denial that treatment or the worker was important. It is difficult to grow up, and children may feel that support will be left behind, that they will be on their own, and all the good things they have acquired will be lost. Thus sufficient time is needed to make the termination period as therapeutic as earlier work. This period should be one of integration, of summing up what the child has accomplished, and what the future may hold. The following case illustrates how this can be done:

Marilyn, age 7, was referred because of her bizarre, uncontrollable behavior at home. She would have tantrums and rages and try to destroy things. She would pull down her panties, expose herself, and masturbate in front of her parents and siblings. Away from home, she was mute and frightened. Marilyn was seen for about a year, and during this time she never talked.

When Marilyn began in therapy, her worker gently showed her the toys that were available and allowed her to choose the ones she wanted. At first, only her eyes indicated what she wanted, and the therapist would give it to her. She kneaded clay, making different shapes, many of them long, snake-like forms. Later the shapes became animals. Eventually, Marilyn seemed interested in finger painting, and the worker set this up for her. Marilyn always played alone. From time to time, the worker would make a general comment that was relevant to the child's activity. Usually, the worker sat quietly and knitted while the child played. At the end of each session, the worker carefully put Marilyn's work away in a special place. Each time Marilyn came, she looked over these things and chose one to play with. Marilyn's mother reported much improvement at home. Marilyn had fewer tantrums and exposed herself less often. Of course, both parents were also in treatment at the same time, so their management improved at home.

At the end of the year, the family moved to another city and was prepared to continue treatment there. After making an appropriate referral, the worker helped the parents prepare Marilyn for this change. The worker told Marilyn that when she moved, she would see someone like the worker. During the last month, the worker counted off the number of times they still had together. Marilyn often looked at the worker as though reassuring herself of the worker's continued attention; she also communicated in this silent way. When Marilyn made these contacts, the worker always verbalized what seemed to be going on.

The last time they met, the worker reminded Marilyn that this was their last time together. Marilyn took from the closet all the things she had made and looked them over. When the worker remarked that she had done a lot of work, Marilyn began to make changes in many of the objects. The worker then noted that Marilyn had learned many things and maybe now there were things she wanted to do differently. Marilyn smiled. The worker said she thought that Marilyn would have a chance to do some things differently with the new worker and told Marilyn she could take home some of the things she had made. Marilyn chose some and returned the others to the closet. When the worker thanked her for leaving part of what she had made, Marilyn smiled again.

Marilyn needed much more work before she would be ready to give up therapeutic help. But as often happens with children, family circumstances dictated plans. In the process of leaving, even this mute child was helped to integrate the past and prepare for the future.

Children should participate as much as possible in planning the termination and deciding when would be the right time. Sometimes it is advisable to taper off by increasing the time between visits. It is often helpful to end before the summer vacation, especially if the child is going to camp. During the termination process, children can be helped to go to camp or to become involved in groups in their communities.

Allen (1964) suggests that termination should be viewed as a graduation and emphasize the positive aspects of the child's current activities. Children need to know that although they may not want to stop, they are ready to do so. In addition, they need to see how they are using what they have learned and that the unsatisfactory experiences of the past are over.

Looking Back

Although the giving and receiving of gifts is helpful in this final stage, the best gift is knowing that it is the child who is leaving and the worker who is staying behind. Children should know that returning is a possibility: "If you need me, I am here." This makes separation less permanent

(Ross, 1964). Allen (1964) suggests that this is similar to a follow-up.

Follow-up visits are often used after brief therapy or crisis intervention to give the client a sense of security and the agency an opportunity to evaluate the effect of therepy. Returning for a follow-up visit can be extremely helpful to a latency-age child. It often is advisable during the final visit to schedule a follow-up visit for only a few months later. Knowing the worker will be available often reduces children's tension and permits them to attend to the business of living. Knowing they can report back is a bridge into the future. It also implies that if they experience a crisis, have a problem, or need to talk things over, it may be possible to return for one visit or several visits. This is a step towards therapeutic prevention and a model geared to life.

This model of returning for help is taken for granted in the private therapy of children and adults. Knowing that one can return is reassuring enough to make the occurrence less necessary.

Agencies that have more clients than they can serve often limit the duration of treatment arbitrarily in an attempt to offer service to as many people as possible. This tends to leave all participants dissatisfied. The model of expected return, however, makes clients feel more certain that their needs will be met.

Parents too may feel more confident about the future knowing that there is a place they can come if new difficulties arise as the child grows older or if life brings new problems. Sometimes it is advisable for parents to continue in treatment after the child has stopped. This may be necessary because many parental problems are not related directly to the child. Continuation may also be a bridge and a partnership between worker and parent in the child's interest.

Some children have long histories of abandonment; their lives have never provided them with reliable objects.

This often pertains to foster children whose placements have not been stable. For them, parents, foster parents, and unfortunately even workers come and go. In these cases, the agency may have to assume forever the role of constant, dependable object. Although relating to a building or a large agency is less conducive to growth than is relating to a person, for some children only the agency and its building are permanent.

Dependency is an important determinant of behavior; it induces development when needs are met appropriately and subverts development when basic needs are not met. Social work intervention with any one child or any one adult cannot completely repair the damage caused by an inadequate environment. But everyone needs someone to turn to for support and comfort in time of need.

References

Abelin, E. L. The role of the father in the separation-individuation process. In J. B. McDevitt & C. F. Settlage (Eds.), *Separation individuation: Essays in honor of Margaret S. Mahler*. New York: International Universities Press, 1971.

Ackerman, N., Papp, P., & Prosky, P. Childhood disorders and interlocking pathology in family relationships. In E. J. Anthony & C. Koupernik (Eds.), *The child in his family*. New York: John Wiley & Sons, 1970.

Adams, P. L. *Obsessive children: A sociopsychiatric study*. New York: Brunner/Mazel, 1973.

Aleksandrowicz, M. The biological strangers: An attempted suicide of a seven-and-a-half-year-old girl. *Bulletin of the Menninger Clinic* 1975, **39**, 163–176.

Allen, F. H. Creation and handling of resistance in clinical practice. *American Journal of Orthopsychiatry*, 1934, **2**, 268–278.

Allen, F. H. The ending phase of therapy. In M. R. Haworth (Ed.), *Child psychotherapy*. New York: Basic Books, 1964.

Alpert, A. Reversibility of pathological fixations associated with maternal deprivation in infancy. *Psychoanalytic Study of the Child*, 1959, **14**, 169–185.

Alschuler, R. H. & Hattwick, L. W. *Painting and personality*. Chicago: University of Chicago Press, 1967.

Amster, F. Differential uses of play in treatment of young children. *American Journal of Orthopsychiatry,* 1943, **13,** 62–68.

Anthony, E. J. The mutative impact of serious mental and physical illness in a parent on family life. In Anthony & C. Koupernik (Eds.), *The child in his family,* Vol. 1. New York: John Wiley & Sons, 1970.

Anthony, E. J. An experimental approach to the psychopathology of childhood: Encopresis. In S. I. Harrison & J. F. McDermott (Eds.), *Childhood psychopathology.* New York: International Universities Press, 1972.

Anthony, E. J. Naturalistic studies of disturbed families. In Anthony (Ed.), *Explorations in child psychiatry.* New York: Plenum Press, 1975. (a)

Anthony, E. J. Childhood depression. In Anthony & T. Benedik (Eds.), *Depression and human existence.* Boston: Little, Brown, 1975. (b)

Appelberg, E. The dependent child and the changing worker. *Child Welfare,* 1969, **48,** 407–412.

Argelander, H. *The initial interview in psychotherapy.* New York: Human Sciences Press, 1976.

Arlow, J. A type of play observed in boys during the latency period. In J. B. McDevitt & C. F. Settlage (Eds.), *Separation-individuation: Essays in honor of Margaret S. Mahler.* New York: International Universities Press, 1971.

Arlow, J. A., & Kaydis, A. Finger painting in the psychotherapy of children. In C. E. Schaefer (Ed.), *Therapeutic use of child's play.* New York: Jason Aronson, 1976.

Arnold, E., & Smeltzer, D. J. Behavior checklist factor analysis for children and adolescents. *Archives of General Psychiatry,* 1974, **30,** 799–804.

Ashton, P. T. Cross-cultural Piagetian research: An experimental perspective. *Harvard Educational Review,* 1975, **45,** 457–506.

Axelrod, S. Comments on anthropology and the study of complex cultures. In W. Muensterberger, (Ed.), *Man and his culture.* New York: Taplinger Publishing, 1969.

Bachrach, H. Diagnosis as strategic understanding. *Bulletin of the Menninger Clinic,* 1974, **38,** 390–405.

Baird, M. Characteristic interaction patterns in families of encopretic children. *Bulletin of the Menninger Clinic,* 1974, **38,** 144–153.

Bank, S., & Kahn, M. D. Sisterhood-brotherhood is powerful: Sibling sub-systems and family therapy. In S. Chess & A. Thomas (Eds.), *Annual progress in child psychiatry and child development.* New York: Brunner/Mazel, 1976.

Beck, D. F., & Jones, M. A. *Progress on family problems.* New York: Family Service Association of America, 1973.

Becker, T. On latency. *Psychoanalytic Study of the Child,* 1974, **29**, 3–12.

Beiser, H. R. Discussion. *Journal of the American Academy of Child Psychiatry,* 1970, **9**, 171–174.

Bender, L., & Schilder, P. Suicidal preoccupations and attempts in children. *American Journal of Orthopsychiatry,* 1937, **2**, 225–233.

Benedek, T. The family as a psychologic field. In E. J. Anthony & T. Benedek (Eds.), *Parenthood: Its psychology and psychopathology.* Boston: Little, Brown, 1970.

Benjamin, L. S., Stover, D. O., Geppert, T. V., Pizer, E. F., & Burdy, J. The relative importance of psychopathology, training procedure and urological pathology in nocturnal enuresis. *Child Psychiatry and Human Development,* 1971, **1**, 215–232.

Berecz, J. M. Phobias of childhood: Etiology and treatment. In S. Chess & A. Thomas (Eds.), *Annual progress in child psychiatry and child development.* New York: Brunner/Mazel, 1969.

Berger, A. S., & Simon, W. Sexual behavior in adolescent males. In S. C. Feinstein & P. Giovacchini (Eds.), *Adolescent psychiatry,* Vol. 4. New York: Jason Aronson, 1975.

Berger, M., & Kennedy, H. Pseudobackwardness in children: Maternal attitudes as an etiological factor. *Psychoanalytic Study of the Child,* 1975, **30**, 279–306.

Bibring, E. The mechanism of depression. In P. Greenacre (Ed.), *Affective disorders.* New York: International Universities Press, 1953.

Billingsley, A. Family functioning in the low-income black community. *Social Casework,* 1969, **50**, 563–572.

Bixler, R. Limits are therapy. In M. R. Haworth (Ed.), *Child psychotherapy.* New York, Basic Books, 1964.

Blaydon, C. C., & Stack, C. B. Income support policies and the family. *Daedalus,* Spring 1977, 147–161.

Blinder, B. J. Sibling death in childhood. *Child Psychiatry and Human Development,* 1972, **2**, 169–175.

Bloch, E. L., & Goodstein, L. D. Functional speech disorders and personality: A decade of research. In S. Chess & A. Thomas (Eds.), *Annual progress in child psychiatry and child development.* New York: Brunner/Mazel, 1972.

Blos, P. Comments on the psychological consequences of cryptorchism: A case study. *Psychoanalytic Study of the Child,* 1960, **15**, 395–429.

Blos, P. *On adolescence.* New York: Free Press, 1962.

Blos, P. The initial stages of male adolescence. *Psychoanalytic Study of the Child,* 1965, **20**, 145–164.

Blos, P. The second individuation process of adolescence. *Psychoanalytic Study of the Child*, 1967, **22**, 162–186.

Blos, P. *The young adolescent.* New York: Free Press, 1970.

Bornstein, B. Emotional barriers in the understanding and treatment of young children. *American Journal of Orthopsychiatry*, 1948, **18**, 691–697.

Bornstein, B. Masturbation in the latency child. *Psychoanalytic Study of the Child*, 1953, **8**, 65–78.

Bornstein, B. On latency. *Psychoanalytic Study of the Child*, 1951, **6**, 279–285.

Bowlby, J. Grief and mourning in infancy and early childhood. *Psychoanalytic Study of the Child*, 1960, **15**, 9–52.

Brant, R. S., & Tisza, V. The sexually misused child. *American Journal of Orthopsychiatry*, 1977, **47**, 80–91.

Bruch, H. The role of the parent in psychotherapy with children. *Psychiatry*, 1948, **11**, 169–175.

Bruch, H. Family background in eating disorders. In E. J. Anthony & C. Koupernik (Eds.), *The child in his family*, Vol. 1. New York: John Wiley & Sons, 1970.

Bruch, H. The constructive use of ignorance. In E. J. Anthony (Ed.), *Explorations in child psychiatry.* New York: Plenum Press, 1975.

Bruner, J. S., & Sherwood, V. *Peekaboo and the learning of rule structures.* In Bruner, A. Jolly, & K. Sylva (Eds.), *Play.* New York: Basic Books, 1976.

Buxbaum, E. The latency period. *American Journal of Orthopsychiatry*, 1951, **21**, 182–198.

Buxbaum, E. Technique of child therapy. *Psychoanalytic Study of the Child*, 1954, **9**, 297–333.

Buxbaum, E. Hair pulling and fetishism. *Psychoanalytic Study of the Child*, 1960, **15**, 243–260.

Buxbaum, E. The parents' role in the etiology of learning disabilities. *Psychoanalytic Study of the Child*, 1964, **19**, 421–447.

Buxbaum, E. *Troubled children in a troubled world.* New York: International Universities Press, 1970.

Campbell, J. D. Peer relations in childhood. In M. L. Hoffman & L. W. Hoffman (Eds.), *Review of child development research*, Vol. 1. New York: Russell Sage Foundation, 1964.

Chapman, M. Salient needs: A casework compass. *Social Work*, 1977, **58**, 343–349.

Chess, S. Marked anxiety in children. *American Journal of Psychotherapy*, 1973, **17**, 390–396.

Chess, S., & Hassibi, M. Behavior deviation in mentally retarded children. *Journal of the American Academy of Child Psychiatry,* 1970, **9**, 282–297.

Chethik, M. Amy: The intensive treatment of an elective mute. *Journal of the American Academy of Child Psychiatry,* 1973, **12**, 482–499.

Cohen, N. *Social work in the American tradition.* New York: Holt, Rinehart & Winston, 1958.

Cole, S. O. Hyperkinetic children: The use of stimulant drugs evaluated. *American Journal of Orthopsychiatry,* 1975, **45**, 28–37.

Coles, R. Violence in ghetto children. *Children,* 1967, **14**, 101–104.

Colm, H. Phobias in children. In H. S. Strean (Ed.), *Approaches in child guidance.* Metuchen, N.J.: Scarecrow Press, 1970.

Comer, J. The black American child in school. In E. J. Anthony & C. Koupernik (Eds.), *The child in his family,* Vol. 3. New York: John Wiley & Sons, 1974.

Connor, F. P., Hoover, R., Horton, K., Sands, H., Sternfeld, L., & Wolinsky, G. F. Physical and sensory handicaps. In N. Hobbs (Ed.), *Issues in the classification of children,* Vol. 1. San Francisco: Jossey-Bass, 1975.

Coolidge, J. C., & Brodie, R. D. Observations of mothers of 49 school phobic children. *Journal of the American Academy of Child Psychiatry,* 1974, **13**, 275–285.

Coolidge, J., Tessman, E., Waldfogel, S., & Willer, M. L. Patterns of aggression in school phobia. *Psychoanalytic Study of the Child,* 1962, **17**, 319–333.

Cytryn, L., & McKnew, J. Proposed classification of childhood depression. *American Journal of Psychiatry,* 1972, **129**, 149–155.

Davis, I. Advice-giving in parent counseling. *Social Casework,* 1975, **56**, 343–347.

Deutsch, C. Social class and child development. In B. M. Caldwell & H. N. Ricciuti (Eds.), *Review of child development and social policy,* Vol. 3. Chicago: University of Chicago Press, 1973.

Deutsch, F. The application of psychoanalysis to psychosomatic concepts. In M. Heiman (Ed.), *Psychoanalysis and social work.* New York: International Universities Press, 1953.

Deutsch, M. Happenings on the way back to the forum. *Harvard Educational Review,* 1969, **39**, 523–557.

DeVries, R. Relationship among Piagetian IQ and achievement assessment. *Child Development,* 1974, **45**, 746–756.

DiLeo, J. H. *Young children and their drawings.* New York: Brunner/Mazel, 1970.

Dowling, A. S. Psychosomatic disorders of childhood. In S. L. Copel (Ed.), *Behavior pathology of childhood and adolescence.* New York: Basic Books, 1973.

Dudek, S. Z., & Lester, E. P. The good child facade in chronic underachievers. *American Journal of Orthopsychiatry,* 1968, **38,** 153–160.

Ekstein, R., & Friedman, S. W. A technical problem in the beginning phase of psychotherapy with a borderline psychotic child. In G. E. Gardner (Ed.), *Case studies in childhood emotional disabilities,* Vol. 2. New York: American Orthopsychiatric Association, 1956.

Ekstein, R., & Friedman, S. The function of acting out, play action and play acting in the psychotherapeutic process. In Ekstein (Ed.), *Children of time and space, of action and impulse.* New York: Appleton-Century-Crofts, 1966.

Ekstein, R., & Wallerstein, J. Observations in the psychotherapy of borderline and psychotic children. *Psychoanalytic Study of the Child,* 1956, **11,** 303–311.

Ekstein, R., & Wallerstein, J. Choice of interpretation in the treatment of borderline and psychotic children. In Ekstein (Ed.), *Children of time and space, of action and impulse.* New York: Appleton-Century-Crofts, 1966.

Enzer, N., & Stackhouse, J. A child guidance approach to the multi-problem family. *American Journal of Orthopsychiatry,* 1968, **38,** 527–538.

Erikson, E. Sex differences in the play configurations of pre-adolescents. *American Journal of Orthopsychiatry,* 1951, **21,** 66–67.

Erikson, E. Growth and crises of the healthy personality. In C. Kluckhohn, H. A. Murray, & D. M. Schneider (Eds.), *Personality in nature, society, and culture.* New York: Alfred A. Knopf, 1953.

Erikson, E. *Childhood and society.* (2nd ed.) New York: W. W. Norton, 1963.

Erikson, E. *Identity, youth and crisis.* New York: W. W. Norton & Co., 1968.

Erikson, E. Play and actuality. In M. Piers (Ed.), *Play and development.* New York: W. W. Norton, 1972.

Erikson, K. T. *Everything in its path: Destruction of community in the Buffalo Creek flood.* New York: Simon & Schuster, 1976.

Esman, A. H. Nocturnal enuresis: Some current concepts. *Journal of the American Academy of Child Psychiatry,* 1977, **16,** 150–158.

Essman, C. S. Sibling relations as socialization for parenthood. *Family Coordinator,* 1977, **26,** 259–262.

Evans, N. S. Mourning as a family secret. *Journal of the American Academy of Child Psychiatry,* 1976, **15,** 502–509.

Ewalt, P., & Kutz, J. An examination of advice giving as a therapeutic intervention. *Smith College Studies in Social Work,* 1976, **47,** 3–19.

Fanshel, D., & Shinn, E. B. *Dollars and sense in the foster care of children: A look at cost factors.* New York: Child Welfare League of America, 1972.

Fanshel, D., & Shinn, E. *Children in foster care.* New York: Columbia University Press, 1977.

Feldman, Y. A casework approach toward understanding parents of emotionally disturbed children. *Social Work,* 1958, **3** (3), 23–29.

Feldman, Y. Listening and understanding. *Clinical Social Work Journal,* 1975, **3,** 85–89.

Fenichel, O. *The psychoanalytic theory of the neurosis.* New York: W. W. Norton, 1945.

Foster, R. M. Intrapsychic and environmental factors in running away from home. *American Journal of Orthopsychiatry,* 1962, **32,** 486–491.

Fraiberg, S. A therapeutic approach to reactive ego disturbances in children in placement. *American Journal of Orthopsychiatry,* 1962, **32,** 18–31.

Fraiberg, S. The origins of identity. *Smith College Studies in Social Work,* 1968, **38,** 79–101.

Fraiberg, S. Some characteristics of genital arousal and discharge in latency girls. *Psychoanalytic Study of the Child,* 1972, **27,** 439–475.

Fraiberg, S., Adelson, E., & Shapiro, V. Ghosts in the nursery. *Journal of the American Academy of Child Psychiatry,* 1975, **14,** 387–421.

Frank, M. C. Modifications of activity group therapy: Response to ego-impoverished children. *Clinical Social Work Journal,* 1976, **4,** 102–109.

Frankl, L. Self-preservation and the development of accident proneness in children and adolescents. *Psychoanalytic Study of the Child,* 1963, **18,** 464–483.

Freud, A. *The ego and the mechanisms of defense.* New York: International Universities Press, 1936.

Freud, A. The role of bodily illness in the mental life of children. *Psychoanalytic Study of the Child,* 1952, **7,** 69–81.

Freud, A. The concept of developmental lines. *Psychoanalytic Study of the Child,* 1963, **18,** 245–265.

Freud, A. *Normality and pathology in childhood.* New York: International Universities Press, 1965.

Freud, A. *The writings of Anna Freud,* Vol. 4. New York: International Universities Press, 1968. (a)

Freud, A. *The writings of Anna Freud,* Vol. 5. New York: International Universities Press, 1968. (b)

Freud, A. The symptomatology of childhood: A preliminary attempt at classification. *Psychoanalytic Study of the Child*, 1970, **25**, 19–44.

Freud, S. 1909 (a). Analysis of a phobia in a five year old boy. In J. Ernest (Ed.), *Collected papers*, Vol. 3. New York: Basic Books, 1955.

Freud, S. 1909 (b). Family romance. In J. Ernest (Ed.), *Collected papers*, Vol. 5. New York: Basic Books, 1955.

Freud, S 1917 Mourning and melancholia. In J. Ernest (Ed.), *Collected papers*, Vol 4. New York: Basic Books, 1955.

Fuller J. S. Duo therapy. *Journal of the American Academy of Child Psychiatry*, 1977 **16**, 469–476.

Furman, E. *A child's parent dies*. New Haven, Conn.: Yale University Press, 1974.

Futterman, E. H., & Hoffman, I. Crisis and adaptation in the families of fatally ill children. In E. J. Anthony & C. Koupernik (Eds.), *The child in his family*, Vol. 2. New York: John Wiley & Sons, 1970.

Galdston, R. Mind over matter: Observation on 50 patients hospitalized with anorexia nervosa. *Journal of the American Academy of Child Psychiatry*, 1974, **13**, 246–263.

Galenson, E. A consideration of the nature of thought in childhood play. In J. B. McDevitt & C. F. Settlage (Eds.), *Separation-individuation: Essays in honor of Margaret S. Mahler*. New York: International Universities Press, 1971.

Ganter, G., Yeakel, M., & Polansky, N. A. *Retrieval from limbo: The intermediary group treatment of inaccessible children*. New York: Child Welfare League of America, 1967.

Gardner, R. *Therapeutic communication with children: The mutual storytelling technique*. New York: Jason Aronson, 1971.

Gerard, M. Psychogenic tics in ego development. *Psychoanalytic Study of the Child*, 1947, **2**, 133–161.

Gerard, M. Enuresis: A study in etiology. In *The emotionally disturbed child*. New York: Child Welfare League of America, 1957.

Giarretto, H. The treatment of father-daughter incest: A psychosocial approach. *Children Today*, 1976, **5**, 4.

Gil, D. Unraveling child abuse. *American Journal of Orthopsychiatry*, 1975, **45**, 346–356.

Gilpin, D. C. Psychotherapy of the oppositional child. In E. J. Anthony (Ed.), *Three clinical faces of childhood*. New York: Spectrum Publishers, 1976.

Gittelman-Klein, R., & Klein, D. School phobia: Diagnostic considerations in the light of imipramine effects. In Klein & Gittelman-Klein (Eds.), *Progress in psychiatric drug treatment*. New York: Brunner/Mazel, 1975.

Glaser, K. Masked depression in children and adolescents. *Journal of Psychotherapy*, 1967, **21**, 565–574.

Glaser, K. Suicidal children—management. *American Journal of Psychotherapy*, 1971, **25**, 27–36.

Glaser, P., & Navarre, E. Structural problems of the one-parent family. *Journal of Social Issues*, 1965, **21**, 98–109.

Glick, J. Cognitive development in cross-cultural perspective. In F. D. Horowitz (Ed.), *Child development research*. Chicago: University of Chicago Press, 1975.

Goffman, E. *Stigma: Notes on the management of strained identity*. Englewood Cliffs, N.J.: Prentice-Hall, 1963.

Golan, N. Crisis theory. In F. J. Turner (Ed.), *Social work treatment: Interlocking theoretical approaches*. New York: Free Press, 1974.

Goldings, H. Jump-rope rhymes and the rhythm of latency development in girls. *Psychoanalytic Study of the Child*, 1974, **29**, 431–450.

Gondor, L. Use of fantasy communications in child psychotherapy. In M. R. Haworth (Ed.), *Child psychotherapy*. New York: Basic Books, 1964.

Goode, W. J. Force and violence in the family. *Journal of Marriage and the Family*, 1971, **33**, 624–636.

Gottesfeld, H. Tests as predictors of behavior. *Year Book: New Jersey Secondary School Teachers' Association*, 1966, 53–55.

Gottesfeld, H. *In loco parentis*. New York: Jewish Child Care Association of New York, 1970.

Greenacre, P. Differences between male and female adolescence: Sexual development as seen from longitudinal studies. In S. C. Feinstein & P. Giovacchini (Eds.), *Adolescent psychiatry*, Vol. 4. New York: Jason Aronson, 1975.

Greenberg, L. M., & Stephans, J. H. Use of drugs in special syndromes: Enuresis, tics, school refusal, and anorexia nervosa. In J. M. Wiener (Ed.), *Psychopharmacology in childhood and adolescence*. New York: Basic Books, 1977.

Grinspoon, L., & Singer, S. B. Amphetamines in the treatment of hyperkinetic children. *Harvard Educational Review*, 1973, **43**, 515–555.

Group for the Advancement of Psychiatry. *Psychopathological disorders in childhood: Theoretical considerations and a proposed classification*, Report No. 620. New York: Author, 1966.

Group for the Advancement of Psychiatry. *The field of family therapy*, Report No. 78. New York: Author, 1970.

Group for the Advancement of Psychiatry. *From diagnosis to treatment: Planning for the emotionally disturbed child*, Report No. 87. New York: Author, 1973.

Guttman, H. A. The child's participation in conjoint family therapy. *Journal of the American Academy of Child Psychiatry*, 1975, **14**, 490–499.

Hallowitz, D. Individual treatment of the child in the context of family therapy. *Social casework*, 1966, **47**, 82–86.

Hallowitz, D., & Cutter, A. V. A collaborative diagnostic treatment process with parents. *Social Work*, 1958, **3**, 90–95.

Halpern, W., Hammond, J., & Cohen, R. A therapeutic approach to speech phobia: Elective mutism reexamined. *Journal of the American Academy of Child Psychiatry*, 1971, **11**, 94–107.

Hamilton, G. *Psychotherapy in child guidance.* New York: Columbia University Press, 1963

Harley, M. Some reflections on identity problems in prepuberty. In J. B. McDevitt & C. F. Settlage (Eds.), *Separation-individuation: Essays in honor of Margaret S. Mahler.* New York: International Universities Press, 1971.

Harlow, H. F., & Harlow, M. Learning to love. *American Scientist*, 1966, **54**, 244–272.

Harre, R. The conditions for a social psychology of childhood. In M. P. M. Richards (Ed.), *The integration of a child into a social world.* London: Cambridge University Press, 1974.

Harris, O. C. Day care: Have we forgotten the school-age child? *Child Welfare*, 1977, **56**, 440–448.

Hartmann, H. *Ego psychology and the problem of adaptation.* New York: International Universities Press, 1958.

Hartmann, H. Developmental psychology. In Hartmann (Ed.), *Essays on ego psychology.* New York: International Universities Press, 1964.

Hartrup, W. W. Peer interaction and social organization. In P. H. Mussen (Ed.), *Carmichael's manual of child psychology*, Vol. 2. New York: John Wiley & Sons, 1970.

Haworth, M. R. Limits and the handling of aggression. In Haworth (Ed.), *Child psychotherapy.* New York: Basic Books, 1964.

Herzog, E., & Lewis, H. Children in poor families: Myths and realities. *American Journal of Orthopsychiatry*, 1970, **40**, 375–387.

Herzog, E., & Sudin, C. Family structure and composition: Research considerations. *In Race, research and reason: Social work perspectives.* New York: National Association of Social Workers, 1969.

Hirsch, K. de. Speech and language disturbances. In A. M. Freedman & H. I. Kaplan (Eds.), *The child: His psychological and cultural development*, Vol. 1. New York: Atheneum Press, 1972.

Hirsch, K. de. Language deficits in children with developmental lags. *Psychoanalytic Study of the Child*, 1975, **30**, 95–126.

Hoag, J. M., Noriss, N. G., Himeno, E. T., & Jacobs, J. The encopretic child and his family. *Journal of the American Academy of Child Psychiatry,* 1971, **10,** 242–256.

Hobbs, N. *The futures of children.* San Francisco: Jossey-Bass, 1975.

Hollis, F. Casework: *A psychosocial therapy.* New York: Random House, 1964.

Humphrey, I. L., Knipstein, R., & Bumpass, E. R. Gradually developing aphasia in children. *Journal of the American Academy of Child Psychiatry,* 1975, **14,** 652–665.

Jacobson, E. Superego formation and the period of latency. In Jacobson, *The self and the object world.* New York: International Universities Press, 1964.

Jacobson, E. The return of the lost parent. In M. Schur (Ed.), *Drives, affects and behavior,* Vol. 2. New York: International Universities Press, 1965.

Jacobson, E. A special response to early object loss. In Jacobson, *Depression.* New York: International Universities Press, 1971.

Jenkins, S., & Norman, E. *Filial deprivation and foster care.* New York: Columbia University Press, 1972.

Jenkins, S., & Norman, E. *Beyond placement: Mothers view foster care.* New York: Columbia Press, 1975.

Jensen, A. R. How much can we boost IQ and scholastic achievement? *Harvard Educational Review,* 1969, **39,** 1–123.

Jessner, L., Blom, G. E., & Waldfogel, S. Emotional implications of tonsillectomy and adenoidectomy in children. *Psychoanalytic Study of the Child,* 1952, **7,** 126–169.

Johnson, A. M. Collaborative psychotherapy: Team setting. In M. Heiman (Ed.), *Psychoanalysis and social work.* New York: International Universities Press, 1953.

Johnson, A., Falstein, E. I., Szurek, S. A., & Svendesen, M. School phobia. *American Journal of Orthopsychiatry,* 1941, **11,** 702–711.

Johnson, A., & Giffen, M. E. Some applications of psychoanalytic insights to the socialization of children. *American Journal of Orthopsychiatry,* 1957, **27,** 462–474.

Johnson, A., Szurek, S., & Falstein, E. Collaborative psychiatric therapy of parent-child problems. *American Journal of Orthopsychiatry,* 1942, **12,** 511–516.

Joint Commission on Mental Health of Children. *Report of crisis in child mental health.* New York: Harper & Row, 1969.

Justice, B., & Justice, R. *The abusing family.* New York: Human Sciences Press, 1976.

Kagan, J. Acquisition and significance of sex typing and sex role identity. In M. L. Hoffman & L. W. Hoffman (Eds.), *Review of child development research*, Vol. 1. New York: Russell Sage Foundation, 1964.

Kagan, J. Inadequate evidence and illogical conclusions. *Harvard Educational Review*, 1969, **39**, 274–277.

Kagan, J. The psychological requirements for human development. In N. B. Talbot (Ed.), *Raising children in modern America.* Boston: Little, Brown & Co., 1976.

Kagan, J. The child in the family. *Daedalus*, Spring 1977, 33–56.

Kahn, J. H., & Nursten, J. P. School refusal: A comprehensive view of school phobia and other failures of school attendance. *American Journal of Orthopsychiatry*, 1962, **32**, 707–718.

Kamerman, S., & Kahn, A. J. *Social services in the United States.* Philadelphia: Temple University Press, 1976.

Kamin, L. J. The science and politics of IQ. *Social Research*, 1974, **41**, 387–425.

Kanner, L. The children haven't read those books: Reflections on differential diagnosis. In S. Chess & A. Thomas (Eds.), *Annual progress in child psychiatry and child development.* New York: Brunner/Mazel, 1970.

Kaplan, E. B. Reflections regarding psychomotor activities during the latency period. *Psychoanalytic Study of the Child*, 1965, **20**, 220–338.

Kaplan, S. L., & Escoll, Philip. Treatment of two silent adolescent girls. *Journal of the American Academy of Child Psychiatry*, 1973, **12**, 59–72.

Kaplan, S. L., & Poznanski, E. Child psychiatric patients who share a bed with a parent. *Journal of the American Academy of Child Psychiatry*, 1974, **13**, 344–356.

Katan, A. Some thoughts about the role of verbalization in early childhood. *Psychoanalytic Study of the Child*, 1961, **16**, 184–186.

Kay, P. Psychoanalytic theory of development in childhood and preadolescence. In B. W. Wolman (Ed.), *Handbook of child psychoanalysis.* New York: Van Nostrand Reinhold, 1972.

Kaydis, A. L., Krasner, J. D., Wiener, M. F., and Foulkes, S. H. *Practicum of group psychotherapy.* (2nd ed.) Hagerstown, Md.: Harper & Row, 1974.

Keith-Lucas, A. Ethics in social work. In *Encyclopedia of social work*, Vol. 1. New York: National Association of Social Workers, 1971.

Kellam, S. G., Branch, J. D., Agoawal, K., & Ensminger, M. E. *Mental health and going to school.* Chicago: University of Chicago Press, 1975.

Kelly, J. B., & Wallerstein, J. S. The effects of parental divorce: Experiences of the child in early latency. *American Journal of Orthopsychiatry*, 1976, **46**, 20–32.

Kestenberg, J. *Children and parents: Psychoanalytic studies in development.* New York: Jason Aronson, 1975.

Kissel, S., & Arkins, V. Anorexia nervosa reexamined. *Child Psychiatry and Human Development,* 1973, **3**, 255–263.

Kleeman, J. A. The peek-a-boo game: Part I. Its origins, meanings and related phenomena in the first year. *Psychoanalytic Study of the Child,* 1967, **22**, 239–274.

Klein, E. Psychoanalytic aspects of school problems. *Psychoanalytic Study of the Child,* 1949, **3–4**, 369–390.

Kolansky, H. Some psychoanalytic considerations on speech in normal development and psychopathology. *Psychoanalytic Study of the Child,* 1967, **22**, 274–295.

Koupernik, C. The roots of hypochondriasis. In E. J. Anthony & C. Koupernik (Eds.), *The child in his family,* Vol. 2. New York: John Wiley & Sons, 1973.

Krugman, D. C. Working with separation. *Child Welfare,* 1971, **50**, 528–537.

Lackie, B. Mahler applied. *Clinical Social Work Journal,* 1975, **3**, 24–31.

Lamont, J. H. Interpretation in therapy with children. *Smith College Studies in Social Work,* 1958, **28**, 139–150.

Lane, H. *The wild boy of Aveyron.* Cambridge, Mass.: Harvard University Press, 1976.

La Vietes, R. L. Crisis intervention for ghetto children: Contraindications and alternative considerations. *American Journal of Orthopsychiatry,* 1974, **44**, 720–727.

Lebovicci, S. Children who torture and kill. In E. J. Anthony & C. Koupernik (Eds.), *The child in his family,* Vol. 2. New York: John Wiley & Sons, 1973.

Lester, D. Self-mutilating behavior. *Psychology Bulletin,* 1972, **78**, 119–128.

Le Vine, R. A. *Culture, behavior and personality.* Chicago: Aldine Publishing Co., 1973.

Levinson, H. Termination of psychotherapy: Some salient ideas. *Social Casework,* 1977, **58**, 480–489.

Levitt, M., & Rubinstein, B. O. The fate of advice: Examples of distortion in parental counseling. *Mental Hygiene,* 1957, **41**, 213–216.

Lewis, M. The latency child in a custody conflict. *Journal of the American Academy of Child Psychiatry,* 1974, **13**, 635–646.

Lewis, M. Transitory or pseudo-organicity and borderline personality in a 7-year-old child. *Journal of the American Academy of Child Psychiatry,* 1976, **15**, 131–138.

Lidz, T. *The person.* New York: Basic Books, 1968.

Lieberman, F. Transition from latency to prepuberty in girls: An activity group becomes an interview group. *International Journal of Group Psychotherapy,* 1964, **14,** 455–464.

Lieberman, F., & Gottesfeld, M. L. The repulsive client. *Clinical Social Work Journal,* 1973, **1,** 22–31.

Lieberman, F., & Taylor, S. S. Combined group and individual treatment of a schizophrenic child. *Social Casework,* 1965, **46,** 80–85.

Liebman, R., Minuchin, S., & Baker, L. The role of the family in the treatment of anorexia nervosa. *Journal of the American Academy of Child Psychiatry,* 1974, **13,** 264–274.

Lindemann, E. Symptomatology and management of acute grief. In H. J. Parad (Ed.), *Crisis intervention: Selected readings.* New York: Family Service Association of America, 1965.

Littner, N. *Some traumatic effects of separation and placement.* New York: Child Welfare League of America, 1956.

Littner, N. Violence as a symptom of childhood emotional illness. *Child Welfare,* 1972, **51,** 208–219.

Long, H. Parents' reports of undesirable behavior in children. *Child Development,* 1941, **12,** 43–62.

Loof, D. H. Psychophysiologic and conversion reactions in children. *Journal of the American Academy of Child Psychiatry,* 1970, **9,** 318–331.

Loomis, E. The use of checkers in handling certain resistances in child therapy and child analysis. *Journal of the American Psychoanalytic Association,* 1957, **5,** 130–135.

Love, S., & Mayer, H. Going along with the defenses in resistant families. *Social Casework,* 1959, **40,** 69–74.

Lubove, R. *The professional altruist.* Cambridge, Mass.: Harvard University Press, 1965.

Lystad, M. *A child's world.* Publication No. 74-118. Rockville, Md.: National Institute of Mental Health, 1974.

Lystad, M. Violence at home: A review of the literature. *American Journal of Orthopsychiatry,* 1975, **45,** 328–345.

Maccoby, E. E., & Jacklin, C. N. *The psychology of sex differences.* Stanford, Calif.: Stanford University Press, 1974.

Maclennan, B. Modifications of activity group therapy for children. *International Journal of Group Psychotherapy,* 1977, **27,** 85–96.

Mahler, M. A psychoanalytic evaluation of tic in psychopathology of children: Symptomatic and tic syndrome. *Psychoanalytic Study of the Child,* 1949, **3–4,** 279–310.

Mahler, M. Thoughts about development and individuation. *Psychoanalytic Study of the Child,* 1963, **18,** 307–324.

Mahler, M. A study of the separation-individuation process. *Psychoanalytic Study of the Child,* 1971, **26,** 403–424.

Mahler, M. S., Pine, F., & Bergman, A. *The psychological birth of the human infant.* New York: Basic Books, 1975.

Malmquist, C. P. Depression in childhood and adolescence. In S. Chess & A. Thomas (Eds.), *Annual progress in child psychiatry and child development.* New York: Brunner/Mazel, 1972.

Malone, C. A. Some observations on children of disorganized families and problems of acting out. In E. Rexford (Ed.), *A developmental approach to problems of acting out.* Monograph No. 1. New York: Journal of the American Academy of Child Psychiatry, 1966.

Malone, C. A. Developmental deviations considered in the light of environmental forces. In E. Pavenstedt (Ed.), *The drifters.* Boston: Little, Brown, 1967.

Mann, J. *Time-limited psychotherapy.* Cambridge, Mass.: Harvard University Press, 1973.

Martino, M. S., & Newman, M. B. Siblings of retarded children: A population at risk. *Child Psychiatry and Human Development,* 1974, **4,** 168–177.

Mattsson, A., Seese, L. R., & Hawkins, J. W. Suicidal behavior as a child psychiatric emergency: Clinical characteristics and follow-up result. *Archives of General Psychiatry,* 1969, **20,** 100–109.

McDermott, J. F., & Char, W. F. The undeclared war between child and family therapy. *Journal of the American Academy of Child Psychiatry* 1974, **13,** 422–436.

McDonald, M. *Not by the color of their skin.* New York: International Universities Press, 1970.

McLaughlin, M. M. Survivors and surrogates: Children and parents from the ninth to the thirteenth centuries. In L. de Mause (Ed.), *The history of childhood.* New York: Psychohistory Press, 1974.

Meeks, J. E. Children who cheat at games. *Journal of the American Academy of Child Psychiatry,* 1970, **9,** 157–174.

Meers, D. Contributions of a ghetto culture to symptom formation. *Psychoanalytic Study of the Child,* 1970, **25,** 209–230.

Meers, D. Precocious heterosexuality and masturbation: Sexuality in the ghetto. In I. M. Marcus & J. I. Francis (Eds.), *Masturbation from infancy to senescence.* New York: International Universities Press, 1975.

Mendelson, M. *Psychoanalytic concepts of depression.* New York: Spectrum Publications, 1974.

Millar, S. *The psychology of play.* New York: Jason Aronson, 1974.

Millar, T. Peptic ulcers in children. In J. C. Howells (Ed.), *Modern perspectives in international child psychiatry.* New York: Brunner/Mazel, 1971.

Miller, D. *Adolescence: Psychology, psychopathology and psychotherapy.* New York: Jason Aronson, 1974.

Miller, J. B. M. Children's reactions to the death of a parent: A review of the psychoanalytic literature. *Journal of the American Psychoanalytic Association,* 1971, **19**, 697–719.

Miller, R. R. Disappointments in therapy: A paradox. *Clinical Social Work Journal,* 1977, **5**, 17–28.

Miller, S. M., & Mishler, E. G. Social class, mental illness, and American psychiatry: An expository review. In F. Riessman, J. Cohen, & A. Pearl (Eds.), *Mental health of the poor.* Glencoe, Ill.: Free Press, 1964.

Minuchin, S. The use of an ecological framework in the treatment of a child. In E. J. Anthony & C. Koupernik (Eds.), *The child in his family,* Vol. 1. New York: John Wiley & Sons, 1970.

Minuchin, S., Montalvo, B., Guerney, B., Rosman, B. L., & Schumer, F. *Families of the slums.* New York: Basic Books, 1967.

Mitchell, C. A. Duo therapy: An innovative approach to the treatment of children. *Smith College Studies in Social Work,* 1976, **46**, 236–247.

Mittelman, B. Motility in the therapy of children and adults. *Psychoanalytic Study of the Child,* 1957, **12**, 284–319.

Mizio, E. Impact of external systems on the Puerto Rican family. *Social Casework,* 1974, **55**, 76–83.

Moore, J. G. Yo-yo children—victims of matrimonial violence. *Child Welfare,* 1975, **54**, 557–566.

Moore, W. T. The impact of surgery on boys. *Psychoanalytic Study of the Child,* 1975, **30**, 529–548.

Moustakas, C. *Children in play therapy.* New York: Jason Aronson, 1973.

Murphy, L. B. Problems in recognizing emotional disturbance in children. *Child Welfare,* 1963, **42**, 473–487.

Murphy, L. B. Longterm foster care and its influence on adjustment in adult life. In J. E. Anthony & C. Koupernik (Eds.), *The child in his family,* Vol. 3. New York: John Wiley & Sons 1974.

Nagelberg, L., & Spotnitz, H. Strengthening the ego through the release of frustration-aggression. *American Journal of Orthopsychiatry,* 1958, **28**, 794–801.

Nagelberg, L., Spotnitz, H., & Feldman, Y. The attempt at healthy insulation in the withdrawn child. *American Journal of Orthopsychiatry,* 1953, **23**, 238–251.

Nagera, H. *Early childhood disturbances, the infantile neuroses and the adult disturbances.* New York: International Universities Press, 1966. (a)

Nagera, H. Sleep and its disturbances approached developmentally. *Psychoanalytic Study of the Child,* 1966, 21, 393–447. (b)

National Council of Organizations for Children and Youth. *America's children,* 1976. Washington, D.C.: Author, 1976.

National Institute of Child Health and Human Development. *Perspectives on human deprivation: Biological, psychological and sociological.* Washington, D.C.: U.S. Department of Health, Education & Welfare, 1968.

National Institute of Mental Health. *Child abuse and neglect programs: Practice and theory.* Washington, D.C.: U.S. Department of Health, Education & Welfare, 1977.

National Research Council, Advisory Committee on Child Development, Assembly of Behavioral and Social Sciences. *Toward a national policy for children and families.* Washington, D.C.: National Academy of Sciences, 1976.

Neubauer, P. Review of Augusta Alpert's corrective object relations program. *Psychosocial Process,* **1,** 1970, 7–13.

Neubauer, P. Early sexual differences and development. In E. Adelson (Ed.), *Sexuality and psychoanalysis.* New York: Brunner/Mazel, 1975.

Newberger, E. H. Child abuse and neglect: Toward a firmer foundation for practice and policy. *American Journal of Orthopsychiatry,* 1977, **47,** 374–376.

Newman, C. J., Dember, C. F., & Krug, O. He can but he won't: A psychodynamic study of so-called gifted underachievers. *Psychoanalytic Study of the Child,* 1973, **28,** 83–130.

Norlin, J., & Ho, M. K. A co-worker approach to working with families. *Clinical Social Work Journal,* 1974, **2,** 127–134.

Offer, D., & Vanderstoep, E. Indications and contraindications for family therapy. In S. C. Feinstein & P. Giovacchini (Eds.), *Adolescent psychiatry,* Vol. 3. New York: Basic Books, 1974.

Olden, C. On adult empathy with children. *Psychoanalytic Study of the Child,* 1953, **8,** 111–126.

Opie, I., & Opie, P. *The lore and language of school children.* Oxford: Eng.: Oxford University Press, 1959.

Orfandis, M. M. Children's use of humor in psychotherapy. *Social Casework,* 1972, **53,** 147–155.

Padilla, A., & Ruiz, R. A. *Latino mental health: A review of the literature.* Rockville, Md.: National Institute of Mental Health, 1973.

Paonessa, J. J., & Paonessa, M. W. The preparation of boys for puberty. *Social Casework,* 1971, **53,** 39–44.

Parad, H. Crisis intervention. In *Encyclopedia of social work,* Vol. 1. New York: National Association of Social Workers, 1971.

Parens, H., & Saul, L. J. *Dependence in man.* New York: International Universities Press, 1971.

Paternite, C. E., Loney, J., & Longhorne, J. E. Relationships between symptomatology and SES-related factors in hyperkinetic MBD boys. *American Journal of Orthopsychiatry,* 1976, **46,** 291–301.

Patterson, J. H., & Pruitt, A. W. Treatment of mild symptomatic anxiety states. In J. Wiener (Ed.), *Psycho-pharmacology in childhood and adolescence*. New York: Basic Books, 1977.

Pearson, G. H. A survey of learning difficulties in children. *Psychoanalytic Study of the Child*, 1952, **7**, 322–386.

Peller, L. Libidinal phases, ego development and play. *Psychoanalytic Study of the Child*, 1954, **9**, 178–198.

Peller, L. Daydreams and children's favorite books. *Psychoanalytic Study of the Child*, 1959, **14**, 414–433.

Perlman, H. H. *Social casework*. Chicago: University of Chicago Press, 1957.

Perlman, H. H. Children in exile. *Social Work*, 1977, **22**, 137–139.

Piaget, J. *Play, dreams and imitation in childhood*. New York: W. W. Norton, 1945.

Piaget, J. *The origins of intelligence in children*. New York: W. W. Norton, 1963.

Piaget, J. Piaget's theory. In P. H. Mussen (Ed.), *Carmichael's manual of child psychology*, Vol. 1. (3rd ed.) New York: John Wiley & Sons, 1970.

Piaget, J., & Inhelder, B. *The growth of logical thinking from childhood to adolescence*. New York: Basic Books, 1958.

Piaget, J., & Inhelder, B. *Psychology of the child*. New York: Basic Books, 1969.

Piggott, L. R., & Simson, C. R. Changing diagnosis of childhood psychosis. *Journal of Autism and Childhood Schizophrenia*, 1975, **5**, 239–245.

Pine, F. On the concept "borderline" in children. *Psychoanalytic Study of the Child*, 1974, **29**, 341–368.

Plionis, E. M. Family functioning and childhood accident occurrence. *American Journal of Orthopsychiatry*, 1977, **47**, 250–263.

Polansky, N. A., Borgman, R., & Saix, C. *Roots of futility*. San Francisco: Jossey-Bass, 1972.

Poznanski, E., & Zrull, J. P. Childhood depression: Clinical characteristics of overtly depressed children. In S. Chess & A. Thomas (Eds.), *Annual progress in child psychiatry and child development*. New York: Brunner/Mazel, 1971.

Proskauer, S. Focused time-limited psychotherapy with children. *Journal of the American Academy of Child Psychiatry*, 1971, **10**, 619–639.

Provence, S. A., & Lipton, R. C. *Infants in institutions: A comparison of their development with family-reared infants during the first year of life*. New York: International Universities Press, 1962.

Prugh, D. G., Engel, M., & Morse, W. C. Emotional disturbances in children. In N. Hobbs (Ed.), *Issues in the classification of children*, Vol. 1. San Francisco, Jossey-Bass, 1975.

Prugh, D. G., Wermer, H., & Lord, J. P. On the significance of the anal phase in pediatrics and child psychiatry. In G. E. Gardner (Ed.), *Case studies in childhood emotional disabilities,* Vol. 2. New York: American Orthopsychiatric Association, 1956.

Rank, B. Aggression. *Psychoanalytic Study of the Child,* 1949, **3–4,** 43–48.

Rapoport, L. The state of crisis: Some theoretical considerations. In H. J. Parad (Ed.), *Crisis intervention: Selected readings.* New York: Family Service Association of America, 1965.

Reilly, M. *Play as exploratory learning.* Beverly Hills, Calif.: Sage Publications, 1974.

Reiner, B. S., & Kaufman, I. *Character disorders in parents of delinquents.* New York: Family Service Association of America, 1959.

Renshaw, D. *The hyperactive child.* Chicago: Nelson-Hall, 1974.

Richmond, M. *What is social casework.* New York: Russell Sage Foundation, 1922.

Rie, H. E., Rie, E. D., Steward, S., & Ambuel, S. P. Effects of ritalin on underachieving children: A replication. *American Journal of Orthopsychiatry,* 1976, **46,** 313–322.

Riese, H. *Heal the hurt child.* Chicago: University of Chicago Press, 1962.

Ripple, L. *Motivation, capacity and opportunity.* Social Service Monograph, 2nd series. Chicago: School of Social Service Administration, University of Chicago, 1964.

Robins, L. N. Antisocial behavior disorders of childhood: Prevalence, prognosis and prospects. In E. J. Anthony and C. Koupernik (Eds.), *The child in his family,* Vol. 3. New York: John Wiley & Sons, 1974.

Rochlin, G. The dread of abandonment. *Psychoanalytic Study of the Child,* 1961, **16,** 451–470.

Rock, N. Conversion reactions in childhood: A clinical study on childhood neuroses. *Journal of the American Academy of Child Psychiatry,* 1971, **10,** 65–93.

Rose, J. A. Relation of therapy to the reality of parental connection with children. *American Journal of Orthopsychiatry,* 1949, **19,** 351–357.

Rosenfeld, A. A., Nadelson, C. C., Krieger, M., & Backman, J. H. Incest and sexual abuse of children. *Journal of the American Academy of Child Psychiatry,* 1977, **16,** 327–339.

Rosenthal, L. Child guidance. In S. R. Slavson (Ed.), *The fields of group psychotherapy.* New York: International Universities Press, 1956.

Rosenthal, L. Qualifications and tasks of the therapist in group therapy with children. *Clinical Social Work Journal,* 1977, **5,** 191–199.

Ross, A. O. Interruptions and termination of treatment. In M. R. Haworth (Ed.), *Child psychotherapy.* New York: Basic Books, 1964.

Ross, H. The teachers game. *Psychoanalytic Study of the Child,* 1965, **20,** 288–297.

Rossi, A. S. A biosocial perspective on parenting. *Daedalus,* Spring 1977, 1–31.

Rutter, M., Lebovicci, S., Eisenberg, L., Sneznevsky, A. V., Sadoun, R., Brooke, E., & Lin, T-Y. A tri-axial classification of mental disorders in childhood. *Journal of Child Psychology and Psychiatry,* 1969, **10,** 4–61.

Sacken, D. H., & Roffee, I. H. Multiproblem families: A social-psychological perspective. Sometimes I feel like a motherless child. *Clinical Social Work Journal,* 1976, **4,** 34–43.

Sandler, J. Sexual fantasies and sexual theories in childhood. In *Studies in child psychoanalysis: Pure and applied.* Psychoanalytic Study of the Child, Monograph, Series No. 5. New Haven: Yale University Press, 1975.

Sandoval, J., Lambert, N. M., & Yandell, W. Current medical practice and hyperactive children. *American Journal of Orthopsychiatry,* 1976, **46,** 323–334.

San Martino, M., & Newman, M. B. Family mythology. *Journal of the American Academy of Child Psychiatry,* 1975, **14,** 422–435.

Sapir, S. G., & Nitzburg, A. C. *Children with learning problems.* New York: Brunner/Mazel, 1973.

Sarnoff, C. *Latency.* New York: Jason Aronson, 1976.

Schamess, G. Group treatment modalities for latency-age children. *International Journal of Group Psychotherapy,* 1976, **26,** 455–473.

Scheidlinger, S. Experimental group treatment of seriously deprived latency-age children. *American Journal of Orthopsychiatry,* 1960, **30,** 356–368.

Schonfeld, W. Adolescent development: Biological, psychological and sociological determinants. In S. C. Feinstein, P. L. Giovacchini, & A. A. Miller (Eds.), *Adolescent Psychiatry.* New York: Basic Books, 1971.

Schowalter, J. E. Parent death and child bereavement. In Schoenberg, B., Gerber, I., Wiener, A., Kutscher, A. H., Peretz, D., & Carr, A. C. (Eds.), *Bereavement: Its psychosocial aspects.* New York: Columbia University Press, 1975.

Schrag, P., & Divorky, D. *The myth of the hyperactive child.* New York: Pantheon Books, 1975.

Schultz, L. G. The child sex victim: Social, psychological and legal perspectives. *Child Welfare,* 1973, **52,** 147–157.

Sears, R. R., Raus, L., and Alpert, R. *Identification and child rearing.* Stanford, Calif.: Stanford University Press, 1965.

Selig, A. L. The myth of the multiproblem family. *American Journal of Orthopsychiatry,* 1976, **46,** 527–532.

Selvini-Palazzoli, M. The families of patients with anorexia nervosa. In

E. J. Anthony & C. Koupernik, (Eds.), The child in his family, Vol. 1. New York: John Wiley & Sons, 1970.

Shafu, M., Salguero, C., & Finch, S. Anorexia a deux: Psychopathology and treatment of anorexia nervosa in latency-age siblings. *Journal of the American Academy of Child Psychiatry*, 1975, **14**, 617–645.

Shane, M. Encopresis in a latency boy: An arrest along a developmental line. *Psychoanalytic Study of the Child*, 1967, **22**, 296–314.

Sherman, E. A., Phillips, M. H., Haring, B., & Shyne, A. W. *Service to children in their own homes: Its nature and outcome.* New York: Child Welfare League of America, 1973.

Sherman, S. N. Family treatment: An approach to children's problems. *Social Casework*, 1966, **47**, 368–372.

Sherman, S. N. Family therapy. In F. J. Turner (Ed.), *Social work treatment: Interlocking theoretical approaches.* New York: Free Press, 1974.

Shugart, G. Anxiety in siblings upon separation. *Social Work*, 1958, **3**, 30–36.

Silver, L. The playroom diagnostic evaluation of children with neurologically based learning difficulties. *Journal of the American Academy of Child Psychiatry*, 1976, **15**, 240–256.

Skeels, H. M. *Adult status of children with contrasting early life experiences.* Society for Research in Child Development, Chicago, Ill., 1966, **31** (3, Whole No. 105).

Slavson, S. R., & Schiffer, M. *Group psychotherapies for children.* New York: International Universities Press, 1975.

Smolen, E. M. Nonverbal aspects of therapy with children. *American Journal of Psychotherapy*, 1959, **13**, 872–881.

Sobey, F. Orientation to change in roles in social work practice. In Sobey (Ed.), *Changing roles in social work practice.* Philadelphia: Temple University Press, 1977.

Solnit, A. J., & Stark, M. H. Mourning the birth of a defective child. *Psychoanalytic Study of the Child*, 1961, **16**, 523–537.

Sperling, M. School phobias: Classification, dynamics and treatment. *Psychoanalytic Study of the Child*, 1967, **22**, 375–401.

Sperling, M. The clinical effects of parental neuroses on the child. In E. J. Anthony & T. Benedek (Eds.), *Parenthood: Its psychology and psychopathology.* Boston: Little, Brown, 1970.

Sperling, M. Sleep disturbances in children. In J. G. Howells (Ed.) *Modern perspectives in international child psychiatry.* New York: Brunner/Mazel, 1971.

Sperling, M. *The major neuroses and behavior disorders in children.* New York: Jason Aronson, 1974.

Sperling, M. Somatic symptomatology in phobia: A psychoanalytic study. In J. A. Lindon (Ed.), *Psychoanalytic forum*, Vol. 5. New York: International Universities Press, 1975.

Spitz, R. A. Hospitalism. *Psychoanalytic Study of the Child*, 1945, **1**, 53–74.

Spitz, R. A. Anaclitic depression. *Psychoanalytic Study of the Child*, 1946, **2**, 313–342.

Spitz, R. A. *The first year of life: A psychoanalytic study of normal and deviant development of object relations.* New York: International Universities Press, 1965.

Spotnitz, H., Nagelberg, L., & Feldman, Y. Ego reinforcement in the schizophrenic child. *American Journal of Orthopsychiatry*, 1956, **26**, 146–162.

Stein, Marvin. The what, how and why of psychosomatic medicine. In D. Offer & D. Freedman (Eds.), *Modern psychiatry and clinical research.* New York: Basic Books, 1972.

Stein, Myron. The function of ambiguity in child crises. *Journal of the American Academy of Child Psychiatry*, 1970, **9**, 462–476.

Steward, M., & Regalbuto, G. Do doctors know what children know? *American Journal of Orthopsychiatry*, 1975, **45**, 146–149.

Stimbert, V. E., & Coffey, K. R. Obese children and adolescents: A review. In *Research relating to children*, Bulletin No. 30. Washington, D.C.: Clearing House on Early Childhood Education, 1972.

Sugar, M. Interpretive group psychotherapy with latency children. *Journal of the American Academy of Child Psychiatry*, 1974, **13**, 648–666.

Sullivan, H. S. *The interpersonal theory of psychiatry.* New York: W.W. Norton, 1953.

Surgeon General's Scientific Advisory Committee on Television and Social Behavior. *Television and growing up: The impact of television violence.* Rockville, Md.: National Institute of Mental Health, 1972.

Szurek, S. A. Childhood origins of psychopathic personality trends. In Szurek & I. N. Berlin (Eds.), *The antisocial child: His family and his community.* Palo Alto, Calif.: Science & Behavior Books, 1969.

Szurek, S. A. Elements of psychotherapeutics with the schizophrenic child and his parents. In Szurek & I. N. Berlin (Eds.), *Clinical studies in childhood psychoses.* New York: Brunner/Mazel, 1973.

Tanner, J. M. Physical growth. In P. H. Mussen (Ed.), *Carmichael's manual of child psychology*, Vol. 1. (3rd ed.) New York: John Wiley & Sons, 1970.

Tarjin, G., Wright, S. W., Eyman, R. K., & Keeran, C. V. Natural history of mental retardation: Some aspects of epidemiology. In S. Chess & A. Thomas (Eds.), *Annual progress in child psychiatry and child development.* New York: Brunner/Mazel, 1974.

Temple-Trujillo, R. E. Conceptions of the Chicano family. *Smith College Studies in Social Work*, 1974, **45**, 1–20.

Thomas, A., Chess, S., Birch, H. G., Herzig, M. E., & Korn, S. B. *Behavioral individuality in childhood.* New York: New York University Press, 1963.

Thomas, A., Hertzig, M. E., Dryman, I., & Fernandez, P. Examiner effect in IQ testing of Puerto Rican working-class children. *American Journal of Orthopsychiatry,* 1971, **41,** 809–821.

Thornburg, H. D. Educating the preadolescent about sex. *Family Coordinator,* 1974, **23,** 35–39.

Titchener, J. L., Riskin, J., Emerson, R. The family in psychosomatic process. In J. G. Howells (Ed.), *Theory and Practice of family psychiatry.* New York: Brunner/Mazel, 1971.

Tolstrup, K. The necessity for differentiating eating disorders: Discussion of Hilde Bruch's paper on the family background. In E. J. Anthony & C. Koupernik (Eds.), *The child in his family.* New York: John Wiley & Sons, 1970.

Tooley, K. The role of geographic mobility in some adjustment problems of children and families. *Journal of the American Academy of Child Psychiatry,* 1970, **9,** 366–378.

Toolon, J. M. Depression in children and adolescents. In G. Caplan & S. Lebovicci (Eds.), *Adolescence: Psychosocial perspectives.* New York: Basic Books, 1969.

Travis, G. *Chronic illness in children: Its impact on child and family.* Stanford, Calif.: Stanford University Press, 1976.

Van Dam, H., Heinicke, C. M., & Shane, M. On termination in child analysis. *Psychoanalytic Study of the Child,* 1975, **30,** 443–474.

Voyat, G. IQ: God-given or man-made? In J. Helmuth (Ed.), *Disadvantaged child,* Vol. 3. New York: Brunner/Mazel, 1970.

Wallach, H. D. Termination of treatment as a loss. *Psychoanalytic Study of the Child,* 1961, **16,** 538–548.

Wallerstein, J. S., & Kelly, J. B. The effects of parental divorce: Experiences of the child in later latency. *American Journal of Orthopsychiatry,* 1976, **46,** 256–269.

Warson, S. R., Caldwell, M. R., Warinner, K. A. J., & Jensen, R. A. The dynamics of encopresis: Workshop 1953. In G. E. Gardner (Ed.), *Case studies in childhood emotional disabilities,* Vol. 2. New York: American Orthopsychiatric Association, 1956.

Wax, D. E., & Haddox, V. G. Enuresis, fire setting and animal cruelty: A useful danger signal in predicting vulnerability of adolescent males to assaultive behavior. *Child Psychiatry and Human Development,* 1974, **4,** 151–156.

Weisman, A. D. Coping with untimely death. *Psychiatry,* 1973, **36,** 366–373.

White, R. W. Strategies of adaptation: An attempt at systematic description. In G. Coelho, D. A. Hamburg, & J. E. Adams (Eds.), *Coping and adaptation.* New York: Basic Books, 1974.

Whiteman, M. The development of conceptions of psychological causality. In J. Hellmuth (Ed.), *Cognitive studies,* Vol. 1. New York: Brunner/Mazel, 1970.

Whiting, B., & Edwards, C. P. A cross-cultural analysis of sex differences in the behavior of children aged 3 through 11. In S. Chess & A. Thomas (Eds.), *Annual Progress in Child Psychiatry and child development.* New York: Brunner/Mazel, 1974.

Whittaker. J. K. Causes of childhood disorders: New findings. *Social Work,* 1976, **21,** 91–96.

Wiener, J. M. Identical male twins discordant for anorexia nervosa. *Journal of the American Academy of Child Psychiatry,* 1976, **15,** 523–534.

Williams, M. Problems of technique during latency. *Psychoanalytic Study of the Child,* 1972, **27,** 598–620.

Winnicott, C. Communicating with children. *Child Care Quarterly Review,* 1964, **18,** 65–80.

Winnicott, D. W. *Therapeutic consultations in child psychiatry.* New York: Basic Books, 1971.

Winnicott, D. W. Transitional objects and transitional phenomena. In Winnicott, *Through paediatrics to psycho-analysis.* New York: Basic Books, 1975.

Wolfenstein, M. A phase in the development of children's sense of humor. *Psychoanalytic Study of the Child,* 1951, **6,** 336–349.

Wolfenstein, M. Children's understanding of jokes. *Psychoanalytic Study of the Child,* 1953, **8,** 162–176.

Wolff, S. *Children under stress.* London: Allen Lane, Penguin Press, 1969.

Wolkenstein, A. S. The fear of committing child abuse: A discussion of eight families. *Child Welfare,* 1977, **56,** 249–257.

Wynne, L. C. Some guidelines for exploratory conjoint family therapy. In J. Haley (Ed.), *Changing families.* New York: Grune & Stratton, 1971.

Yalom, I. D. *The theory and practice of group psychotherapy.* New York: Basic Books, 1970.

Yandell, W. Therapeutic problems related to the expression of sexual drives in psychotic children. In S. A. Szurek & I. N. Berlin (Eds.), *Clinical studies in childhood psychoses.* New York: Brunner/Mazel, 1973.

Yorukuglu, A. Children's favorite jokes and their relation to emotional conflicts. *Journal of the American Academy of Child Psychiatry,* 1974, **13,** 677–690.

Young, L. An interim report on an experimental program of protective service. *Child Welfare,* 1966, **45,** 373–387.

Zentall, S. Optimal stimulation as the theoretical basis of hyperactivity. *American Journal of Orthopsychiatry,* 1975, **45,** 549–562.

INDEX

Abbot, Edith, 233
Abelin, E. L., 21, 185
Ability problems, 160–163
Accidents, as a self-preservation disorder,
    210–211
Ackerman, N., 43
Adams, P. L., 276
Adams, Paul, 13
Adaptation reaction, defined, 242
Addams, Jane, 233
Adelson, E., 47, 265
Adolescence, 36–39
    child abuse, 48
    cognitive ability, 36–37, 38
    crisis of, 37–39
    defined, 37
    divorce of parents, 46
    education, 36–37
    the ego, 38
    the id, 38
    identity, sense of, 36, 37
    language, 38
    love, 38
    peer relations, 37
    play, 38
    preparation for, 117
    puberty, 37
    racial awareness, 37
    sexuality, 37
    as a transition period, 36
Adults
    behavior disturbing to, 134
    complaints by, 133–136
    infant dependency on, 20–21
    racial prejudice, 30–31
    See also Parents
Advice, giving, 268–271
Ages 6 to 12, see Early latency; Late
    latency; Middle latency
Aggression, 147–153
    anger and, 147–148
    anxiety and, 148
    class and, 149–150
    the community and, 149, 150
    culture and, 149
    early latency, 73–74, 81, 89
    the ego and, 147
    elimination disorders and, 202–203
    the family and, 147–152
    fantasies and, 148, 149
    fear and, 148
    late latency, 123–124
    love and, 147–148, 152
    as normal, 147
    in play, 147
    self destructive acts as, 152
    sex hormones and, 81
    sexuality and, 149
    socioeconomic status and, 149–150
    the superego and, 147

symptoms, 147–153
    television and, 150
    underachievement and, 166
    violence and, 148, 149, 150
Aid to Dependent Children, 12
Aleksandrowicz, M., 210
Allen, F. H., 261, 307, 308
Alpert, A., 275
Alpert, R., 231
Alschuler, R. H., 77
Amphetamines, 157–158
Amster, F., 288
Anal stage, 23, 200
Androgens, 109, 111
Anger
    aggression and, 147–148
    depression and, 144
    phobias and, 178
    underachievement and, 166–169
Animism, 200
Anorexia, 136, 194–198
    the family and, 196–198
    fear and, 195
Anthony, E. J., 61, 62, 147, 200, 203
Anti-immigration movements, 233–234
Antisocial behavior, 148–149
Anxieties, 134
    absence from school, 173–175
    aggression and, 148
    depression and, 144
    early childhood, 27–28, 30
    early latency, 31–32, 87
    foster care, 53
    infancy, 21
    late latency, 112, 124–129
    panic and, 243–244
    phobias and, 173–175, 177
    psychosomatic concept, 184, 186–187
    sleep disorders and, 207–208
    symptoms, 137–139
Aphasia, 216
Appelberg, E., 55
Argelander, H., 55
Arkins, V., 195, 196
Arlow, J. A., 74, 293
Arnold, E., 135
Ashton, P. T., 66
Atomism, spontaneous, 84
Axelrod, S., 66

Bachrach, H., 233
Baird, M., 200, 204
Baker, L., 196
Bank, S., 43
Beck, D. F., 246
Becker, T., 104
Bed-wetting, 134
Beginnings of treatment, 219–258
    biopsychosocial diagnosis, 229–244
    clinical diagnosis, 240–244

diagnostic formulation, 238–240
    the facts, 231–238
concrete services, 256
duration of treatment, 252–256
expectations, 219–220
family diagnostic interviews, 223–229
    children as collaborators, 227–228
    the contract, 228–229
    parents as collaborators, 224–227
first contact, 221–223
goals, 245–247
teamwork, 256–258
types of treatment, 247–252
Being left, 295–304
    illness, 299–301
    transfers, 303–304
    vacations, 299–301
    worker leaves agency, 301–303
    See also Leaving
Beiser, H. R., 292
Bender, L., 210
Benedek, T., 40–41
Benjamin, L. S., 203
Berecz, J. M., 177
Berger, M., 129, 170
Bergman, A., 21, 185, 296
Berlin, I. N., 284
Bibring, E., 143
Billingsley, A., 43
Biopsychosocial diagnosis, 229–244
    clinical diagnosis, 240–244
    diagnostic formulation, 238–240
    the facts, 231–238
Bixler, R., 284
Blacks
    extended family, 43
    IQ, 233, 234
    religion, 145
Blaydon, C. C., 63
Blinder, B. J., 59
Bloch, E. L., 215
Blom, G. E., 61
Blos, P., 36, 105, 107, 108, 111, 113, 114,
    117, 120, 122, 123, 124, 129, 220,
    296
Borderline personality, defined, 243
Borgman, R., 48
Bornstein, B., 87, 104, 105, 107, 274, 275
Bowlby, J., 142
Brain dysfunctions, 160
Brant, R. S., 51
Brodie, R. D., 175
Bruch, H., 191, 193, 260
Bruner, J. S., 286
Bumpass, E. R., 187, 216
Buxbaum, E., 147, 148, 171, 211, 273

Campbell, J. D., 79
Castration fears, 87
Categorization, appropriate use of, 241
Cerebral palsy, 160
Chapman, M., 263
Char, W. F., 251
Chess, S., 138, 164
Chetnik, M., 216, 276
Child abuse, 47–52
    adolescence, 48

defined, 48
    as a developmental interference,
        139
    early childhood, 48
Child neglect, 47–52
    as a developmental interference,
        139
Childhood, early, 23–31
    as the anal stage, 23
    anxieties, 27–28, 30
    child abuse, 48
    cognitive ability, 24–26
    daydreams, 26
    death, 56–57
    the ego, 28, 30
    fantasy, 26–29
    love, 29
    oedipal conflicts, 28–29
    parents, 23–24, 29–30
    play, 26–29
    preoperational stage, 24–25
    racial differences, coping with, 30–31
    sexuality, 26, 28
    sexual differences, coping with, 29–30
    verbalization, 23–24
Class
    aggression and, 149–150
    effects of, 66–67
    late latency, 120
    peer relations and, 81
    symptoms and, 145–146
Classification of disorders, 241–244
Clinical diagnosis, 240–244
Coffey, K. R., 192, 193
Cognitive ability
    adolescence, 36–37, 38
    early childhood, 24–26
    early latency, 74–75, 83–86, 91
    late latency, 117–119
    middle latency, 99–103
    trauma and, 142
Cohen, N., 233
Cohen, R., 216
Cole, S. O., 156, 158
Coles, R., 145
Colm, H., 177
Comer, J., 145
Communication, 259–294
    with children, 271–287
        hide-and-seek, 286–287
        listening, 277–281
        resistance, 275–277
        talking, 281–286
        worker's problems, 273–275
    with parents, 259–271
        giving advice, 268–271
        listening, 263–264
        play, 264–268
        resistance, 260–262
    play as, 287–294
        cheating at games, 291–293
        equipment and setting, 289–291
        fantasy, 293–294
        with parents, 264–268
        therapy and, 287–289
Communication disorders, 212–216
    mutism, 215–216
    stuttering, 214–215

Community, the
  aggression and, 149, 150
  sense of, 43–44
Concrete services, 256
Connor, F. P., 214
Contracts for treatment, 228–229
Coolidge, J., 175
Creativity, 118–119
Crisis intervention, 252–253
Crying, 135, 213
  avoidance of, 144–145
Culture, 65–68
  aggression and, 149
  the environment and, 65–66
  parents and, 65, 68
  peer relations and, 81
  sexuality and, 66, 106
  symptoms and, 145–146
Cutter, A. V., 227
Cytryn, L., 144

Dancing, 106
Davis, I., 269
Day care facilities, 63
Daydreams
  depression and, 146
  early childhood, 26
  late latency, 118, 119
Death, 56–59
  as a developmental interference, 139
  early childhood, 56–57
  early latency, 57–59, 87
  late latency, 57–59
  middle latency, 57–59
  parents, 59
  siblings, 58–59
Defense mechanisms, 88
Dember, C. F., 171
Department of Labor, 63
Depression, 142–147
  anger and, 144
  anxiety and, 144
  daydreams and, 146
  duration of, 146–147
  love and, 143–144
  masochistic activities and, 145
  parents and, 142–143
  as reaction to loss, 142–143
  sadness and, 144
  symptoms, 142–147
  violence and, 145
Desmond, Mrs. Jill, 25
Deutsch, C., 67
Deutsch, F., 181
Deutsch, M., 235
Developmental interferences, 139–142
DeVries, R., 235
Diagnostic formulation, 238–240
DiLeo, J. H., 77
Disobedience, 134, 135
Divorce, 44–46
  increase in, 64
Divorky, D., 156
Dowling, A. S., 181
Drawings
  early latency, 76–78
  middle latency, 95

Drugs
  adverse effects of, 158
  emotions and, 159
  See also names of drugs
Dudek, S. Z., 166

Early childhood, see Childhood, early
Early latency, 31–32, 71–91
  achievements of, 32–36
  aggression, 73–74, 81, 89
  anxieties, 31–32, 87
  cognitive ability, 74–75, 83–86, 91
  death, 57–59, 87
  defense mechanisms, 88
  drawings, 76–78
  education, 72, 75–76, 79, 82–83
  the ego, 32, 72, 74, 76, 77, 83, 87, 90–91
  fantasies, 31–32, 73, 74, 90
  games, 72–76
  growth, 71–72
  language, 73–74, 78, 83, 84
  masturbation, 87–88
  oedipal conflicts, 82, 87, 88
  parents, 88–89
  peer relations, 76, 79–80, 91
  physical development, 71–72
  play, 31–32, 72–76, 89
  psychological development, 86–91
  repetitive behavior, 32
  separation by sex, 88
  sexuality, 80–83
  stories, 78, 89–90
  studiousness, effeminacy and, 83
  the superego, 83, 90–91
  teachers, 89
Eating disorders, 191–198
  anorexia, 136, 194–198
    the family and, 196–198
    fear and, 195
  obesity, 192–194
    the family and, 193
    symptoms, 193
Economic pressures of the family in society, 62–64
Education, 19
  adolescence, 36–37
  early latency, 72, 75–76, 79, 82–83
  emphasis on IQ, 66
  late latency, 118, 129
  middle latency, 101
  minorities, 66
Edwards, C. P., 106
Effeminacy, studiousness and, 83
Ego, the, 137
  adolescence, 38
  aggression and, 147
  early childhood, 28, 30
  early latency, 32, 72, 74, 76, 77, 83, 87, 90–91
  functioning of, 239
  late latency, 32, 125–127, 129
  middle latency, 32, 101, 104–105, 107
  underachievement and, 171
Ejaculation
  first experience of, 109–110
  late latency, 109–111, 126
  onset of, 37

Ekstein, R., 281, 283, 287
Elimination disorders, 199–206
  aggression and, 202–203
  encopresis, 203–206
    three types of, 203
  enuresis, 201–203
  the family and, 199–206
Emerson, R., 186
Emigration, 63, 233–234
Emotional overcontrol, 136
Encopresis, 203–206
  three types of, 203
Engel, M., 240
Enuresis, 201–203
Enzer, N., 266
Erikson, E., 19–20, 23, 33, 37, 65, 103,
    114, 125, 230, 288, 289
Erikson, K. T., 43
Escoli, Philip, 216, 276
Esman, A. H., 201
Essman, C. S., 42
Estrogen, 109, 110, 111
Evans, N. S., 58
Ewalt, P., 269
Extended family, 43–44
  geographic mobility, 64
  minorities, 43
  sense of community, 43–44

Falstein, E., 138
Family, the, 40–44, 105
  aggression and, 147–152
  anorexia and, 196–198
  elimination disorders and, 199–206
  extended, 43–44
    geographic mobility, 64
    minorities, 43
    sense of community, 43–44
  mental retardation and, 164–165
  multiproblem, 46–47
  obesity and, 193
  peer relations and, 79
  as a psychological field, 41
  psychosomatic concept, 183–186
  underachievement and, 169–171
  version of reality in, 41
  See also Parents; Siblings
Family crisis, 56–61
  death, 56–59
    mourning, 57, 58
    siblings, 58–59
  illness, 59–61
    hospitalization, 60–61
    long-term, 6?
    siblings, 59
Family diagnostic interviews, 223–229
  children as collaborators, 227–228
  the contract, 228–229
  parents as collaborators, 224–227
Family problems, 44–56
Family in society, the, 62–68
  changing families, 64–65
  economic pressures, 62–64
  societal influences, 65–68
Family therapy, 250–252
Famshel, D., 52, 54
Fantasies, 148
  aggression and, 148, 149

early childhood, 26–29
  early latency, 31–32, 73, 74, 90
  late latency, 112, 114, 119, 123–129
  middle latency, 105
  symptoms, 137, 142, 146
Fantasy play, 293–294
Fathers, see Parents
Fears, 134, 135
  aggression and, 148
  anorexia and, 195
  castration, 87
Feldman, Y., 226, 261, 263, 268, 276, 285
Fenichel, O., 24, 281
Finch, S., 196
Food stamp policies, 63
Foster, R. M., 209
Foster care, 52–56, 140
  anxieties, 53
  long-term placement, 55–56
  reasons for placement in, 52
  regular visits, 53–54
  stress from, 182–183
Foster parents, 53–55, 271
Fraiberg, Selma, 13, 22, 47, 88, 109, 124,
    265, 285
Frank, M. C., 248
Frankl, L., 211
Freud, A., 27, 37–38, 90, 95, 105, 123,
    127, 136, 137, 147, 152, 166, 189,
    206, 207, 208, 209, 220, 240, 261,
    275, 288
Freud, S., 28, 128, 176, 297
Friedman, S., 287
Fuller, J. S., 249
Furman, E., 58
Futterman, E. H., 60

Galdston, R., 196
Galenson, E. A., 74
Games
  cheating at, 291–293
  cruelty in, 147
  early latency, 72–76
  hide-and-seek, 286–287
  late latency, 112–114, 128–129
  middle latency, 100, 103
  See also Play
Ganter, G., 248
Gardner, R., 293
Geographic mobility, 64
Gerard, M., 191, 200, 202
Giaretto, H., 52
Giffen, M. E., 41
Gil, D., 50
Gilpin, D. C., 277, 285
Gittelman-Klein, R., 174
Glaser, K., 143, 210
Glaser, P., 65
Glick, J., 66
Goals of treatment, 245–247
Goffman, E., 66
Golan, N., 253
Goldings, H., 73
Gonadotropins, 109, 110
Gondor, L., 288
Goode, W. J., 50
Goodstein, L. D., 215
Gottesfeld, H., 55, 234

Gottesfeld, M. L., 47
Greenacre, P., 129
Greenberg, L. M., 201
Grinspoon, L., 156, 158, 159
Group for the Advancement o. Psychiatry,
    149, 181, 242, 243, 252
Group therapy, 247–250
Growth, 32
    early latency, 71–72
    late latency, 109–112
    middle latency, 92–94
Guttman, H. A., 250

Haddox, V. G., 202–203
Hallowitz, D., 227, 251
Halpern, W., 216
Hamilton, G., 230, 241
Hammond, J., 216
Harley, M., 108, 118, 124
Harlow, H. F., 20
Harlow, M., 20
Harre, R., 68
Harris, O. C., 63
Hartmann, Heinz, 15, 68, 238
Hartrup, W. W., 116
Hassibi, M., 164
Hattwick, L. W., 77
Hawkins, J. W., 210
Haworth, M. R., 284
Heinicke, C. M., 305
Herzog, E., 46
Hide-and-seek game, 286–287
Hirsch, K. de, 72, 214
Ho, M. K., 257
Hobbies
    late latency, 112, 113
    middle latency, 94–95
Hobbs, N., 154, 235, 240
Hoffman, I., 60
Hollis, F., 229, 241
Homosexuality, 113, 120–121, 123, 128
Hormonal processess, 81, 109, 110, 126
Hospitalization, 60–61
Humphrey, I. L., 187, 216
Hyperactivity, 155–157
Hyperkinesis, 156–160
Hypochondriasis, 189–190
Hypothyroidism, 193

Id, the
    adolescence, 38
    middle latency, 105
Illness, 59–61
    being left because of, 299–301
    as a developmental interference, 139
    hospitalization, 60–61
    long-term, 60
    parents, 60, 61
    siblings, 59
    treatment and, 299–301
Incest, 51–52
Income, 62–64
    minorities, 64
Indians (American), IQ, 233, 234
Infancy, 19–23
    anxieties, 21
    autonomy, struggle to achieve, 22–23
    basic trust in, 19–20

capacity to adapt in, 20
dependence on adults, 20–21
explorations, 20–22
food during, 20
parents, 20–22
rapprochement stage, 22
sensorimotor stage, 22
sexuality, autoerotic activities, 19
siblings, 21
vocalization, 21
Inferiority, feelings of, 103–105
Inhelder, B., 21, 25, 38, 74, 83, 84, 98,
    100, 117, 118
Interviews for treatment
    family diagnostic, 223–229
        children as collaborators, 227–228
        the contract, 228–229
        parents as collaborators, 224–227
    the first, 221–223
IQ, 223–235
    emphasis on, 66
    mental retardation and, 163
    minorities, 233–235

Jacklin, C. N., 66, 81
Jacobson, E., 104, 143, 254
Jenkins, S., 54
Jessner, L., 61
Johnson, A., 41, 138, 173, 257
Johnson-Lodge Immigration Act, 233
Joint Commission on Mental Health of
    Children, 13
Jokes, 277–278
    late latency, 114, 119
    middle latency, 96–97
Jones, M. A., 246
Justice, B., 49
Justice, R., 49

Kagan, J., 62, 65, 82, 106, 235
Kahn, A. J., 48
Kahn, J. H., 172
Kahn, M. D., 43
Kamerman, S., 48
Kamin, L. J., 233
Kanner, L., 241
Kaplan, E. B., 94
Kaplan, S. L., 208, 216, 276
Katan, A., 213
Kaufman, I., 47, 149
Kay, P., 89
Kaydis, A. L., 250, 293
Keith-Lucas, A., 67
Kellam, S. G., 134
Kelly, J. B., 44, 254
Kennedy, H., 170
Kestenberg, J., 87, 88, 89, 106, 109, 110,
    112, 113, 123
Kissel, S., 195, 196
Kleeman, J. A., 21, 286
Klein, D., 174
Klein, E., 170
Knipstein, R., 187, 216
Kolansky, H., 214
Koupernik, C., 190
Krug, O., 171
Krugman, D. C., 55
Kutz, J., 269

La Vietes, R. L., 254
Lackie, B., 267
Lambert, N. M., 156
Lamont, J. H., 281
Lane, H., 213
Language, 32–33, 36
  adolescence, 38
  early latency, 73–74, 78, 83, 84
  late latency, 118, 119
  middle latency, 96
Late latency, 108–130
  achievements of, 32–36
  aggression, 123–124
  anxieties, 112, 124–129
  class, 120
  cognitive ability, 117–119
  creativity, 118–119
  daydreams, 118, 119
  death, 57–59
  education, 118, 129
  the ego, 32, 125–127, 129
  fantasies, 112, 114, 119, 123–129
  feeling of loss, 127
  games, 112–114, 128–129
  grooming interests, 114
  growth, 109–112
  hobbies, 112, 113
  hormonal processes, 109, 110, 126
  jokes, 114, 119
  language, 118, 119
  love, 113, 120, 128
  narcissism, 126–127
  oedipal conflicts, 128
  parents, 127–129
  peer relations, 112–117, 120, 126
  physical development, 32
  play, 112–117, 119
  psychological development, 125–130
  sexuality, 119–124
    class, 120
    development of, 109–112
    ejaculation, 109–111, 126
    homosexuality, 113, 120–121, 123, 128
    masturbation, 111, 120, 123, 124
    menstruation, 109–110, 112, 120, 126
    nocturnal emissions, 120
    orgasm, 111
    venereal disease, 120
  the superego, 116, 126–127
Laws, The (Plato), 13–14
Le Vine, R. A., 65
Learning problems, 154–179
  ability problems, 160–163
  absence from school, 172–179
    school phobia, 173–176
    truancy, 172
  clues suggesting, 162
  hyperactivity, 155–157
  hyperkinesis, 156–160
  mental retardation, 163–166
  minimal brain damage, 156–160
    diagnosis of, 158–159
  underachievement, 166–171
  tests, 162–163
Leaving, 295, 296, 304–309
  looking back, 307–309
  planning a termination, 304–305

  process of, 305–307
  See also Being left
Lebovicci, S., 147
Lester, D., 211
Lester, E. P., 166
Levinson, H., 302
Lewis, H., 46
Lewis, M., 44, 159
Lieberman, F., 47, 121, 248
Liebman, R., 196
Lindemann, E., 56
Lipton, R. C., 20
Listening
  to children, 277–281
  to parents, 263–264
Littner, N., 53, 148, 149, 150
Loney, J., 149
Long, H., 134
Longhorne, J. E., 149
Loof, D. H., 186
Loomis, E., 291
Lord, J. P., 200, 201
Loss
  depression as reaction to, 142–143
  feeling of, 127
  psychosomatic concept, 184
Love
  adolescence, 38
  aggression and, 147–148, 152
  depression and, 143–144
  early childhood, 29
  late latency, 113, 120, 128
Love, S., 262
Lubove, R., 233
Lystad, M., 51, 78

Maccoby, E. E., 66, 81
McDermott, J. F., 251
McDonald, M. M., 212
McKnew, J., 144
Maclennan, B., 249
Mahler, M. S., 21, 24, 185, 190, 296
Malmquist, C. P., 145
Malone, C. A., 47, 149, 210
Mann, J., 252
Martino, M. S., 165
Masochistic activities, depression and, 145
Masturbation
  early latency, 81–88
  inhibition of, 87 88
  late latency, 111, 120, 123, 124
  middle latency, 107
  underachievement and, 170
Mattson, A., 210
Mayer, H., 262
Meeks, J. E., 291, 292
Meers, D., 145 146
Mendelson, M 144
Menstruation
  first experience of, 109–110
  late latency, 109–110, 112, 120, 126
  onset of, 37
Mental retardation, 163–166
  the family and, 164–165
  IQ and, 163
  siblings and, 165

Mexican-Americans
  extended family, 43
  IQ, 233, 234
Middle latency, 92–107
  achievements of, 32–36
  cognitive ability, 99–103
  death, 57–59
  drawings, 95
  education, 101
  the ego, 32, 101, 104–105, 107
  fantasies, 105
  games, 100, 103
  group activities, 98–99
  growth, 92–94
  heroes and heroines, 96
  hobbies, 94–95
  the id, 105
  inferiority, feelings of, 103–105
  jokes, 96–97
  language, 96
  motivational processes, 101
  parents, 105
  peer relations, 95, 98–99, 105
  physical development, 92–94
  play, 94–98
  psychological growth, 103–105
  pubertal growth, 93
  riddles, 97
  sexuality, 105–107
    masturbation, 107
  shame, feelings of, 103–105
  socialization, 98–100
  solitary activities, 95
  stories, 95–96
  the superego, 107
  superstitions, 97
  television, 96, 107
Millar, S., 76, 119
Millar, T., 186
Miller, D., 108
Miller, J. B. M., 57
Miller, R. R., 270
Miller, S. M., 255
Minimal brain damage (MBD), 156–160
  diagnosis of, 158–159
Minorities
  disturbing behavior by, 134–135
  education, 66
  extended family, 43
  family problems, 46, 48, 51–52
  income, 64
  IQ, 233–235
  religion, 145
Minuchin, S., 42, 62, 196
Mishler, E. G., 255
Misunderstandings, 137
Mitchell, C. A., 249
Mittelman, B., 285, 286
Mizio, E., 43
Mobility, geographic, 64
Mood changes, 135, 136
Moore, J. G., 44, 51
Moore, W. T., 61
Morse, W. C., 240
Mothers, see Parents
Mourning, 57, 58
Moustakas, C., 289
Multiproblem families, 46–47

Murphy, L. B., 53, 239
Mutism, 215–216
Myopia, 94

Nagelberg, L., 285
Nagera, H., 139, 206, 207, 208, 238
Narcissism, 126–127
National Council of Organizations for Children and Youth, 63
National Institute of Child Health and Human Development, 46
National Institute of Mental Health, 48
National Research Council, 62, 63, 64
Navarre, E., 65
Neubauer, P., 66, 135–136, 275
Neurosis, defined, 242–243
Newberger, E. H., 48
Newman, C. J., 171
Newman, M. B., 41, 165
Nightmares, 207–208
Night terrors, 207
Nitzburg, A. C., 155
Nocturnal emissions, 120
Norlin, J., 257
Normal variation, defined, 242
Norman, E., 54
Nursten, J. P., 172

Obesity, 192–194
  the family and, 193
  symptoms, 193
Oedipal conflicts
  early childhood, 28–29
  early latency, 82, 87, 88
  late latency, 128
  underachievement and, 170
Offer, D., 251
Olden, C., 274
Opie, I., 73, 96
Opie, P., 73, 96
Orfandis, M. M., 277
Orgasm, 111
Overdependency, 136

Padilla, A., 235
Panic, anxiety and, 243–244
Paonessa, J. J., 111
Paonessa, M. W., 111
Papp, P., 43
Parad, H., 253
Parens, H., 20, 105
Parents, 33, 41–42
  basic trust in, 19–20
  as collaborators, 224–227
  communication with, 259–271
    giving advice, 268–271
    listening, 263–264
    play, 264–268
    resistance, 260–262
  complaints by, 133–136
  coping and adapting by, 237–238
  culture and, 65, 68
  death, 59
  depression and, 142–143
  divorce, 44–46
    increase in, 64
  early childhood, 23–24, 29–30
  early latency, 88–89

family problems and, 46, 49–52, 54
foster, 53–55, 271
illness, 60, 61
infancy, 20–22
infant dependency on, 20–21
late latency, 127–129
middle latency, 105
mother's feeling of isolation, 63–64
school phobia and, 174–176
separation of, 44
single, 64–65
working mothers, 63
Paternite, C. E., 149
Patterson, J. H., 207
Pearson, G. H., 155
Peer relations, 33
    adolescence, 37
    class and, 81
    culture and, 81
    early latency, 76, 79–80, 91
    family and, 79
    late latency, 112–117, 120, 126
    middle latency, 95, 98–99, 105
Peller, L., 29, 76, 90, 98
Perlman, H. H., 54, 229, 241
Personality
    borderline, defined, 243
    psychosomatic concept, 184
    school phobia and, 175
    symptoms and, 145
Personality disorders, defined, 243
Phallic symbols, 176–177
Phobias, 173–179
    anger and, 178
    anxiety and, 173–175, 177
    play and, 178
    psychosomatic concept, 185
    school, 173–176
        parents and, 174–176
        personality and, 175
    transient, 177
Physical development
    early latency, 71–72
    late latency, 32
    middle latency, 92–94
Physical examinations, 237
Piaget, J., 21, 22, 24, 25, 38, 74, 75, 83, 84, 98, 100, 117, 118, 200
Piggott, L. R., 243
Pine, F., 21, 185, 243, 296
Plato, 13–14
Play
    adolescence, 38
    aggression in, 147
    as communication, 287–294
        cheating at games, 291–293
        equipment and setting, 289–291
        fantasy, 293–294
        with parents, 264–268
        therapy and, 287–289
    early childhood, 26–29
    early latency, 31–32, 72–76, 89
    late latency, 112–117, 119
    middle latency, 94–98
    with parents, 264–268
    phobias and, 178
    symbolic, 74–75
    See also Games

Plionis, E. M., 210, 212
Polansky, N. A., 48, 248
Poverty, 64
    economy poverty level, 62–63
    family problems and, 46, 48
    food stamp policies, 63
    intellectual and academic retardation, 146
    public assistance budgets, 63
    religion and, 145
    welfare policies, 63
Poznanski, E., 146, 208
Preoperational stage, 24–25
Prepuberty, see Late latency
Proskauer, S., 254
Prosky, P., 43
Provence, S. A., 20
Prugh, D. G., 200, 201, 240
Pruitt, A. W., 207
Pseudobackwardness, 170
Psychiatric examinations, 236
Psychological development
    early latency, 86–91
    late latency, 125–130
    middle latency, 103–105
Psychosomatic concept, 181–189
    anxiety, 184, 186–187
    the family, 183–186
    loss, 184
    personality, 184
    phobias, 185
    symptoms, 184, 187
Psychotic disorders, defined, 243
Puberty, 37
Public assistance budgets, 63
Puerto Ricans
    extended family, 43
    IQ, 234

Questionnaires, use of, 135

Racial awareness, adolescence, 37
Racial differences, coping with, 30–31
Racial prejudice, adults, 30–31
Rank, B., 148
Rapoport, L., 56, 125
Rapprochement stage, 22
Raus, L., 231
Reactive disorders, defined, 242
Reading disorders, 136
Regalbuto, G., 86
Reiner, B. S., 47, 149
Religion
    minorities and, 145
    poverty and, 145
Remarriage, 64
    rate of, 64
Renshaw, D., 156, 157
Richmond, Mary, 12–13, 234
Riddles, middle latency, 97
Rie, H. E., 159
Riese, H., 226
Ripple, L., 220
Riskin, J., 186
Ritalin, 159
Robins, L. N., 149
Rochlin, G., 53
Rock, N., 186, 187

Rose, J. A., 271
Rosenfeld, A. A., 51
Rosenthal, L., 248
Ross, A. O., 308
Ross, H., 75
Rossi, A. S., 64
Ruiz, R. A., 235
Rutter, M., 242

Sadness, depression and, 144
Saix, C., 48
Salguero, C., 196
San Martino, M., 41
Sandoval, J., 156
Sapir, S. G., 155
Sarnoff, C., 19, 118
Saul, L. J., 20, 105, 143
Schamess, G., 249
Scheidlinger, S., 249
Schiffer, M., 249
Schilder, P., 210
Schonfeld, W., 110
School
    absence from, 172–179
        school phobia, 173–176
        truancy, 172
    first attendance, 138, 139
School phobia, 173–176
Schowalter, J. E., 58
Schrag, P., 156
Schultz, L. G., 51
Sears, R. R., 231
Seese, L. R., 210
Self-destructive acts, aggression and, 152
Self-esteem, 33
Self-mutilation, as a self-preservation
        disorder, 211–212
Self-preservation disorders, 209–212
    accidents, 210–211
    self-mutilation, 211–212
    suicide, 209–210
Selig, A. L., 46
Selvini-Palazzoli, M., 196
Sensorimotor stage, 22
Separation of parents, 44
Separation by sex, early latency, 88
Sexuality
    adolescence, 37
    aggression and, 149
    culture and, 66, 106
    early childhood, 26, 28
        sexual differences, coping with, 29–30
    early latency, 80–83
    infancy, autoerotic activities, 19
    inhibition, 19
    late latency, 119–124
        class, 120
        development of, 109–112
        ejaculation, 109–111, 126
        homosexuality, 113, 120–121, 123,
            128
        masturbation, 111, 120, 123, 124
        menstruation, 109–110, 112, 120, 126
        nocturnal emissions, 120
        orgasm, 111
        venereal disease, 120
    middle latency, 105–107
        masturbation, 107

Shafu, M., 196
Shame, feelings of, 103–105
Shane, M., 203, 305
Shapiro, V., 47, 265
Sherman, E. A., 263
Sherman, S. N., 224, 251
Sherwood, V., 286
Shinn, E., 52, 54
Shugart, G., 55
Siblings, 34–36, 42–43
    death, 58–59
    illness, 59
    infancy, 21
    many roles of, 42–43
    mental retardation and, 165
Silver, L., 161, 162
Singer, S. B., 156, 158, 159
Single parents, 64–65
Skeels, H. M., 164
Slavson, S. R., 249
Sleep disorders, 206–208
    anxiety and, 207–208
Smeltzer, D. J., 135
Smolen, E. M., 285
Social work, defined, 67
Socialization, 67–68
    middle latency, 98–100
Societal influence, 65–68
Solnit, A. J., 165
Speech, 135, 136, 160, 212–216
    mutism, 215–216
    stuttering, 214–215
Sperling, M., 174, 175, 183, 185, 202,
        206, 207
Spitz, R. A., 20, 142, 164, 212–213
Spontaneous atomism, 84
Spotnitz, H., 262, 276, 285
Stack, C. B., 63
Stackhouse, J., 266
Stark, M. H., 165
Stein, Marvin, 181
Stein, Myron, 170, 253
Stephans, J. H., 201
Steward, M., 86
Stimbert, V. E., 192, 193
Stories
    early latency, 78, 89–90
    middle latency, 95–96
Stress, 181–189
    from foster care, 182–183
Studiousness, effeminacy and, 83
Stuttering, 214–215
Sudin, C., 46
Sugar, M., 249
Suicide, as a self-preservation disorder,
        209–210
Sullivan, H., 33, 108
Superego, 239
    aggression and, 147
    early latency, 83, 90–91
    late latency, 116, 126–127
    middle latency, 107
    unreasonable conditions imposed by,
        143
Superstitions, middle latency, 97
Surgeon General's Scientific Advisory
        Committee, 150
Surgery, 61

Symbolic play, 74–75
Symptomatology, 136–142
Symptoms, 133–153
  adult complaints and, 133–136
  aggression, 147–153
  anxiety, 137–139
  class and, 145–146
  culture and, 145–146
  depression, 142–147
  fantasies, 137, 142, 146
  misunderstandings, 137
  obesity, 193
  personality and, 145
  psychosomatic concept, 184, 187
  symptomatology, 136–142
  threats, 139
Szurek, S., 138, 284

Tanner, J. J., 72, 93
Tarjin, G., 163
Taylor, S. S., 248
Teachers, 75, 89
Teamwork in treatment, 256–258
Television
  aggression and, 150
  middle latency, 96, 107
Temper tantrums, 134
Temple-Trujillo, R. E., 43
Testosterone, 111
Thomas, A., 231, 235
Thornburg, H. D., 120
Threats, symptoms, 139
Thumb-sucking, 134
Tics, 190–191
Time-limited therapy, 254–255
Titchener, J. L., 186
Toilet training, 199–200, 202
Tolstrup, K., 192, 195
Tooley, K., 64
Toolon, J. M., 143
Transferred clients, 303–304
Trauma, 142, 144
Travis, G., 60
Truancy, 172

Underachievement, 166–171
  aggression and, 166
  anger and, 166–169
  the ego and, 171
  the family and, 169–171

  masturbation and, 170
  oedipal conflicts and, 170
Unemployment, 62

Vacations, treatment and, 299–301
Van Dam, H., 305
Vanderstoep, E., 251
Venereal disease, late latency, 120
Verbalization
  behavior and, 136–137
  early childhood, 23–24
Violence
  aggression and, 148, 149, 150
  depression and, 145
Vocalization, infancy, 21
Voyat, G., 234

Waldfogel, S., 61
Wallach, H. D., 301
Wallerstein, J., 281, 283
Wallerstein, J. S., 44, 254
Warson, S. R., 204
Wax, D. E., 202–203
Weisman, A. D., 59
Welfare policies, 63
Wermer, H., 200, 201
White, R. W., 88
Whiteman, M., 85, 101
Whiting, B., 106
Whittaker, J. K., 238
Wiener, J. M., 195
Wife abusers, 50–51
Williams, M., 272
Winnicott, C., 272, 276
Winnicott, D. W., 21, 231, 281, 293
Wolff, S., 253
Wolkenstein, A. S., 50, 96
World Health Organization (WHO), 242
Wynne, L. C., 250

Yalom, I. D., 250
Yandell, W., 156, 274
Yeakel, M., 248
Yorukuglu, A., 278
Young, L., 256

Zentall, S., 156
Zrull, J. P., 146